No Letter in Your Pocket

MIROLAND IMPRINT 42

Canada Council **Conseil des Arts**
for the Arts **du Canada**

ONTARIO ARTS COUNCIL
CONSEIL DES ARTS DE L'ONTARIO

an Ontario government agency
un organisme du gouvernement de l'Ontario

Canadä

Guernica Editions Inc. acknowledges the support of the Canada Council
for the Arts and the Ontario Arts Council. The Ontario Arts Council
is an agency of the Government of Ontario.

We acknowledge the financial support of the Government of Canada.

No Letter in Your Pocket

How a daughter chose love and forgiveness to heal from incest

HEATHER CONN

GUERNICA EDITIONS
TORONTO · CHICAGO · BUFFALO · LANCASTER (U.K.)
2023

Guernica Founder: Antonio D'Alfonso

Connie McParland, Michael Mirolla, series editors
Michael Mirolla, editor
David Moratto, cover design and interior design
Guernica Editions Inc.
287 Templemead Drive, Hamilton, ON L8W 2W4
2250 Military Road, Tonawanda, N.Y. 14150-6000 U.S.A.
www.guernicaeditions.com

Distributors:
Independent Publishers Group (IPG)
600 North Pulaski Road, Chicago IL 60624
University of Toronto Press Distribution (UTP)
5201 Dufferin Street, Toronto (ON), Canada M3H 5T8
Gazelle Book Services
White Cross Mills, High Town, Lancaster LA1 4XS U.K.

First edition.
Printed in Canada.

Legal Deposit—First Quarter
Library of Congress Catalog Card Number: 2022945179
Library and Archives Canada Cataloguing in Publication
Title: No letter in your pocket : how a daughter chose love and forgiveness to
heal from incest / Heather Conn.
Names: Conn, Heather, author.
Description: "MiroLand imprint; 42"--Page preceding title page.
| Includes bibliographical references.
Identifiers: Canadiana (print) 2022042098X | Canadiana (ebook) 20220423946
| ISBN 9781771837873 (softcover) | ISBN 9781771837880 (EPUB)
Subjects: LCSH: Conn, Heather. | LCSH: Incest victims—Canada—Biography.
| LCSH: Adult child sexual abuse victims—Canada—Biography. | LCSH: Conn,
Heather—Travel—India. | LCSH: Forgiveness. | CSH: Authors, Canadian
(English)—Biography. | LCGFT: Autobiographies.
Classification: LCC HV6570.9.C3 C66 2023 | DDC 306.877092—dc23

*This manuscript is dedicated
to my late husband Frank McElroy (1954–2019),
whose unending love and support
soared far beyond this story*

*and to Georgeanna Joy Drew (1948–2015),
whose caring, wisdom, and clear spirit
helped nurture and heal me in deep ways*

Author's Note

EVEN AFTER MANY decades of healing and more than a decade since my father's death, this was not an easy story to write. At times, it felt too overwhelming to recreate my emotional conflict over incest. Like a dejected cold-case detective with a box of dusty old case files, my literal-minded journalist brain slowly awoke to the truth. A resistant investigator, it wanted indisputable proof beyond the memories that had stayed with me since childhood. For a long time, it seemed that only validating words from an outsider would make me a believer. I did not want to accept what lay within me. I had no enthralling Perry Mason moment, no stumbled-upon written confession or third-party admission: "One night, he took me aside and shared this disturbing story ..." No one took a DNA swab of semen stains on my childhood sheets or underwear. All I had were unwanted recollections and compelling circumstantial evidence.

I recognized my inherent conflict: as much as I wanted to wrap up the case with a guilty verdict, so to speak, I still felt an urge to burn the files and find my father innocent.

I wanted to think that his determined touches, our bedroom romps, made little difference—but they did. Because my incest incidents were not violent, extensive or extreme and did not occur on a regular basis, I sometimes feel like I don't merit the term "incest survivor." Part of me thinks: I haven't suffered enough. Others were abused far worse than me. But that's part of the insidiousness of parental seduction. You can try to make incest, whether it's emotional or physical, feel as insignificant as dandruff, yet, you still can't brush it off.

My father's actions, done under the guise of love and caring, and solely for his secret pleasure, left me a crumpled wreck for too long. As one therapist friend says: "Integration sucks."

Until my early thirties, I had no idea that I had shut out so much buried pain. As a result, deep love with anyone seemed impossible. Judgments and fear separated me from the true core of people, events, and my own being. Through my twenties, kind, caring men had expressed interest in me yet I turned them away, attracted to "bad boys." I blamed men for my own unbridled lust and longings. For too long, I viewed them far too harshly, bearing a self-righteous assumption that they would ultimately betray me.

An acquaintance recently told me that she had wondered how long it would take me to realize that my dad had sexually abused me. She recognized that reality during a writing workshop when I shared my dreams and confusion at age thirty-three.

My slow awakening process seems so protracted now. Like getting revived after years in a coma, things felt familiar and unreachable at the same time. Denial and awareness co-existed effortlessly. It's a bit like the time I camped alone, in my forties, in Ucluelet on Vancouver Island in British Columbia. One morning, hearing sniffs and a growl just outside my tent, I told myself it was a dog, even though no campers in the isolated wilderness spot had one. It's my stomach, I insisted. But my heart and body knew: it was a bear. The night before, I had found fresh bear scat close by. A black bear had walked through the campsite next to me.

Awakening slowly to my secret took me on a long, misguided search for love, although I didn't know that's what lay beneath my quest. I had no idea then that I was looking for answers to questions that I had barely even formulated.

Now in my early sixties, I still remember my father with ambivalence. My dumbfounded disdain mixes with love, acceptance, and gratitude. The rage is gone. Although I denounce my father's actions and those of all abusers, it was tough to hold condemnation and love for him at the same time.

Almost all incest memoirs label the abuser an evil monster and do little to examine or understand his motives. They focus on horror, which the mainstream media, in turn, can sensationalize and serve as titillating trash. However, demonizing someone as "the other" will never allow us to see beyond judgments to true understanding. We all have a dark side; *how* we manifest it makes the difference.

My story is a conscious journey to find forgiveness. I chose this approach because holding onto grief, rage, and bitterness kept me miserable and chronically ill. I wanted to put compassion into practice even though I have heard strident judgment of others who, in some people's eyes, have appeared too soft towards their abuser. Let me be clear: rage and condemnation are wholly necessary and appropriate responses to acts of sexual violence. That's where I began with my father. It took decades for me to move beyond that to seek true understanding and find some semblance of emotional peace and acceptance. My forgiveness does not ignore or minimize what he did. It is simply a personal choice in healing.

Hopefully, after reading my memoir, you will understand how someone can grapple past denial, anger, and shame to find forgiveness and compassion. Ultimately accepting my father's betrayal, I chose unconditional love. This approach drew on another man's love for me plus decades of meditation, mindfulness, contemplative texts, and the teachings of Zen master Thich Nhat Hanh. Yoga and contemplative practices not only helped me overcome depression, debilitating pain, and near-suicide, but reconcile with a perpetrator. I hope my memoir makes my redemptive act feel accessible to almost anyone, even if the idea of forgiveness for this terrible behaviour initially seems off-putting and impossible. I certainly do not condone attempts at reconciliation with all abusers. Again, it is a personal choice.

I hope to inspire you and survivors of any family secret, but particularly incest and sexual abuse, to thrive, honour your bodies, and, if desired, find a spiritual practice as a healing foundation. As a privileged western white woman, I was lucky to have enough resources and support to process my experiences therapeutically in a variety of ways, including through trauma-informed counselling.

This book is my attempt to explain how denial, ambivalence, and a trauma bond can cause abuse survivors to act in ways that might not make sense to outside observers. Although this memoir shows how damaging both sexual and covert (emotional/psychological) incest are, it reveals how someone can recover from them.

"You had no boundaries," one acquaintance told me. I wish I could draw straight lines that clearly connect my search for love with incest memories, leading to "aha" moments of new awareness regarding how my dad truly related to me. But that is not how the process unfolded. My life is full of splayed lines: detours rather than direct routes. You can't show the truth of something by addressing it directly, a writing professor of mine once said. Now I know what she means—a long series of encountering "not-its" can help reveal what "it" is.

To evoke my adult confusion while in India, I present flashbacks and piercing, unassembled snippets of memory that seem to be whispering: "You're not going to ignore us this time." I have tried to present my incest-related memories, strange body sensations, and dream fragments as close to the same order and time in which they originally occurred; however, in a few places, for narrative flow, I have compressed these into a shorter time frame. In recreating how my remembering unfolded, I wanted to show how intrusive and out of context my wisps of incest memories were. They seemed to exist beyond the "normal" linear, logical framework of thought and time. As Stephen King advises readers about his childhood events in *On Writing*: "[D]on't look for a through-line. There are *no* lines—only snapshots, most out of focus."

Part of my personal evolution has been learning to accept and integrate my incest-related memories with "regular" memories, and I share that process in this book.

While writing, it was challenging to convey my young self in

India as sexually liberated yet still desperate for male validation, oblivious to what deeper reality lay beyond her actions. Similarly, I present my unknowing child self, who thought intimate encounters with her dad were a sign of loving closeness—the sought-after warmth she couldn't experience with her mom—yet still sensed something was "off."

As someone who passionately believes "The personal is political," I show ways to fight back with a peaceful heart and words, seeking respect and accountability, not revenge. If you want to take your abuser to court, go for it. Just make sure that you have a strong support network and are ready to handle possible condemnation from loved ones and others.

After confronting my father in person, I sought, and received, an apology. Many incest survivors never get that satisfaction: their perpetrator has died or denies the facts, they have cut off all contact, or they don't have enough support to face their abuser.

I hope that such a victory can inspire others, as peaceful warriors, to speak out and challenge the blame-the-victim mentality still entrenched in today's beyond-#MeToo society. We need more stories from survivors.

Heather Conn
January 2022

WARNING: This book deals with sexual assault, incest, and emotional trauma and might cause disturbance and anxiety for some readers. Be advised that for some survivors, reading these descriptions of incest could trigger memories of your own abuse.

Contents

Sample everything in life, except incest and folk dancing.
  —Advice from playwright **George S. Kaufman** to
    his daughter

*To discern the patterns of a life, we must become time
amphibians, swimming backward and forward through the
temporal seas. Time is ... a fluid medium in which
everything is interconnected and in which each apparently
unique happening is also a metaphor for other happenings,
past and future.*
  —**Jean Houston**, *A Mythic Life*

Burn all the maps to your body.
  —**Richard Brautigan**

*To see how incest can shred and divide a Being is the scariest
thing I've witnessed in my life.*
  —**Tori Amos**, *Piece by Piece*

PROLOGUE

GONE

With death comes honesty.
—**Salman Rushdie,** *The Satanic Verses*

OCTOBER 2, 2010. The middle-aged undertaker, in a natty suit and open black overcoat, wheels in the steel gurney so that it lies parallel to a deluxe bed in the hospice room.

I stand, alone, by the door in the corner of the plush, semi-dark room. After the undertaker raises the gurney so that it is roughly the same height as the bed, he counts "One, two, three." Two nurses, one at my father's head and one at his feet, lift his eighty-five-year-old body, with its blood-mottled arms and legs and flimsy hospital gown, onto the gurney.

His right arm flops off his chest and falls to the side, a useless weight. The undertaker quickly puts it back at his side and glances at me, the fifty-one-year-old youngest daughter. It is just past eight p.m. My dad has been dead for little over an hour.

The undertaker methodically wraps a white sheet over him, like a head waiter folding a large, fancy napkin on a long table. When he covers my father's face and head, with its clumps of white hair, the nurse standing at the head of the gurney says: "We don't do that here." Again, the undertaker looks at me. No one says anything. His back blocks my view as he zips my father into a crinkly body bag, the white sheet disappearing under the black cover.

It's just like those true-crime TV shows that I watch, except he has no ligature marks around his neck, no gunshot wounds—just bones and organs ravaged by terminal cancer.

The nurse covers his body with a gold patchwork quilt, specially made for the hospice for this purpose.

Under a clear, starry night, I follow two nurses, the undertaker, and the body out the front double doors of the hospice into the parking lot. The undertaker pushes the gurney into the back of a sleek black SUV. He's placed a square of carpet beneath the gurney, on top of the rear bumper, to save his paint job from scratches. My dad would have liked that practical touch of prizing an automobile, the same way he used to coddle his red 1960 MGA sports car.

Before my father disappears into the car interior, a nurse removes the quilt from his body and folds it over her arm. Teary, I hug both nurses.

"I liked your dad," one of them says as I walk towards my father's cushy silver Honda sedan. "He always had a smile."

Crying softly, I sit in the unfamiliar car in the dark, wondering if I can find my way back to my parents' gated community, a prominent fixture in this city of 90,000 southwest of Toronto. Thousands of kilometres from my west-coast home, I imagine myself lost beneath this star-flecked night, circling the manicured, generic streets within their spotless complex, trying to find my way to the right house.

That same night, back at my parents' home, I find strange comfort wearing a clean set of my father's huge, navy-blue pajamas under a white, terrycloth robe that he bought for guests. My mother goes to bed. My dad's wing chair in the den stands empty. I'm tired but abuzz with adrenaline, feeling guilty for not sobbing.

As he was dying, I held his left hand and arm, feeling his arm vibrate while energy flew through it, on final escape. His last breath, a short wheeze, left his chest in a low, deep tone. When I struggled to pull the gold ring with the Egyptian hieroglyphics off his wedding finger, my mother, at his bedside, said: "At least he won't feel it."

* * *

My father filled a basement room with maps, books, artwork, and souvenirs from Burma and India like a miniature Taj Mahal. After multiple visits there, he considered Myanmar a second home, calling the Burmese "the Irish of Asia" for their sense of humour. He admired Nobel laureate Aung San Suu Kyi, Myanmar's leader, who was placed under house arrest for "endangering the state" as a pro-democracy activist in July 1989, seven months before the two of us travelled there. (I wonder now what he would have thought of her regime's much-later violence against Myanmar's Rohingya Muslims.) He sent me books like *Outrage: Burma's struggle for democracy*, replacing his usual conservatism with a spirit aghast at the injustice of the nation's brutal military dictatorship.

I had spent a month in Southeast Asia with my father before starting to explore Thailand, Nepal, and India on my own. My parents had instilled their love of travel in all four children. While many in their twenties or early thirties are contemplating parenthood, I was thinking: *Where to next?* The lure of freedom has always tugged at me. As an early reader, I remember a rabbit in a book named *Pookie*. Long ears hit by a walloping wind, he stood atop a hill, dwarfed by sky and cloud. His only belongings lay wrapped in a bindle, a red kerchief at the end of a stick. As a child, this symbol of the lone nomad stayed with my bold spirit, beyond greedy Mr. Toad in *The Wind in the Willows*, the poetic lilt of Robert Louis Stevenson, and the delight and mystery of Beatrix Potter's practical Mrs. Tiggywinkle.

On the night my dad died, I surveyed the row of mouthwash and toiletries and his eyeglasses that my mom had placed on the counter in the bathroom. Above them, behind the door, hung a framed print of *Before the Bath*, an 1892 painting by Canadian artist Paul Peel. Only visible when the bathroom door was closed, it showed two children cowering behind a partition. One crouched, naked, while the other stood with a bare chest, only one sleeve of a thin white gown still in place. A burly nursemaid in white cap and apron beckoned at them. While I was growing up, this image had hung in my dad's office, presumably as wholesome as a Norman Rockwell tableau.

In his home office, in the basement, I read my dad's diary, found in his desk drawer. Most of it focused on his non-stop demands at the hospital. I was amazed at how he juggled high-pressure duties, from staff crises and doing rounds to mentoring interns, hosting visiting doctors, and writing many papers for conferences. He confided, at one point, that he was trying not to panic over having to write three medical papers in ten days. He attended regular meetings in areas from surgery to pharmacology.

On the small, lined pages he confessed to drinking too much at social events and complained of hangovers.

My dad's home office contained large, framed photos of his medical certificates and him with groups of colleagues over the years but none of his wife or kids. His desk bore a sign that said: "When you're right no one remembers, when you're wrong, no one forgets."

Colleagues will remember my father's many accomplishments and awards as an anesthesiologist, professor emeritus, and former director of an intensive care unit at a children's hospital. He saved thousands of lives and developed a technique that brought back kids from otherwise cold-water drowning; they recovered without suffering brain damage. Yet, his medical expertise could not save him from multiple myeloma, a painful bone cancer. His diagnosis dragged him from healthy cheer to death in about six months. Twenty years earlier, when we were in Burma together, he told me that people invented heaven so they wouldn't think that it was "the end" when they died. I wonder: *What does he think now?*

I picture him in his home library in his favourite chair, a book in his lap, puffing on his pipe, nodding his bald head and tapping his foot to an LP of Benny Goodman's sextet playing *Bei Mir Bist Du Schon* from 1937. Martha Tilton sings: *It means you're the fairest in the land* ... As a child, I didn't understand the meaning of the words, but his pleasure in them made me think they must be special, special like how he treated me.

Family photo #1: In a studio headshot of my father, used for his funeral service notice, he appears as a middle-aged man of success in a navy suit jacket and pale blue shirt. His navy tie bears repeated crests. Head slightly tilted, he looks confident, glancing just off-camera through large, clear-framed glasses. His smile shows a gap between his two front teeth.

I want to remember him this way, robust and happy. I feel shocked that the image doesn't repulse me, that I don't want to tear it up. This photo says: Life is fine, he is fine, we are all fine. I wanted to believe that.

For my father's funeral, I chose some of the swing jazz that he loved so much, like Glenn Miller's *Mood Indigo* and Louis Armstrong singing *It's a Wonderful World*. One of his female friends, who spoke at the event in his honour, characterized him as a perpetual "ladies' man." Even in his final weeks, confined to a bed, he told her that he could smell her perfume, when she wasn't wearing any.

At the reception in the church basement afterwards, a woman mentioned how upset my dad was when the all-boys' private school in Toronto, which he had attended for grade thirteen, allowed girls to enroll. He once told me that male gynecologists were better than female ones and that a husband had no place being in the delivery room when his wife was giving birth. He followed the strict gender rules of a previous era too outdated for me.

One of his medical colleagues said my father was the only one who could sit through hours of administrative meetings at the hospital and still come out laughing and telling jokes. Another mentioned that he was the most generous person he had ever met. (I later learned that my dad donated to about fifty organizations.) A woman praised him for saving her child's life. A man from my dad's men's group said that my father never bragged about his accomplishments. John Coutlee, a retired medical engineering technologist whom he hired after a ten-minute interview in the early 1960s, wrote about him: "[T]he great staff that he assembled ... indicated the talent he had for recognizing good people with many skills ... He was a good leader who could come up with ideas and then sell people on them, including hospital administrators ... No department head or administrator whom I worked with in my later career was as supportive as he was."

I could let in this praise: "He was able to bring out the best in people ... To me he was a great man and one to whom I owe my career." Yet, these words from Coutlee held different resonance for me: "He was very adept at maneuvering people to do his will."

* * *

Alone in the den that night of my father's death, I watched the television documentary *Tiger Woods: the Rise and Fall*. An exotic dancer displayed two tattoos of a tiger on her lower back, representing the two pregnancies she had had with the married golf great; one ended with a miscarriage, the other, an abortion. This show reinforced a theme that has always fascinated me: How do high-profile, outwardly successful people compartmentalize their lives, committing horrific deeds like rape, incest or murder that remain secret for years? What prompts and enables such folk, who aren't outwardly psychotic, to lead such double lives?

Such deceptions and corresponding public adulation of someone's façade, with no repercussions for the person's actions, still trouble me profoundly.

This Tiger Woods video formed a symbolic bookend to my father's death. Only two days earlier, after receiving word that he was "in the process of dying," I had rushed to get on a red-eye flight. At the airport in Vancouver, waiting for my flight east to Toronto, I had watched a television news report. Toronto police had charged an anesthetist with twenty-six counts of sexual assault, allegedly committed while his female patients were anesthetized, undergoing surgery.

When my father's middle brother Keith died, his eldest daughter, my cousin Jan, told me that she wrote loving messages to him and placed them in the pockets of the jacket that he was buried in. I liked that. Three days after my dad died, I wrote him a quick letter on a narrow pad that bore his name above a seaside image with a lighthouse. During the funeral home visitation, I had planned to put this note in his suit pocket but his closed casket was already on display. I tried lifting the lid but it seemed bolted shut. Too fearful to try and open it, and immersed in the details of funeral preparations, I never followed up.

For those who can't comprehend at all how I could feel love towards an abuser, read on. These conflicting parallel realities began to converge and collide twenty years earlier in Southeast Asia. Back then, I had mostly buried what had transpired between my dad and me, preferring to remain oblivious.

PART ONE

ADRIFT IN ASIA
(1990–91)

The past is not a package one can lay away.
—Emily Dickinson

CHAPTER ONE

CONFUSED

I'm not confused, I'm just well mixed.
—**Robert Frost**

WHITE AND SLEEK, the *Oriental Queen*, a luxury, double-deck tour boat, was cruising down the 370-kilometre-long Chao Phraya River in Bangkok. I lounged on the top stern deck. On this one-day excursion in early March 1990, I spurned the vessel's air-conditioned interior to experience the sticky 33-degrees-Celsius heat and sun, and partly to escape the inane tour guide. Unfortunately, his bad jokes and trivia, delivered in a thick Thai accent, remained piped throughout the boat; a Muzak version of "Lara's Theme," activated when he took a break, gave surprising reprieve.

Thin, red-haired, and thirty-one, I felt too young and tall in this throng of middle-agers and seniors in starched white shirts, lipstick, white hair, and too-white legs. Yet, in a floppy-brimmed bamboo hat, dripping under the long-sleeved shirt stuck to my skin, I couldn't ditch my tourist appearance. Others made no effort to hide theirs. A man with a video camera recorded everything, static or moving: pagodas (*wats*); rows of flimsy wooden float homes; large swathes of water hyacinths; a floating market; noisy, two-stroke long-tail passenger boats that looked like blunt-nosed barracudas; the tapered, golden spires of the Royal Palace; and a seven-storey replica of a Pepsi can.

My sixty-four-year-old companion, paunchy and bald, looked

ready for safari in his khaki Tilley Endurables outfit. He pointed to a row of scows towed by tugboats.

"They make me think of elephants following each other from nose to tail," he said at high volume; he tended to yell when he talked because he couldn't hear well.

Later, below deck, I chatted with Abe and Elaine, a down-to-earth, middle-aged couple from California, while munching on prawns during a great buffet.

"Have you known him long?" Elaine asked, referring to the man accompanying me.

"All my life," I replied. "He's my dad."

My father had invited me to accompany him for a month, at his expense, to Hong Kong, Malaysia, Singapore, Thailand, and Burma (now Myanmar). He was revisiting a holiday from 1983, pleased to return to his favourite places in Asia. My mom had chosen not to go with him.

I had already saved for a year of solo travel in Southeast Asia, drawn to some notion of Eastern mystique. Meditation, yoga, and Buddhism interested me far more than my Judeo-Christian heritage. Longing to backpack in Asia, I felt determined to end my inner turmoil from the previous six months.

Something unknown was troubling me. While growing up, I had dreamt repeatedly that someone was trying to kill me and I needed to tell people. In the dreams, I would run out into the street, waving my arms, hoping to flag down a car and get help. Usually, no one stopped. If they did, I would blurt out an explanation, but they never believed me. Thinking me crazy, they just drove off. Until my forties, many of my dreams took place in my childhood home, even though I lived thousands of kilometres away and felt little kinship to the place.

Cynical and tough at thirty-one, I was still trying to define myself outwardly. Yet, the material world seemed devoid of answers; I wanted to go more deeply within. Not counting summer jobs, I had worked mostly with stories, visual or otherwise: as a newspaper reporter, magazine editor, assistant photo editor, freelance writer, researcher, writing instructor, and oral historian. Although I felt passionate about writing and working with words, no career niche felt right. This left me feeling less than worthy within my family's parameters for success, where it was a given that you would excel.

Beyond my parents' stereotypical gender roles, I wanted to believe that I would find and fall in love with a sensitive, caring, loving man who had a kind, generous heart.

Essentially, I was willfully planning to meet a life mate, having just read the love story *The Bridge Across Forever* by Richard Bach. At the same time, I was hoping to get clear on whether to have a child or not.

Was I confused? Hell, yes. An anxious mess.

I was clear on one thing: I wanted to travel solo for a year in Southeast Asia, exploring my spirituality without a guru, ashram, or drugs. Wary of communities based around an authority, I didn't want anyone regulating my choices or decisions. I had already heard enough stories about male spiritual leaders who had seduced female followers, and had met several, including my own mentor, whose egos were more than healthy. Nor did I want to become a "bliss ninny," lost in a cult. Stumbling and bumbling, I was creating my own version of "Heal yourself, heal the world": Deal with your own baggage first; then you have more to offer others.

Before arriving in Asia, I had found myself attracted to the compassion and nonviolence of Tibetan Buddhism, to the belief that our attachment to anything—money, achievement, possessions—creates needless suffering. Taoist thought also appealed: Follow the middle way, the path without extremes. Surrender to the natural flow of life. Trust the process. Let go. If I could release ambitions, would I be happier? I was trying to find an absolute answer, some path with a one-way sign to an obvious destination point beyond the usual scramble for status and wealth. But I felt terrified to let go of control.

Like centuries of spiritual seekers, like the Beatles, like thousands of backpackers before me in the 1960s and '70s, I sought to tramp through India. This dust-and-deities nation, suffused with saffron, mysticism, ritual, the *Kama Sutra*, temples, and tantra, has produced some of the world's greatest spiritual adepts from Patanjali and Buddha to Krishnamurti. Surely, I could progress in a country where some people almost literally survive on religion and spirituality. Hindu *saddhus* or holy pilgrims, for example, with no home or possessions, depend completely on alms from strangers.

My spiritual mentor in Canada reinforced a belief that I maintain today: nothing external will ever bring me happiness. Can I find loving peace within and accept what is without resistance? For me, that means choosing not to lash out at every perceived slight or so-called failure, not railing over people and events that do not comply with my desires and goals. Isn't that what maturity is supposed to look and feel like?

* * *

At a family wedding, at age fifteen, I remember my embarrassment when my father, still sober, openly ogled and made suggestive remarks in front of guests about my sister's busty friend who wore a low-cut dress. He and a medical colleague, in front of a tween me, once verbally drooled over women's bikinied bodies at a hotel swimming pool. My dad liked to wear a navy tie with a repeat motif of small pink pigs and the acronym MCP for "male chauvinist pig." My young, sensitive heart didn't know how to interpret this. Did he respect women, including me, or not?

One evening, he and I, at twenty-three, went out drinking in San Antonio, Texas, where he was on a medical sabbatical. When we were both drunk, he told me that I had "luscious" breasts. Strangely, I felt proud and flattered. Only when a boyfriend later reacted with shock did I realize that such intimate camaraderie was wrong.

In my late twenties, my father invited me to dine with him at a dimly lit, lakefront restaurant in Toronto. He remarked: "This is the kind of place you'd take your mistress to." He did the same with my eldest sister, Nancy, who's ten years older than me. She remembers him taking her for lunch several times, when she was a teenager, to

Le Provençal, an expensive Toronto restaurant. He wouldn't allow her to wear pants; she had to get dressed up for the occasion. When he saw somebody he knew during lunch, he pretended he didn't see him.

"He liked the idea of having a woman on his arm," Nancy says. "It was as if seeing me with him, people would think that I was a mistress. He liked to give the impression of a man about town. He always thought of himself as a bit of a lover boy."

By then, I only half-realized that my dad treated me like a surrogate partner, not knowing this was part of covert incest. When a parent-child relationship is inappropriately sexualized, the parent makes a child the object of his or her "affection, love, passion, and preoccupation," psychologist Kenneth M. Adams says in *Silently Seduced*. This often occurs to avoid the pain and dissatisfaction of a marriage.

As my father and I began our trip together in southeast Asia, I still believed that gaining his attention, like when he confided in me about his work and spoke to me as an intellectual peer, reinforced a sense of respect. But my view on that quickly changed.

At hotels, my dad pointedly told reception clerks and others that I was his daughter, wanting to avoid the assumption that we were lovers. Except when staying in a five-star hotel, we had separate rooms.

Eight days after our stay in Bangkok, on a muggy evening in Kuching, the fourth-largest city in Malaysia, I hurriedly dressed to get ready for dinner at the Hilton Hotel.

The door to my father's room was ajar. Inside, a porter was just leaving. My dad was in the bathroom with the door closed. Leaning back on my elbows, I sprawled on the bed to wait for him.

When my father opened the bathroom door, he smiled and asked: "How did you get in here?" He added: "And you have your clothes on." Stunned, I remained on the bed, still propped on my elbows.

I must have misheard him or misunderstood. Too shocked to ask him to repeat it, I blotted out the comment.

Several months later, while I was travelling solo in India, his remark evoked an odd childhood memory that had never left me.

I am lounging on the bed at home in our guest room, in a wrinkly cotton nightgown, around age five. Leaning back on my elbows, I rest one outstretched leg over the other, toes touching. My eyes look straight at the camera, serious and questioning, under bangs and a bowl of red hair. My dad is taking a picture of me. I don't know why a male hospital employee—I think it was an intern—whom he's hired to do odd jobs around the house, is in the room.

"Look at that pose," my dad says to him. "She's already got the moves down." I don't know what he means and badger him to explain.

"I want to play doctor." My father ignores my comment. I repeat it, more insistently. The other man grimaces, looking staggered. My dad explains: "She doesn't know what she's saying."

Family photo #2: A precocious five-year-old, I sprawl across the guest room bed in my nightgown. The black-and-white photo in my family album captures this memory into timelessness. The prone position I had adopted on the bed in Malaysia, twenty-six years later, was exactly the same.

The other man's look of horror, within a context I didn't comprehend, stayed with me into adulthood. I remember my dad later telling me that our games were something special, just for him and me, not for others to know.

My logical adult mind wants to retain something sharp and solid as proof. But I can't recall specific visual details like wallpaper or colours. Such memories are like celluloid ghosts, mere wisps of a former presence.

Decades later, a feminist mentor tells me: "Don't be innocent. Your behaviour was repressed. You were provocative and didn't know it." Her comments confuse the adult me even more.

More than fifty years after my dad photographed me, at five, on the bed, I tracked down the man who I believed had been in the room with us and told him about the incest. Hugely loyal to my father, he told me via a long-distance phone call, "Kids say all kinds of things. I think you should forget about the whole thing [trying to identify that adult in the room]."

Three years before this Asia trip with my dad, while visiting my parents in Toronto, I had experienced a series of fast dream images that suggested sexual behaviour between my father and me. In one, he had ended up in my bed. But I had dismissed them as mere Freudian fantasy. In my journal, I had written: *[R]eally bizarre— don't know where on earth those came from—certainly not something I'm aware of on any external level.* At the time of the dream, at age twenty-eight, I had felt depressed and deeply troubled. After seeking counselling, I thought that my parents would be supportive. Instead, my mom seemed defensive and surly.

"I suppose you're going to blame us for everything," she said.

Before arriving in Asia with my father, a memory had wafted through me.

Floating near the ceiling of my bedroom, I look down at my five-year-old body. It lies, face up, in my white four-poster bed. Being up high feels exciting, like the swoops and whirls of Peter Pan flight. What fun, what freedom. I want to do this again.

But when I tell my mommy, she looks alarmed. I don't understand. Why doesn't she want me to have fun?

I flew away when Daddy put his fingers inside my private place. Does he do this to her? I want to do it again. I think we were playing doctor. Does he play doctor with her? Then Daddy was moving, moving, jerking the bed. It scared me. I remember a wet spot on the bed.

I want my mommy to be happy. She doesn't believe me. I insist it's true and show her the wet stain on the sheet.

"Have you told anyone else about this?"

"No, Mommy. It's just Daddy and I. I thought that you—"

"Promise me you won't tell anyone?"

"I promise. Why, Mommy? Why?"

I want to fly again.

This memory had to be a dream. My father loved me. A fun-loving jokester, he liked to tease me as a child. He took me to the Santa Claus parade and seemed to have as much fun as I did watching the Simpson display windows of Christmas scenes with mechanized animals and elves. He often drove me to a lakefront park in Toronto so that I could play on my favourite tall spiral slide, the one I called "twirly."

In the summer, we went together to the Mosport track in Ontario to watch Formula One races; I marvelled at this world of speed and driving finesse. While I was in my teens, my dad gave me driving tips and explained many things I didn't know, from British history to basic physics. We were kindred rebel spirits. He was the one who spoiled me. I loved him.

More than two decades later, I learned that out-of-body experiences are extremely common among those who have been sexually abused in childhood.

Before leaving for Southeast Asia, I had felt more apprehension than excitement and wasn't sure why. Other than memories I had dismissed as fantasy, I had no conscious awareness then, at all, of incest. Referring only to our family's lack of openness and emotional expression, I had written in my journal: *Will I or can I break the wall of our family silence?*

Family photo #3: Our six-member family poses in a photographer's studio in October 1964. I am five, with a pixie smile, half of my bangs down, half held back with a barrette. My dad, in black-rimmed glasses, suit and tie, sits to my right. I lean into him, in easy comfort, my elbow on his lap, hand on his knee. On the left side of the photo, he and I appear joined, a cozy unit. The rest of the family, not touching each other at all, look almost separate from us. My sisters stand behind us, in descending order, based on height. My mom sits at the end, on the right. Everyone is smiling.

This photo was taken around the same time as the one my dad took of me stretched out on the bed in my nightgown, resting back on my elbows.

CHAPTER TWO

STUBBORN

Be stubborn and persist, and trust yourself on what you love.
You have to trust what you love.
 —Carolee Schneemann

ALTHOUGH MY DAD and I spent almost twenty-four hours a day together in Asia, we spoke surprisingly little. We had quiet, delectable meals, mostly at the restaurant in each of our hotels, or ordered room service. One Bangkok dinner was chicken wrapped in banana leaves, pork curry with water spinach, honey chicken, and fresh vegetables.

Daddy insists that I, age five, eat a bowl of soupy rhubarb placed before me on the dining room table for dessert. I refuse, recoiling from its smell. The sweet-sickly taste and pulpy fibers in pink goo make me think of vomit.

Holding the bowl of rhubarb, he drags me to the basement and locks me, alone, into his small corner workshop. He finds disobedience in any of his children intolerable.

I play with his mini-vise on the thick wooden counter, opening and closing it again and again, twirling its small, straight handle. Hammers and other tools hang in a neat row on the wall, too high up for me to reach.

One by one, I open the tiny square drawers inside the first two rows of stacked clear-plastic shelves. So many different sizes and shapes of nails and screws, rusty and new. I gaze up at the mounted head of a deer with shiny brown eyes and faded-looking skin, and draw patterns with my shoes in the thin layer of sawdust on the floor.

After more than four hours of confinement, I hold my nose and swallow each mushy spoonful of the ghastly muck. At last, I'm allowed back upstairs.

"I had to show you who was boss," my father explained, many years later, branding me stubborn. I remember feeling power—not fear.

Was I trying to be the boss of my own body and spirit? Decades later, I cringed while reading an account by actor Lupita Nyong'o of her interactions with predatory Hollywood producer Harvey Weinstein. In one incident, when she wouldn't have an alcoholic beverage with him and in another, refused to have sex with him, she said he called her "stubborn" both times.

My sister Wendy told me how she remembered our family's Sunday rhubarb incident, which occurred when she was ten: "It was awful. He was out-of-control dominating. He grabbed you and yanked you down there and locked the door and made us all go away. We [mom and sisters] were all crying. We were horrified. I thought you were going to be dead when he opened the door. I was traumatized." She adds: "He was the most powerful person in the wrong way. I don't think he ever felt that he had done anything wrong. Mom wouldn't stand up to him. She wouldn't say 'boo.'"

This episode became part of our family lore. My dad sometimes mentioned it with a laugh. He thought it would teach me obedience, but it made me more rebellious and resentful than ever. I never ate another piece of rhubarb for probably twenty years.

* * *

During a fifteen-and-a-half-hour train ride through Thailand, my dad and I shared only snippets of dialogue, often with him re-counting his knowledge of the Second World War, in which he never fought.

One afternoon, he said to me: "Your mother was the one who raised you kids. I can't do anything about that now."

Throughout our trip, we toured temples, museums, and historic sites with a guide, and shopped. In tourist groups, like schools of fish lured to bait, we swam around pagodas and pillars and Buddha statues with a sense of "must-see" obligation while hawkers tried to snag us with displays of tacky hats, vertical arrays of postcards, pseudo silks, and questionable gems. In the humid heat, my overweight dad tired easily when walking; it usually didn't take long before he was back in his room, downing a small bottle of gin with mix from the mini-bar.

"I can't wait to get a glass in my hand," he told me.

One afternoon, sitting in my dad's hotel room, I found the courage to ask him something I had wanted to know for a while: "How did you deal with daily life-and-death issues at the hospital and telling parents that their child wasn't going to make it? Didn't that affect you emotionally?"

He didn't reply and focused on watching television.

Finally, he said: "A good doctor doesn't get emotionally involved with his patients. If you do, you lose your effectiveness."

"But you had to have reactions, didn't you? You're not a robot. How did you handle them?"

He made some comment about the movie *Moonlighting*, in English, that was on TV. He kept looking at the screen.

"You're so busy thinking fast and fighting to guarantee survival that you don't get time to be emotional," he said. After a few moments, he added: "That's why so many doctors drink and commit suicide."

As a doctor, my dad had received calls from distraught mothers who hoped that he could somehow reverse their child's brain damage from near-drowning years after an incident. "By then, it's too late to do anything," he told me. "It all depends on what treatment these kids get at the scene." He told me when I was young: "An anesthetist can kill you faster than any surgeon can."

To cope with work stress, my father had used booze. On this trip, I saw first-hand his dependence on alcohol: his desperation to find a drink when he learned that our hotel bar was closed after a too-long train ride; his repeated requests on the plane for my free mini-bottles of liquor; his persistent need for alcohol every day; his daily maintenance of wine at meals. He got edgy and irritable when he had not had a drink for extended hours. He usually carried a pocket flask of Beefeater gin and sought out places to find mix for it. After ordering too many bottles of wine at a meal, he could drink to the point of slurring his words. On a plane trip, after downing three quick glasses of champagne and two Drambuie, he told me that he never thought my mom would turn into her own mother, whom he characterized as rigid and critical. In his view, she had.

I wanted to gain a deeper connection with my dad, yet saw how his daily needs and desires usurped mine: when I was watching a movie on television in a hotel room and went to the bathroom, he would switch the channel to something he wanted to watch. Whenever we entered a shared hotel room, he was always first to put his luggage in the storage area, leaving no room for mine. At a dinner, after three glasses of white wine, he urged me to have another glass. "One for me," he said.

Stunned, I realized, for the first time, that he was an alcoholic—or, in today's therapeutic parlance, he suffered alcohol use disorder.

* * *

I wonder now: Did my dad's alcoholism, combined with a tiny cluster of rogue DNA, make him more susceptible to committing incest? The journalist in me is not trying to rationalize his behaviour, only determine its origins. The son of a general practitioner, he was the pampered youngest of three boys. He was doted on as his mother's favourite—"the centre of attention from day one," my sister Mary Ann says. I have wondered: Was *he* sexually abused? I'll never know. Sexual abuse often repeats down a generational line, as if through some twisted genetic code.

Like my father, two of his ancestors overindulged in bottled spirits; today, they'd be called alcoholics. John Conn, his great-great-grandfather, moved north from the rural township of Garafraxa, Ont. to the Thornbury area to avoid the temptations of cheap alcohol offered at many local taverns. My dad's third great-grandfather, William Heather, died from "intemperance."

No wonder my father always seemed to have a drink in his hand at home.

* * *

I felt grateful for the supreme comfort of our travel and my dad's generosity, but recognized how much our bond had fallen short for me. I would have readily traded our travel opulence for bare rooms and a bench if it meant that we connected more deeply and he could truly "see" me. Instead, he regularly steered any talk back to himself or his past medical work. If we were discussing something esoteric or of interest to me that he knew little about, he would usually introduce a medical comment to return to familiar ground. His habit, decades old, of monopolizing conversations was too entrenched for him to even notice.

At the family dinner table, my father had assumed that whatever topic most fascinated him, whether Second World War battles that he never fought or struggles to save a child in intensive care, equally intrigued the rest of us. (After longing to join the air force in the Second World War, he was turned down, due to his eyesight. Instead, he was a captain on reserve with the Royal Canadian Army Medical Corps, from 1948 to 1952, then served as a reserve squadron leader with the Royal Canadian Air Force, from 1954 to 1960.)

He frequently rattled off tales of battles with vigour and detail as if he had fought them first-hand. My dad seemed to have read every book on the First and Second World Wars and watched just as many movies about them, both documentaries and dramas. Such vicarious living gave him a detached sense of solace, he explained. Any emergencies he faced as director of an intensive care unit paled in comparison to what grisly tasks wartime medics had to perform in the field.

Rarely did he ask how my school day went or how we, his children, felt about something. My blurted-out ideas, questions, and challenges about anything off-topic or oblique often brought on a few-seconds' lull in conversation, a quick comment or lack of response, then everything else disappeared under his ongoing monologue. At times, I felt like smashing my fist on the table and yelling, "Shut up!" but, of course, never did.

Still, I felt proud of his accomplishments, including his arrangements for a set of conjoined twins in Burma to come to Toronto to receive an operation that successfully separated them. In 1983, at age twenty-four, I had watched some of the operation with my dad on closed-circuit television at the hospital; it received considerable media attention. (When I proudly showed him my first photograph published in a book, he pulled out a copy of *Life* magazine, which contained *his* photo of the yet-to-be-separated twins transported onto a plane in a milk crate.) On our trip to Asia, we had visited the twins in Burma, then healthy, happy seven-year-olds.

I remember as a child feeling awe and wonder at my father's power, skill, and ability to know what tiny, controlled amounts of drugs to administer to keep an infant or tot asleep and alive while on the operating table. He wasn't just a doctor—he was an "M. Deity": a middle-aged acquaintance described her medical ex-husband that way.

I would sometimes awaken and hear my dad get ready for work. He would zoom off in his peppy MGA like a gallant rescuer. How could such a healing hero commit incest?

* * *

For at least a decade, my father was on call twenty-four hours a day. As busy as he was, though, he could always escape for a weekend alone; my mother never did. I tried. My sister Mary Ann, eight years my senior, remembers me, as a youngster, leaving a note that read, "I have gone to seek my fortune." I have no idea how much distance I travelled—likely no farther than the end of the block.

As my father and I travelled in Asia together, I admired how this consummate world-traveller, who had seen many of the planet's natural and historic wonders, still expressed joy at, and appreciation of, a simple meal, a sunset, or people-watching. He easily engaged strangers in conversation, his curious mind always wondering, analyzing, assessing. When I was navigator in our rental car, he took it in stride when we got lost and never blamed me.

As a thrill-seeking four-year-old who joined my father on road-trip adventures, I had rarely ridden in the passenger seat of his red MGA two-seater. Instead, I squeezed into the narrow storage area behind the seats, lying lengthwise, and looked out the back window, watching the road's white centre lines flash by. I could watch the world rush past from over his shoulder, where he sat with a seat belt made from the buckle and straps of a parachute harness. My dad usually kept the driver's-side window down, so the wind rushed in and blew through my hair. I loved how low to the ground the MGA stood, and my dad proudly demonstrated how we could drive right under certain horizontal parking barriers with space to spare. He tested this out slowly at the parking lot of the downtown hospital where he worked, inching towards and then under the impeding lever, rather than barging at it head-on.

At times, my dad would ask me if I wanted to sit up front with him. Safe in my own private compartment, I said no. We shared ice cream cones, free from my mom's scolding and rules. On the surface, he and I were like two kids in an in-between place, fun and frivolous. Decades later, a therapist friend told me: "Your father sees you as a peer. He doesn't acknowledge the parent-child relationship, the disparity of power he had over you."

* * *

To touch someone or something is to express connection, to gain a tactile sense of their being. Touch can be a boon to the soul. Through ritual, story, and socializing, we grant power to the act of touch. A sword taps a shoulder during knighthood. A schoolgirl fawns: "He touched me." Touching can validate our own presence, inviting transformation. A fairy tags a child with her magic wand. Eager hands rub a bottle to generate a genie. But the English language uses the pejorative term "touchy-feely." If a subject deals with sensitive matters, it's called "touchy." While someone is "touched" if incapacitated or shell-shocked, a touchstone reverberates with positive meaning and significance.

If a child says, "He touched me" and an adult says: "Where?" the word takes on darker implications. With a young one, there can be no consent. How does a single incident, made light of, dismissed or ignored by those in authority, affect a young victim?

Who wants to conjure some sleazy guy with greasy hair and booze on his breath pawing an innocent child in a back room with the door shut? An incest encounter often begins in the open, with a chuckle, a tickle, a look, a stroke, a hand that lingers too long. Then it changes—and the child, one like me, doesn't know why.

My family never gave spontaneous hugs, only a peck on the lips and quick clasp around the waist as a snap greeting. I envied my best friend Persephone, whose Greek family next door never hesitated to envelop someone in their arms, pinch a cheek or sling an arm around a shoulder. They had lavish home-cooked meals on Sunday, vibrant with music, laughter, and rollicking relatives. On most Sundays, while our family sat hushed on rigid pews in our local United Church, hers huddled over cards and poker chips.

Sometimes Persephone's father danced with outstretched arms and a kerchief to a lively Greek tune. Love and affection in her family's home seemed so freewheeling and frequently expressed. At their place, I never felt as if I had to earn it. My sister Wendy remembers: "Their home just flowed love. It was wonderful." When staying overnight with Persephone's family, I often didn't want to leave.

* * *

"I miss your mother," my father told me one day on our trip. "I'm glad you're here with me or I'd be lonely. Aren't you going to be lonely travelling by yourself?"

"No. It's something I want and need to do."

He told me about "Rain," one of his favourite W. Somerset Maugham short stories. In this tale, a missionary on a ship in the South Pacific disdains a supposed prostitute on board. Yet, he ultimately has sex with her and kills himself, unable to reconcile his behaviour. *Why is he telling me this?*

Coming out of the bathroom in his hotel room one night, my father had tears in his eyes. Having never seen him cry before, I felt too astonished to say anything.

We were ending our journey in Bangkok, at the sumptuous, five-star Oriental Hotel, where writers from W. Somerset Maugham and Ian Fleming to Graham Greene have stayed. I had only a week or so left of poolside service, travel by chauffeur-driven, air-conditioned Mercedes, and sleeping in a bed turned down each night with flowers and a different card printed with a quote ranging from Bob Dylan to Shakespeare: "To sleep—perchance to dream …" After that, I would start my more familiar form of travel: cheap meals and guest houses, haggling for reduced fares, and hefting my belongings through sweaty streets.

When he and I said goodbye in Bangkok, we gave each other an affectionate hug and a quick kiss. Feeling awkward and oddly detached, I thanked him for the generous trip. I was ready to move on: forward to the future, not plodding through my past. India was pulling me to her.

Chapter Three

SHARDS

We have to be utterly broken before we can realize that it is impossible to better the truth. It is the truth that we deny which so tenderly and forgivingly picks up the fragments and puts them together again.
—**Laurens Van der Post**

THREE MONTHS AFTER leaving my dad in Bangkok, and backpacking through Thailand and Nepal, I arrived in New Delhi, ill-prepared for the city's smoggy June heat of 42°C. Joining almost nine million people in this northern Indian city, my sweaty body became racked with a bout of bacterial dysentery, known as "Delhi belly." (I had contracted it in Nepal after buying a popsicle, a reckless snack, from a street vendor on my final day in Kathmandu. Avoiding giardia and other common travel illnesses in Nepal had given me a ridiculous sense of super-immunity.)

On the rickety public bus that clattered away from the airport to Connaught Place, Delhi's urban hub, I found a stencilled warning on the back of my wooden seat: "Look under your Seat/There could be a Bomb/Raise Alarm/Earn Reward." A charming welcome.

After wobbling into Ringo's Guest House, I lay flattened on a grungy cot for five days, cramped and nauseous. In a crowded room lined with twenty cots, other backpackers with similar afflictions groaned, muttered, and farted; some curled into a fetal position like unwanted infants. As heat seeped into our airless, windowless room, we all lay near-nude on sweat-soaked sheets. I only left my bed to perch on the crooked seat of a leaky toilet.

Bloated and feverish, I decided to opt for relative comfort and share a two-bed room with a broken toilet and near-broken fan with a Brit broken by dysentery. This extroverted soccer fan, a fast-talking salesman back home, was planning a quick trip to the Taj Mahal before zipping back to London in time for World Cup soccer on the telly.

Miserable, I lay on my sweaty back, gazing at the spindly ceiling fan that wavered like the wings of a sick dragonfly. In the draining temperature, I fantasized about Canadian winters, inspired by the incongruous snowflake wallpaper, and wrote lyrics to my own composition *I Got the Diarrhea Blues*. Four months on the road had reduced me to a weakened heap, yet, I still secretly hoped to find a special kindred spirit in this mystical land. But how could I find love and the meaning of life from a toilet seat?

I decided to give the country a chance, like a first date that wasn't going well but still suggested a vague hint of promise. After a week of sickness, I ventured outdoors. Attempting to walk, my body fell into awkward jerks like a robot lurching on low batteries. After teetering down the dark guest-house stairs, I slowly opened the door into the absorbing oven sun of Delhi.

Urine-soaked street corners, exhaust fog, and the din of manic traffic swirled around me in multi-sensory overdrive. Turbaned autorickshaw drivers yelled and shoved at each other, waving fists. They were among the men who drove India's many motorized, three-wheeled cabs, usually head-on into traffic like a kamikaze golf cart. Men yanked at their crotches, gawking at me and clicking their tongues as if appraising a heifer at auction. Cars and crowds and cows and street peddlers and screeching horns jarred me into chaos. Child beggars, girls and boys, tugged at my clothes, pleading for coins. "*Baksheesh, baksheesh* (coins or a handout)," they cried.

* * *

I left the main-street cacophony and entered an alley, seeking somewhere to try and keep down my first meal in a week. I entered Vikram restaurant, a quiet, clean spot behind glass windows, and sat at the back, among a row of long, empty tables.

A short, meek man with dark glasses, who looked like an Arab version of Paul Simon, sat down beside me.

"I am an antiquities dealer," he said with a smile. "I am from Afghanistan. I have no money." His accent sounded like a weird cross between southern U. S. twang and high-class British English.

We shook hands. He pulled out a photo of a grim-looking, bearded man and told me: "He is my youngest brother. I have not seen him in ten years. I love my brother very much. I have no money." He raised his sunglasses to peer at me.

"I was a gems dealer in Kathmandu for six months," he said, "but now I work with a friend in town who owns a jewellery shop." I kept sipping delicious, freshly squeezed pineapple juice through a straw. "Would you like to visit his shop to look at some semi-precious stones?" He put away the photo in his shirt pocket.

"No thanks. I'm not into jewellery."

Undeterred, he reached into his jeans pocket and pulled out a small paper bundle the size of a chocolate bar. Delicately, he uncrinkled the white paper and laid out its contents: three pieces of broken green glass.

"These were once a whole jar, eighteen hundred years old," he said solemnly, "until I had a most misfortunate accident. It makes me very sad. I was bringing the jar to a museum here in New Delhi. The jar broke accidentally on a bus trip from Kathmandu. Now I have only these pieces."

He then went on to assure me: "They are still worth very, very much money. I will sell them to you for only one hundred and fifty dollars."

"Sorry, not interested."

He wanted to meet me that night at Nirula's, which offered Indian and western food. New Delhi's equivalent of a TGI Friday's, the restaurant can serve as a popular antidote to culture shock for western travellers. I had no plans to be there. The would-be sales-man left.

Throughout southeast Asia, I had heard outrageous tales from street hawkers and smooth talkers who saw any solo westerner, par-ticularly a woman, as a walking cash register or brash neon sign that blinked SUCKER, SUCKER, SUCKER. Today, I can see this wily salesperson with compassion. He was only trying to survive. But back then, a reluctant archaeologist, I was sifting through my own shards: family snippets of unwanted memory and strange dreams.

I never saw that gems dealer again, but on my eighth day in India, ended up at Nirula's after all. This time, I was with Mukesh, a handsome Brahmin with dimples and a moustache, who was five years younger than me. A salesman for an international courier com-pany, he looked fit under his fashionable shirt and tailored pants. His name was a variation of Shiva, he told me, a supreme god in Hinduism's holy trinity. An all-seeing deity, Shiva encompasses joy, creation, destruction, and transformation. (That's all.) I found out later that temple devotees can worship Shiva by giving offerings to a *lingam* or vertical, phallic-like cylinder. Was he trying to tell me something?

We had met at a photo exhibition in America House, Delhi's air-conditioned public centre and library, where I had retreated to avoid the heat. He had approached me with an explanation, in English, about a framed landscape photo that hung in front of me. At first, I ignored him. I knew that some Indian men sought to snag and marry a western woman, viewing her as their ticket to supposed wealth and escape. When he told me he was a salesman, I thought: *He's pitching me.* Has he got gems in his pocket? Yet, his nervousness seemed refreshing. After a bit of banter, I sensed an appealing play-fulness in him. His polite manner, with soft intonations and kind warmth, drew me in.

Within minutes, I was surprised to find myself discussing with this stranger topics ranging from dreams and the nature of the soul to the role of the family. I threw out a few remarks about male-fe-male relationships to discover his views in that area.

"I think that one of the main problems with the world is how women are treated," he said. *Maybe he thinks that's what you want to hear*, warned my inner cynic. Another part of me thought: *Hmmm. I like that.* A few minutes later, Mukesh remarked: "There is an inner child in all of us who needs love and understanding." *Hmm, I like that even more.*

After three hours of non-stop talk, our words and laughter flowed as if we had been friends for decades. We talked easily of divinity; the interconnectedness of life; feminism; the role of the arts in society; politics; living in the moment; cultural misconceptions; the ironies of life, and on and on. While we teased each other, I found myself repeatedly admiring Mukesh's insights and smarts. I had never felt such rapport so quickly with anyone.

His appreciation of life's ironies reminded me of my dad, who loved the satire of my childhood *Mad* magazines, chuckled at Giles' cartoons from Britain, and laughed heartily over Jim Unger's *Herman* character. Yet, beyond his inspired wit, I felt that Mukesh understood and valued my contemplative self and beliefs, something experienced with only one other man, my spiritual mentor in Vancouver. My heart was skipping into fantasy.

At Nirula's, Mukesh ordered two sets of *thali*, a selection of rice, veggies, *dahl* (lentils) and *naan* (flatbread), which came with curd on a circular steel tray with separate compartments. *Why couldn't I have ordered my own food?* We seemed to have slipped into couple mode too quickly. *Isn't that what you wanted?* barked my inner critic. *You're over-analyzing again.*

While Mukesh shared how much he disdained India's sprint towards materialism, middle-class Indian teenagers flirted and fluttered around us. This glossy, too-bright place seemed obscenely distant from the Indian ascetics and sidewalk peddlers in Delhi who spent hours squatting, unshaded, in relentless sun, selling trinkets, pens, and lock-and-key sets. Or from the barefoot child beggars who swarmed any tourist on the street, clamouring for coins.

Later that day, Mukesh and I rushed through town on his green, four-speed Bajaj scooter, my arms around his waist, his fingers caressing mine as we rode. Whooosh. I was a young girl again, released in the freedom of my dad's red MGA. This time, whizzing along with no helmet on, I tried to feel safe as we zipped through lanes of crazed traffic and brash honks while dodging, within centimetres, cars, buses, and autorickshaws. Statistics then pegged New Delhi as the most dangerous city in the world for road-users.

The bright evening sky was hiding a full moon. Knees tight against the scooter, I leaned against Mukesh's back, content yet still wary. A canopy of tall trees fanned us through an evening breeze as we rode past embassy row, the wide avenue of Shantipath. White mansions, tall gates, and high-walled grounds reinforced my sense of incongruous parallel worlds, where diplomats shared the same polluted air as homeless families with only a rusty scrap of bent tin as their portable roof.

We stopped at the sprawling green parkland southeast of downtown that surrounds India Gate, a looming, stone monument like Paris's Arc de Triomphe. Middle-class Indian families sprawled under willow trees, surrounded by ice cream vendors and balloon-sellers. Lovers strolled, hand-in-hand. As Mukesh and I sat closely together on the grass, he moved a few strands of hair from my face. Nervous and confused, I felt unable to relax. A desire for closeness jarred my usual detachment, yet I held back. Part of me wanted to avoid a kiss, another wanted to be held and loved. Lust lurked somewhere in between.

Indian women were staring at me; some of the men scowled. I had not yet learned a common misconception then: any white woman with an Indian man was likely a prostitute.

Mukesh seemed like a wind-up toy of sexual energy, his hormones overcharged batteries. I could feel his erection through our hugs. Yet, when we kissed, slowly, I found myself loosen. He was gentle and sweet.

Since Mukesh still lived with his parents, he invited me to the home of some friends for privacy. I trusted my intuition and the fluid, soothing energy between us.

When we arrived at a sparse apartment, Mukesh's three buddies gawked at me as if encountering their first extraterrestrial. In a nondescript living room—I remember bland walls and an oversized, square chair—we swapped polite introductions, then Mukesh and I wound up in a small bedroom on a characterless bed with a thin cover. I felt more at ease alone with him, but still unsettled. *Are his friends lurking outside the door? Is this a set-up for a sex video or gang rape?*

"Relax," Mukesh said, while playfully unbuttoning my shirt. I returned the favour. We kissed as a frantic voice inside me screamed: *What are you doing?* I insisted back: *I'm trying to have a good time. Go away.*

Mukesh was pawing at me, panting "I want you" under his breath. A corny turn-off. I was wearing only my bra and panties, he was in his briefs.

"Don't worry—I have protection," he replied. I first thought of bodyguards. No, he meant condoms. (Much later, someone told me that India was the world's top producer of condoms. Their biggest market? My home country, Canada.)

"I don't want to have sex," I told him. *Then what the hell are you doing lying on a bed in your underwear with a near-naked stranger? You're asking for it.*

Mukesh insisted.

"No," I replied.

His face dropped. "Is it because I'm Indian?"

"No!" I said, sitting up. "Even if you were green, I wouldn't care. I just feel like it's too fast."

"But I thought you felt the same way I did," he said, sitting up with a pout. "I wanted us to be one, to share this closeness. I feel so attracted to you. Aren't you attracted to me?"

"Yes, but—" I said nothing more. Mukesh got up, put on his pants, and left the room. *Oh no, he's gone to get his friends. They're going to rape me. What will I do?*

I was backed up against the wall when Mukesh opened the door. He laughed.

"What are you doing?" He had a beer in his hand. "Here, try some of this." He took a swig.

"No." I grabbed at my clothes, wondering if Mukesh would try to yank them from me.

He frowned. "Why do you always refuse me?"

"What?" I took a swipe at his clothes on the bed, thinking: *We've barely met and he's already saying "always"?*

"You assume that I'm going to do exactly what you want whenever you want? Were you planning to get me drunk and then try again? What happened to all of your talk about respect and understanding? I think you wanted me all along just for sex."

Mukesh hung his head, then looked up, his eyes teary.

"How can you say that?" he asked, his voice aquiver. "Please, please don't misunderstand me. I love you. Don't you see? I'm sorry. I got carried away."

Mukesh left the room. Minutes later, he had still not returned. I found out that he had left the house, leaving me with his friends. He didn't tell me he was going or say good-bye. They said that he had to pick up a friend at the airport. How could he just dump me like that?

I didn't even know what part of town this was. I should have been more cautious and careful, waiting longer before a sexual encounter. I could have agreed to meet him only in a public place.

Horrified and feeling marooned, I tried to assess the situation. Mukesh's friends did not seem aggressive; I wanted to trust them. By one-thirty a.m., two of the guys had gone to bed. One, round-faced and nerdish, remained in the living room, sitting in the large armchair. I sat down across from him. We chatted amiably about travel, jobs, and family. He told me how much he respected his mother; he even kept a framed photo of her over his bed. I relaxed.

"Can I kiss you?" he asked.

"No!"

He lunged at me, squeezing me into a tight embrace and soggy kiss. Grappling to get free, I tried to push him off. I couldn't move.

After a few interminable seconds, he released me. I slumped into the chair, wanting to run, but had nowhere to go except into Delhi darkness.

One of the guys offered me his bed, saying that he would sleep on the floor. I didn't trust him, but there seemed no alternative. Helplessly awake, I lay down on the bed. After an hour, this same man had crept onto the bed, inching closer to me. Uneasy, I moved to the floor.

The morning after my bedroom session with Mukesh, his friend, the one who had slithered onto the bed beside me, escorted me back to my guest house by autorickshaw as pink-gold dawn light crept onto the streets.

"I can give you tour of Delhi, as you like," he said with a sudden slobbery kiss. Yuck. My father had kissed me that way too.

"No," I snapped, "and when a woman says no, she means no." I stormed up the stairs of the guest house, feeling ready to retch.

* * *

Hours later, I was waiting downtown to catch a morning private bus to Manali, a forested oasis for trekkers in the Himalayas, a nineteen-hour bus ride north. I shoved Mukesh from my mind and reminded myself: Beware of strange men.

"Hayder. Hetter!" Someone who couldn't pronounce "th" was calling my name. I looked up, and saw Mukesh, in a sweat suit and sneakers, running towards me, grinning.

"I have been waiting for you since six-tertee. I came to fetch you at your guest house but you had gone."

He acted as if nothing had happened, as if everything was fine. In a moment, I slipped into childhood. *My father is grouchy and my mother won't let me see him and she says it's alright and I don't think it's alright and why doesn't dad want to see me? My mother gives me an "Everything's fine" smile like a satin dress slipped over a gash but something feels strange and no one can tell me why.*

"How could you abandon me like that?" I cried in a child's voice. "You're such a hypocrite. All your talk about respect. You just wanted to have sex with me and you leave me with your sleazy friends and I was so afraid it was like a nightmare and you—"

"Don't you think I know?" He clasped my hands in his, hung his head, and withdrew into silence. More silence. Lifting his head, Mukesh revealed tears. "I am so sorry. It was the evil inside me." He kneaded my hands with his fingers.

Don't get fooled again, barked my internal chaperone. *You can't trust him.* When the bus arrived, I hoisted my huge backpack and heavy day pack onto a rear seat, looking at Mukesh through the bus window. I wanted to trust him. He reached up through the window and gave my hand a squeeze. *Don't do it. He'll hurt you again.*

A deeper voice within assured me: *Don't let this man go.* His energy and our astounding ease with each other still drew me to him. Although it made little sense, I trusted that. We agreed to meet in Manali in several days.

* * *

Upon arrival in Manali, I rented an upstairs room in a slightly crumbly but cozy wooden house in the old part of town, surrounded by a forest of tall, feathery pines, a patch of apple trees, and the glacier-fed Beas River. A delightful middle-aged Dutch couple, Premgit and Rohit, had been living there for months. Seated on the warped front porch out of the rain, warmed by fresh mint tea, I listened to their Don Fagen jazz and other music. We shared lively travel stories around a rusty, decrepit wood stove.

At last, I could relish a connection to others who understood my journey. Slow down and still the mind. Meditate twice daily. Absorb nature.

Premgit and I bathed and washed our hair in the frigid river; the water felt like nails driven into my skull. As my numb red hands dunked more and more water over my head, I noticed several bare-chested Indian men in *dhotis* (loincloths) staring at us. They were squatted amidst trees in the forest across from us. "Probably taking a dump," Premgit said.

Ensconced with fellow travellers of a spiritual bent, I decided not to search for Mukesh while in Manali. If we ran into each other, fine; if we didn't, that would work too. Within a day or so, while coming out of a bakery with sugar cookies that I called "love substitutes," I saw his shining face across a crowded market area. As if in clichéd slow motion, but with no wind machine to array my hair suggestively, we approached each other with tentative steps and embraced with a restrained kiss.

Previously, some Indians had already openly scowled at us. Men had glared and sneered, even when we just walked together. Some had mistaken Mukesh for a tanned foreigner and insulted us in Hindi or Punjabi, both of which he understood. The nation frowned on any public demonstrations of affection between the sexes, from kisses to hand-holding. A Hindu man couldn't take off his shirt in public because such displays were deemed obscene. A public kiss between a white woman and an Indian man seemed a double no-no.

We were grateful, then, to head to the Naggar Castle Hotel, a former fort and Raja's (king's) headquarters south of Manali in the Kulu Valley in northern India's Himalayan foothills. We spent a euphoric few days, our first as lovers, at this sixteenth-century hotel of timber and stone, a haven for honeymooners. We fell easily into lazy comfort, spending much of our three-day visit in bed, sharing tales and making love. We laughed at our creaky bed springs within earshot of hotel guests having breakfast on the terrace. We slept little, losing our awareness of daylight or night hours. By day, the sun squeezed brightness through cracks around the door into our dim room. In early morning darkness, we snuggled on the terrace, blinking under mountain silhouettes and the timeless promise of stars.

A western male backpacker had reserved our room and was supposed to move in. But when he saw our mattress with the sheets nearly yanked off and our glowing smiles, he stayed in another room. Embarrassed but pleased, I felt relieved to keep the outside world, with its voyeurism and lechery, at bay.

Mukesh was the first man to beckon my heart into openness. His accepting caresses, tentative with inexperience, provided refuge for my wary trust.

When Mukesh and I dashed to catch our bus to Manali, Indian passengers scowled and uttered "tsks" as we sat side by side, holding hands. Once underway, I ignored their stares and focused on the mountain peaks and sky of cloudless blue. We passed fields of women, straddled calf-deep in rows of mud-soaked rice paddies, leggings hoisted to their knees to keep dry. An old shepherd with a grizzled chin and pillbox-style Kulu cap shooed his flock of goats forward, staff in hand. His other hand clasped the floppy legs of a baby goat, which rode, bleating, across his shoulders.

Once back in Manali, Mukesh had to head to New Delhi for work while I was returning to my forest sanctuary and newfound friends. We disregarded more glares of disapproval as we kissed good-bye, then he mounted the steps of the long-distance bus. Shoved tight against the window, he made a squashed-face imprint on the glass for fun, then waved at me. I watched his bobbing hand and grinning face get smaller and smaller until the bus disappeared behind a noxious puff of exhaust.

Standing alone in a crowd of curious Indians, I felt bereft, as if a dear, close friend had died unexpectedly. He wrote me later: "The day when I left Manali and kissed you goodbye, I felt so alone. In the bus (you won't believe this) I wept like a child. I miss you so much." I had never experienced this kind of emotional expression in my family. It seemed taboo.

CHAPTER FOUR

REMEMBERING

Our sense of worth, of well-being, even our sanity depends upon our remembering. But, alas, our sense of worth, our well-being, our sanity also depend upon our forgetting.
　—Joyce Appleby

AFTER THE SMOG, clatter, and frenetic traffic of New Delhi, soothing comfort came within the open vistas of Ladakh or "Little Tibet" in northern India and the welcoming acceptance of its people. The name Ladakh comes from the Tibetan term *La-Tags*, meaning "the land of the high mountain passes." This stunning territory, shared mostly by Buddhists and Muslims, lies in India's northernmost state of Jammu and Kashmir, north of Nepal. Tibet, which China refuses to acknowledge as an independent nation, shares Ladakh's border in the north.

As I wandered the streets of Leh, the capital, observing Ladakhis in their daily tasks, their welcoming grins prompted a sense of safety in me. The local men, in western-style clothes or brown gowns with thick, wrap-around belts of coarse cloth, did not pester me but often smiled, frequently with missing or capped teeth. They seemed to understand my desire for solitude. In this quiet sprawl of space, far from cities with twitchy men and lingering hands, hordes could not harass me. The slow, welcoming pace of these people strengthened my willingness just "to be" without any schedule or daily markers of an urban identity.

I admired the Ladakhi culture. Traditionally, the people had covered their basic needs without money, growing barley and raising yaks and other animals, and trading for salt with others outside the region. The area had opened to tourism for the first time in 1974; I visited sixteen years later.

Anyone could disappear in this desert vastness, a welcoming hug of space. Upon my arrival in Leh at the end of June, I could barely catch my breath from the altitude at 3,048 metres, even while walking on flat land. For the first two weeks of my six-week stay in the region, I felt winded after only minimal exertion and wanted to stop and rest. This forced me to slow down, to take more measured steps. The altitude gave me mild headaches and brief chest pains and kept me awake at night. But within a month, I felt more acclimatized and could walk easily for hours.

Ladakh invited me to breathe in visual richness and absorb intense weather. With little warning, the air could fill with hail or rain. Arcing in unison, farmers' scythes swept through barley in a flash of sun. The men's dark heads were barely visible over the blond grain tufts, their voices singing in a lilting, three-part cadence. Undulating in long swathes, tan heads of barley fields swayed as if mirroring the paint strokes of Van Gogh. Long rows of hoodoos tucked into hills, their shadow cavities laden with brown and orange like Georgia O'Keeffe landscapes. In early hours, skies fluctuated from brilliant stars to iridescent clouds and the glow of sunrise.

A storm. Stark desert. Seductive light at dusk. Embracing me like giant cupped hands, the area's silhouetted peaks offered daily reassurance, like the Coast Mountains back in Vancouver. A single look of sky and earth and mountains in this tough, tactile place made me ready to renounce my life in the West forever.

My body was remembering how Nature had proven my salvation in childhood. As a child in my suburban Toronto backyard, which had stretched above the unpredictable ways of Lake Ontario, I had watched sleek water rats, fat as marmots, slip across the grass. In the wind, under the whooshing backs of weighty maples, I saw pheasants, Canada geese, rabbits, swans, and little mice with ears that seemed too big for hearing. Laughing, I had laid on my back under blissful blue sky, rolled in grass, sniffed and scrunched dry leaves. Sea gulls squalled, squirrels hurried, robins rode invisible pogo sticks. Animals seemed to have no bedtime, no rules—just endless play. Parents weren't a part of this picture.

The sheer openness of the terrain in Ladakh invited me to surrender and stretch into expanded space, both within and outside myself, and loosen my body. Heidegger has said: "We make a space inside ourselves, so that being can speak." The more I allowed night skies to envelop me, and tiptoed through silent vastness inside me, the more I could feel myself give way to the seamless essence of Great Mystery or All That Is.

While meditating every day in Ladakh, indoors or out, often for an hour at a time, my western gung-ho priorities and desires began to fade into *laissez-faire* drifts of release. My breathing slowed down, introducing flickers of stillness. I sat in the lotus position, palms up on my knees, eyes closed. This inner focus allowed me to see the crazy dance of my "monkey mind": wild leaps of thought, judgments, and criticisms that I mistook for solid "reality." A subtle, vibrant energy of reassurance and deep peace seemed to flow through me here, a barefoot caress compared to my mind's usual boot print to the head.

Buddhists say that the ego must die before awareness begins. I wondered what still tethered me to my old, conditioned self. When any of us strip away our external identity and status markers (career, salary, home, car), what's left?

* * *

The part of me that sought spiritual healing and wholeness had found an ally in Mukesh. But I felt drawn to a second man in India who held unsettling similarities to my father. I saw clearly that he drank too much and surveyed tourist women to decide who to hit on. Such behaviour repelled me, yet I readily overlooked it.

I met Michael (not his real name), a tall, toned British mountain guide in his early forties, while trekking in dusty Markha Valley in Ladakh with a young couple from Canada's Northwest Territories.

This blond, pony-tailed maverick and his eight clients had been hiking back to Leh, returning from a nearby climb. Michael had been far ahead of the group, a lone figure on the horizon. I remember feeling an odd sense of knowingness when one of his clients explained who he was. "Of course, it's him," I thought. There was no logical explanation for this, especially since I had never heard of him. Yet, I felt certain that we were supposed to meet.

Soon, I had caught up with Michael and we agreed to hike together for the rest of the afternoon on a flat, open expanse of cracked, caked earth, under unforgiving sun. We left ahead of my companions and fell easily into talk about Nepal, Tibetans, writing and publishing, mysticism, spirituality, and our sense of affinity with the earth. We soon blended into a smooth, gliding gait across the chalky dryness, through a small canyon of boulders and vertical walls, and along a narrow river valley. We both took long strides simultaneously, finding balance and support on loose rocks, sometimes pivoting before finding a solid foot rest.

Michael had spoken with passion about climbing, sharing stories of his ascents of the tallest peaks in Asia and Europe. Then he had invited me on the Stok Kangri climb. The offer of adventure and challenge had dangled temptation. Michael's down-to-earth ruggedness and lone-wolf mystique were intoxicating. Besides, I found it difficult to ignore his strength and star-athlete physique. At forty-two, when many climbers consider themselves too old for this dangerous sport, he still felt firmly committed to, and inspired by, mountaineering. I eagerly fell into his enthusiasm.

Back in Leh and weeks before the climb, I had watched Michael repeatedly eye female backpackers at a guest house and heard his chortling stories of mountaintop trysts and nubile clients. His behaviour echoed the ribald jokes and comments my father made about well-endowed women. I did not want to become another notch on a bedpost for a global playboy, yet, here I was. Our encounter made me think of Red Riding Hood and the wolf, her basket of crumpets spoiled and scattered. However, I knowingly shared the wolf's path; I could not blame him.

Michael's attunement to wilderness, combined with his simple lifestyle, felt like a refreshing refuge. He had chosen a zeal for climbing over conformity and material gain. He was not saddled to a mortgage and had not lost his soul to a deadening corporate slot.

But Mukesh was waiting for me back in New Delhi, ready to meet me at the airport in two days. I would not be there. Having received no letters from him, I had convinced myself he was just a travel fling, an unrealistic pleasure impossible to continue on the long term. I had written in my journal: *He's too young ... the cultural gap is too great ... long-distance relationships don't work.*

Four days before our climb, I dreamt of a ten-year-old girl in her parents' home in Toronto, one of four siblings, like me. She stood, introverted and numb, in the garage. I prodded her with a long pole like a battering ram, as if to get her to react. She barely responded. In the dream, I felt compassion for her. Who was she and what did her presence mean?

For several days, we acclimatized and practiced ice-axe arrest. Despite a determination to keep Michael at bay, I succumbed to his advances the night before the climb. We wound up making love at base camp, inside his thick, expedition-style sleeping bag while wind slapped at his Eureka Wind River tent. That pre-climb evening, I was supposed to rest and get acclimatized. Instead, in quivering temperatures, we had both wriggled out of layers of thermal underwear, sweaters, and woollens. The thin air at high altitude made normal breathing a challenge. Our prolonged kisses and short, raspy inhalations made us sound like two lechers swapping an obscene phone call. Outside, the tent had felt ready for lift-off in thunderous winds; I wondered if the rocks Michael had placed inside each corner and on the roof would hold.

"I'm scared," I told him.

Surprised, he replied: "Of me?"

I could not explain my fear. Within minutes of our coupling, he was asleep and snoring. Plagued with self-criticism and guilt, I stayed awake for hours. Mukesh and I had made no agreement regarding fidelity, yet, our connection seemed to imply monogamy, at least to me.

Like my father, Michael was well-read with an insightful mind. He used comments identical to ones tossed out by my dad: something to the effect of "agree to disagree" and "If you can't be good, be lucky."

I easily recognized Michael's habit of seeking out alcohol, not resting until some was available, needing excessive amounts to feel tipsy, then imbibing to the point of slurred speech. Beyond my dad, this reminded me of two ex-boyfriends. Yet, I trusted and admired Michael's physical power and climbing expertise, having never met anyone as savvy and at ease in the mountains. Any mistake by a fellow climber can determine whether you live or die. Like my father, he had saved lives. I felt willing to risk my own with him.

We left with a Sherpa at about five a.m., by first daylight, while the snow was still crisp and less prone to avalanches. Our Tibetan cook Jangbu stayed back at base camp at 5,334 metres. After five hours of climbing through snow, rock, and ice, we reached the snow-graced summit. Through exhaustion and awe, I shuddered in the wind, grateful to sit down and rest. Imagining crevasses, dark and deep beneath me, I just wanted to sleep, but we still faced a 762-metre descent back to base camp that afternoon.

Only six weeks after I had left Mukesh in Manali, Michael and I were standing at roughly 6,096 metres on Stok Kangri, a Himalayan peak in Ladakh. He had guided our small climbing group—three clients, including me (all beginners), and two twenty-something U.S. friends of his—to this mountain summit on July 30. (Ten years earlier, I had done a short climb, my first, in the Canadian Rockies as part of an *Edmonton Journal* reporting assignment.) Wearing borrowed Vuarnet mountain glasses, I now squinted in the bright glare. My mammoth snow gloves, pulled on over mitts, made me think of my childhood days stuffed into a too-big, one-piece snowsuit.

"Before us, the sheer and jagged face of Kangri loomed in the afternoon sun, entirely covered with snow, and dazzling," writes Andrew Harvey in *A Journey in Ladakh*. This peak lay south of the Ladakhi capital of Leh.

I sat in snow at the highest place on earth I had ever been, my legs stretched before me. The rocky drop-off left me disoriented with no sense of distance; the way down seemed an infinite white blur. The surrounding rows of staggering white mountaintops, which appeared deceptively close, were multi-kilometres away. Vast cascades of immense clouds, gray and white, tumbled against blue sky like fluid acrobats.

Within this monumental expanse, the space that my body occupied seemed minute and inconsequential, like a forgotten prop at an extraordinary show. Strangely, feeling miniaturized within such seemingly unending space gave me a new sense of freedom and possibilities.

I wanted to swoon in a celebratory, windswept kiss with Michael, but he ignored me. I sensed that he was condemning me, silently, for my weakness at the end of the ascent. Wholly spent, due to lack of sleep and the altitude, I had felt as if I could barely advance. In response, Michael had periodically yanked on the rope around my waist, as if to give me added strength and pull me up. In his world of fierce self-sufficiency, this was akin to cheating or failure. On the way up, he had rebuked two of the male climbers for their slow pace and their decision, at times, to crawl on all fours; he derided them as "grandmothers."

On the summit, our group jostled to pose quickly for photos in our multi-layers of clothes, too exposed to penetrating wind. Our Sherpa helper smoked a cigarette and joked with Michael. I wriggled my toes, wanting to ensure that they had not become inanimate slabs. A Buddhist saying proposes: "When in doubt about where you are meant to be, look down at your feet." I had worried about frostbite on this climb since poor circulation due to Raynaud's disease (constricted blood vessels), even in summer, keeps my feet cold or numb. While dressing for the climb, up at four A. M. in the dark and almost-freezing temperatures, the sane part of my brain had screamed: *What are you doing? You hate the cold and getting up early. Are you nuts? Go back to bed.* Instead, I had pulled on two layers of thick socks and calf-high, rented boots, rigid and shaped like downhill ski boots.

Like almost all climbed Himalayan mountains, the summit we

climbed bore a mound of *mani* (prayer) stones, which contained carved mantras like the Tibetan Buddhist *Om mani padme hum.* ("Praise be to the jewel at the heart of the lotus," which refers to the eternal, divine essence as a gem within our concrete world.) Many Tibetans leave these chiselled prayers as offerings to the gods, testament to their respect for mountaintops as sacred places. Here and across India, they freely practice their religious devotion as refugees, ever since the Chinese government invaded their native land between 1949 and 1951. In Tibet itself, now overtaken by China, such public signs of Buddhism can result in arrest, imprisonment, torture, and death.

Amidst invasion and hardship, many Tibetans had found peace and solace in spirit and nature. I admired their resilience. Since Tibet's invasion by the Chinese, the Dalai Lama has fervently promoted nonviolence, compassion, and forgiveness towards them.

Next to the cairn of stones, between two raised sticks, a row of small, white rectangles on a vertical string flapped in the wind like thin, worn hankies. These tattered Tibetan flags release prayers to the gods and elements, surrendering human will and desire to a greater force. I still had not done this within myself.

I knew that spending time with Michael was reactivating unsavoury aspects of my dad. It was easy to feel disdain for this Brit's frequent drunkenness, yet our shared alcohol-fuelled camaraderie, combined with Michael's emotional distance, felt comfortably familiar. I needed to feel some notion of home, however misguided that atmosphere might have been. If I drank with Michael, I didn't have to feel. With detached sex, I could still feel in control. Wanting to move beyond relationships that relied on destructive habits, I felt disappointed in myself.

On the way down, Michael told us firmly: "Stay focused." He wanted us to walk straight down, feet forward, instead of sidestepping, but I would lose balance and slide on my crampons. For almost the last hour of the two-and-a-half-hour descent, I "skated" down through mushy snow. Drained and lifeless, I was the last person to return to base camp.

That night, after our descent, Michael and I made love again in his tent at base camp, next to a dwindling fire. Once more, he soon fell asleep, snoring. I dreamt. *The room where Elizabeth Barrett Browning wrote: "How do I love thee? Let me count the ways" is crumbling. The stone walls have fallen.*

* * *

"If you don't root yourself more in your body, you're going to die," Michael told me. He figured that a bus would flatten me or I'd fall off a mountain if I didn't pay more attention to my feet. In Ladakh, I was slowly re-remembering how to inhabit my body, what some call "the felt sense." I was reclaiming my physical presence, not only through the climb, but by treading over precarious rocks during treks, hiking in extreme weather, meditating outdoors, and spending time with a man devoted to athletic prowess. As if for the first time, I truly recognized and accepted my body as something that responds directly to my inner and outer environments.

Slowly, I was discovering mindfulness: the practice of bringing attentive awareness to any moment rather than having it rush by, unacknowledged. The more I tapped into this relaxing state, the more I could attune to how feelings revealed themselves in my body through sensations. This, in turn, would enable me to be more responsive to others. This process of checking in with myself, something I had never done while with my father, would allow me to better know how I *truly* felt about a person or situation, rather than letting my mind decide.

* * *

Until I was about nine, my dad and I had a routine. After dinner, with the family still seated at the table, I would crawl onto his lap, and we would "go into our act," as he called it. Encasing me in his arms, my father would stroke my arms and head, sometimes with exaggerated humour and gesture. He never did this with any of my sisters—only me. Beaming, I felt loved and special, inside a safe hollow.

I am on my dad's lap at one end of the dinner table, after a meal. My mother sits at the opposite end, my sisters on either side. I feel something moving under me—my father is getting an erection.

"It feels like a snake," I say. "What have you got in your pocket?"

I try to reach into my dad's pocket, but he stops me.

He must be hiding something for me to find. My mom stares back, my three sisters look blank. No one says anything. My oldest sister Nancy, a teenager, rolls her eyes and exclaims: "Oh, Heather!"

After this incident, my father no longer invited me onto his lap. I didn't understand what had happened or this rejection. Nancy's shock stayed with me to adulthood.

As an adult, one memory of my dad and me remained ingrained, although it had always felt more dream-like than true. Reluctant to give it more credence, it now began to loom with greater significance.

Dad and I are playing on my parents' bed. I feel something move inside his pants. It goes up and down, like a lollipop, and we laugh about it. I like this game, having fun with my father. I sense that my mother is standing just outside the room, watching and waiting. She comes into the room and gently asks me to leave. She wants to talk to my dad.

I wanted to keep playing with my father and didn't understand why my mom had asked me to leave. This felt like punishment for having fun. It seemed to have more to do with my dad than me.

I wanted to believe in an innocent childhood like the lyrics that Shirley Temple sang in *On the Good Ship Lollipop*. I remember my mother's kindness during this exchange; she was not angry at me. I can't recall if I later pestered her to tell me what she wanted to talk to my father about, but that's likely. She would not have responded. I wonder now: How much did she know?

Family photos show my dad and mom in their student years in the 1940s—they met at the University of Toronto—lounging with friends during summers in the cottage country of Bala, Ontario. Their smiles and relaxed poses seem the epitome of carefree leisure. In these images, my beaming mom, with long blonde hair and lipstick, saddle shoes, and pleated skirt, looks ever so much the forties calendar girl.

Raised in a Presbyterian home on a dairy farm in Woodstock, Ont., my mom was close to her dad, a warm-hearted man with a dimple in his chin and kindness in his eyes. He was killed in a car crash, three years before my birth. She was left to grieve this loss mostly on her own, with little emotional support from my father. Her stern, stoic mom had died about ten years earlier.

My mother never lost her innate sense of connection to the natural world. When I was a teen, she gave me a copy of *Gift from the Sea* by Anne Morrow Lindbergh and Thoreau's *Walden*, saying: "You're probably old enough for this now." She read aloud the autobiography of Helen Keller, who made touch a primary form of "seeing" and her understanding of the outside world. My mother knew the names of many birds, able to identify their calls. While growing up, she had a pet crow that liked to ride on her shoulder, and a pet raccoon, which liked to ride on her head. In her sense of harmony with nature, she was a Taoist, although she would never have used that term.

My mother helped me to overcome any fear of indoor spiders by scooping each one in her hand and releasing it outdoors while saying: "They're more afraid of you than you are of them." She introduced me to *Charlotte's Web*, *Stuart Little*, and *The Wind in the Willows*, strengthening my desire to make acquaintances with wild creatures. This sense of connectedness later spilled into my spirituality, reinforcing nature as a source of wonder, an indefinable force of energy, a dance of the divine.

A pacifist, my mom admired the Christian, nonviolent stance of Leo Tolstoy and stayed annoyed at my dad's fascination with war books and movies.

She excelled in domestic skills and baked delicious pies, cookies, and healthy meals with few spices. The *Joy of Cooking, Canada's Food Guide*, and some thick, hardcover etiquette book were her authoritative references. She knew the proper way to fold towels and linens and the corners of bed sheets and could arrange flowers in admirable ways that seemed to whisper: "Please take a photo of me." My mother tried to pass on the folding abilities to me, a reluctant disciple, and even talked about creating a hope chest to prepare me for my seemingly inevitable role as a bride. (Thankfully, after leaving home at seventeen, I heard nothing more about such a chest.)

Since my dad was frequently away at the hospital or a convention—he often worked six days a week—he seemed exotic compared to my familiar, ever-present mom. He hired, trained, and entertained people from around the world. Every day brought him some new challenge to his professional skills or intellect. As a kid, I wanted to live in an exciting realm like his, not in my mother's drudgery.

My mom sometimes travelled with my father to medical conventions. At a conference in Chicago, she wrote her four daughters in October 1960 with characteristic self-deprecation: "I am sitting in the hotel lobby waiting for a lecture to start. This is a special one for the [doctors'] wives. It is on how to bring up your children! Guess if I learn something, Heather at least may benefit!" I was not quite two.

When my sister Nancy was about age ten through sixteen (I was one through five), my mother would cry at the dinner table, roughly twice a year, while my father was eating. "She would get depressed and sob on his shoulder," Nancy recalls, "saying that she works so hard and no one appreciates her." Our dad would continue eating, not comforting her. My sister Wendy says, "Dad would have no sympathy at all. His attitude was 'Buck up and carry on.'"

But one common area my parents shared was their Protestant faith. Both expected my sisters and me to attend our local United Church regularly. Both kept Bibles at home. My mother had received a Bible as a child for perfect attendance at Sunday school. She was horrified when I told her, as a teenager, that I did not want to get confirmed in the church and refused to take the preparatory classes for this.

My sister Mary Ann said: "Dad was very kind, very generous, and very spiritual. He taught Sunday school for many years, fascinated by Saint Paul and the holy land. He stepped out and helped a lot of people."

Yet, within me, I could not excise my dad's DNA, which bore the sacred, profane, and all points in between. As Anais Nin wrote of her father in *Incest*: "I had the essence of his blood in my body."

* * *

While in India, I felt annoyed that unwanted tidbits—dreams, memories, and body sensations that evoked my dad—continued to taunt me, seemingly with a life of their own. *Go away!* I wanted to holler. *You're messing up my life.* I was still denying sexual memories of my dad and me, not wanting more to appear. I needed to open up to them gradually, much like a climber when acclimatizing. Like ascending to a higher altitude by day, then resting lower down by night, I began to inhabit my body at different levels.

I was doing the same with Mukesh and Michael. Michael symbolized my habit of staying guarded and detached. Mukesh represented a more open-hearted way, but this still felt too risky and vulnerable. I had allowed Mukesh's nurturing care to flow into me for short periods until it proved too much, exceeding my comfort level of intimacy. I could then "rest" with Michael. Too much intimacy too fast caused me to suffer the emotional equivalent of altitude sickness.

I laughed at this irony of compartmentalizing Michael and Mukesh, like my father had done with me. Having planned to stay celibate on my Asia trip, I now wanted Michael to let his feelings out, yet I held in mine. He responded with silence and retreat, just like my father. When Michael hinted at joining me later in Canada, I rejected the possibility.

I wonder now how I managed this yo-yoing of relationships, hearts on a string, a quest for love hidden in the palm of my hand. Before meeting Michael, I had craved sexual contact, tired of travelling solo or accompanying loving couples on excursions, always the odd one out. After five months on the road, away from Canada, I missed the rapport of shared slang and quirky cultural references. The dream of a deeper connection with a man still kept me fumbling towards some notion of true intimacy.

After our climb, Michael and I continued a relationship of sorts in Ladakh, sharing a guest house bed and informal get-togethers with other travellers. One night, while performing fellatio on him, I felt deeply rattled. A strange sensation of déjà vu, a tactile body knowingness that felt weirdly familiar but unknown, overcame me. I had never experienced this before during this sexual act. What did it mean?

CHAPTER FIVE

ASSAULT

To be alive is to be vulnerable.
—**Madeleine L'Engle**

SLIDING AND FALLING through mud and downpour, I was cold, tired, and drenched. In early August, a week after our climb, Michael and I were trekking for eight hours on steep unmarked shepherds' paths in the mountains of Kashmir Valley, west of Ladakh. Water squelched through my socks and boots as I skidded on tall grass and slippery rocks. At the occasional boulder-shrouded stream, we forged through numbing, glacier-fed current. At one spot, to traverse a surging river, I had to inch through slowly, supported by Michael and a rope; otherwise, I would likely have been swept away.

I had envisioned this as a rugged, romantic holiday but instead, Michael had invited along at the last minute, without consulting me, thirty-something Carol (not her real name) from Vermont. We had met her at a guest house in Ladakh and knew little about this quiet woman with cropped, sandy hair. She looked like someone who would opt for a Sunday stroll in a park rather than a demanding trek.

We had planned to venture out for almost a week's hike in northern India from the village of Panikar to Gulol Gali pass at about 4,450 metres. But several washouts had forced us to change our route. Upon our night arrival in Panikar, we learned of yet another washout east of us, which further thwarted our plans. We consulted our soggy map and discussed contingencies. After considering our time limitations, food availability, and access to firewood, we decided to head southwest.

We soon came across a family encampment, where a pair of men's shoes with pointed, curled-up toes lay outside a canvas tent. Several mottled, scrawny dogs, which appeared half-wild, barked menacingly at our arrival and came charging towards us. As they snapped and growled, I braced myself for an attack, but a grizzled-faced woman called to them and they retreated. She peered from behind a tent flap and beckoned us inside with a smile. In our condition, such an offer felt like an exotic kiss at an oasis. We tucked inside onto a floor that I remember as heaped with baskets, thin blankets, a few dented pots, and perhaps a trunk. I had never felt so grateful for shelter.

We piled under scratchy blankets and drank plastic cups of bitter dark tea, offered from a bent metal kettle. This woman, whose hard-life wrinkles could have made her anywhere from forty to sixty, was knotting a rope basket. She hunched over a square, open-weave pattern, with her two sons, about eight and twenty-something, respectively, on either side, holding an opposite end. They helped her tie the rows, which looked rough and uneven. For reference, she hauled out a uniformly tied basket as a model and studied it. I marvelled at a family working so cooperatively together. I assumed their dialogue was Urdu, one of India's national languages that incorporates Persian and Arabic, although it could have been Ladakhi. The woman, who laughed and smiled frequently, seemed full of punch.

Outside the tent, the dogs barked through darkness with determined fervour. We went outside and tried to put up our pathetic, soaked tent fly in beating wind. (To keep our loads light, we had decided to forego carrying an entire tent and just take the fly.)

"Whose idea was this anyway?" I muttered. Michael glared at me.

"I can't keep my balance," Carol said. "I'm getting dizzy." We found out that she had had brain surgery only a few months earlier. Michael rolled his eyes at me, as if to say: "How did we get stuck with her?" On this trip, he had disdained both Carol and me as "lambs on the interstate"; since we didn't match his speed and agility, he treated us like bumbling children who hampered his progress, like how my dad had complained about us kids in his diary.

On this trek, Michael distanced himself from me completely. Nothing more than a peck on the lips suggested we had ever been intimate. Forlorn and rejected, I felt as if back with my father: one minute, his special focus, the next, an intrusion. While hiking, it had proven impossible to keep both Michael and Carol within sight. She lagged too far behind while Michael disappeared way ahead with fast, nimble steps. He sometimes timed how long it took him to get between two points, nearly sprinting across rocks.

As we wondered how we would sleep in the cold and wind and if the dogs would get us, the Muslim mother gestured to us. This time, she invited us into the family's smoky stone hut, a roughly three-metre-square space pieced together from piles of large, uneven slabs. Two vertical poles supported the heavy, flat stones that overlapped to form the ceiling. We huddled in the corner next to a fire, under layers of worn blankets. The bearded father arrived and squatted beside the fire next to his family. I envision him now in patched, thick wool pants, although I can't remember what he wore. The family of four laughed and smiled with each other, sipping tea noisily from bowls. The youngest son sang along to folk music on a plastic, portable radio. The BBC news came on, reporting Iraq's invasion of Kuwait, a dissonant reminder of the world beyond our isolation.

Outside, the dogs still bellowed, sounding half-starved and demonic. Their snarls and growls got closer, making me think of the murderous Great Dane in the 1959 movie version of Conan Doyle's *The Hound of the Baskervilles*. The footprints of the terrified female victim-to-be, fleeing from the ever-approaching beast, left only a partial imprint, made by her arched toes.

I snuggled under the wool blankets next to Michael, with Carol lying close by on his other side. I put my arm around him but he didn't respond. The two sons were sleeping under blankets on the floor at the opposite end of the hut, their parents nearby.

Hours later, in a half-awake stupor, I felt something brush lightly around my thighs and crotch. Disoriented, my sleepy mind wondered: Are chickens pecking at me? Is it Michael? The touch stopped and I started to fall back asleep. I rolled over, winding the blankets around me. Minutes later, a hand crept under the layers of blankets and onto my buttock. In the darkness, I couldn't tell who it was or where his body was, but it wasn't Michael.

"You fucking asshole," I yelled, groping for some body part to hit. I found what I thought was a shoulder and squeezed it tightly. I heard a grunt and slight cry. Message delivered. I shook Michael.

"One of these guys grabbed me." Michael did not move. I lay motionless. Within a few minutes, slippery sounds emerged from the corner, then a satisfied sigh. Whoever it was had jerked off. I lay awake for hours, disgusted in the darkness.

When we awoke the next morning, only the mother remained in the hut. I told Michael and Carol what had happened; Carol provided words of comfort. Earlier, around a campfire, she had shared matter-of-factly that her father, a doctor, had thrown her mom, an alcoholic, down the stairs. Alarmed, I listened, fuelled by a silent sense of kinship.

"I'm surprised that you're surprised," Michael told me. "I thought that something like this might happen."

"Then why didn't you do something? You could have at least slept on the outside."

"You're naïve to expect anything else," he said. "What other chance will this guy have to touch a western woman?" Michael implied that he would likely have tried the same thing in that guy's shoes. His words stunned me.

Michael's exposure to suffering did not translate into empathy for my experience. He had seen death in the mountains; he was no stranger to that kind of trauma. He had lost friends to Everest and other peaks. He had described the grisly task of searching for victims after an avalanche and finding body parts, likening the force of impact to getting hit by a freight train. I had tried to get Michael to open up and share the emotional impact such events must have had on him, as I had attempted with my father.

Michael showed me an essay he had started writing about a Sherpa friend who died while on a climb with him. Noticing a weak spot in the rope, he had tied a knot in it as a visual warning. The Sherpa, thinking this was a glitch, had untied it. The rope had broken, sending the Sherpa hurtling down a Himalayan face. Michael had remained with the man until he died, then helped remove his body. Later, he met with the man's widow. Unable to imagine his sense of guilt, I had offered comfort as best I could.

Michael had witnessed a friend's grief following the climbing death of her partner, someone he had known well and liked. He seemed reluctant to elaborate on how he dealt with such feelings on a climb. As with my dad's life-and-death work crises, feelings during tragedy on a peak seemed irrelevant—even foolhardy. But perhaps like me, both men were just unwilling or unable to excavate and articulate their anguish.

Many months later, upon my return to Canada, Michael's lack of empathy regarding my assault still rankled. Although we had had no contact, I wrote him a letter, sharing how abandoned and disappointed I had felt in that mountain hut. "If anything similar happens in the future when you're with a woman, give her loving care and support," I told him, not expecting an answer.

Within a few weeks, Michael replied. To my surprise, he apologized, leaving me heartened and relieved.

More than a month after the trek with Carol, Michael and I reunited at the YMCA in New Delhi. I had released my anger at him for his previous lack of support. Our shared times now seemed more open, our intimacy more tangible, yet, we rarely talked about the future. What did he really think of me? While my dad and I had travelled in Asia, he had said to me, "I don't know what you think of me as a father ..." I had said nothing.

Michael told me that I weighted my outlook too heavily towards spirituality, clinging to childhood pain and family angst. "You could purge it all if you really wanted to and replace it with something else," he said. I cried at his response, seeking solace alone, in the bathroom. Michael made no effort to comfort me; his responses, like my father's, ranged from cold and unreceptive to tender and attentive. He gave me his philosophy: "Get on with life, live it to its fullest, and have fun."

Why was I even contemplating anything more than a fling with Michael? I think now that I was trying to reinvent a new version of my dad through him. My spiritual mentor had said that in my state of questing and uncertainty, wanting a committed, intimate love with a man was like expecting to compete in the Olympics without any training. I was still stuck in little league.

I wrote in my journal: *Now it seems as if neither Michael nor Mukesh are what I need or want. Everything is a mystery because I still don't know who I am.* Only weeks earlier, I had written about Mukesh: *I can easily see us sharing a life together. I would be a fool to let him out of my life.*

About six weeks after the trek, in early October, Michael and I reconnected in Nepal, where I had left him, still asleep, to catch an early bus from Kathmandu to Delhi. Within a week of my departure, he wrote me, disgruntled that I had not woken him to say farewell. I did not think that he cared since we had made no plans to continue our togetherness. Watching his prone form in slumber and releasing him in silence had seemed like an act of respectful surrender. After lounging on a houseboat on Dal Lake under political curfew in Srinagar, Kashmir, amidst crickets and an evening blast of rocket launchers from rebel separatists, we had both chosen diverging paths.

* * *

By that time, men in India had repeatedly groped or pinched me in urban crowds; I didn't know if it would be my breast or back or buttock. A hiking guide had tried to fondle my crotch. Some men had spat or hissed at me while others repeatedly propositioned me. In New Delhi, a pre-teen boy jumped onto the outside of my train, reached in through the window and cupped my breast with his hand, then jumped off in glee, as if on a dare. In some Indian cities, a male stranger would approach me and ask inappropriate questions in English about orgasm or foreplay or suggest what he could try with me. I had even received two earnest marriage proposals from strangers in India. One official-looking gent, in uniform, tried to charge me just to walk through the bustling train station in Bombay! Women-only spaces at some train stations, known as "ladies waiting rooms," were a welcome haven away from gawking male eyes and frequent pestering. Females could relax, smile at each other, and keep the heat at bay.

Yet, even with some women in India, I could not escape stereotyping. Months later, in the state of Sikkim in northeastern India, a female receptionist at a hotel mistook me for a prostitute, even though I wore a long, bulky wool sweater and hiking boots with a scruffy backpack. A proud local resident, a civic official, had toured me around Gangtok, the capital, and suggested better accommodations than the dark, low-cost guest house I was in. When we appeared at the counter of his recommended hotel to enquire about room availability, the receptionist looked at this dignified, middle-aged Indian man, then at me, and assumed that we just wanted a quickie. Even though she apologized, her assumption offended both of us. When I walked alone at dusk in Gangtok, men spat at me and treated me as if I was topless and flaunting myself, even though I wore a thick sweater, hiking boots, and long pants.

Male strangers in India sometimes introduced themselves and asked if I would pose for a quick photo with them and their friends. A few seconds of chit-chat, arms around each other, smiles, laughs, and it was over. Some confided they would pass me off as their girlfriend to their friends. At first, I felt flattered to oblige in these innocent encounters and enjoyed friendly banter. But soon, feeling used, I refused. They seemed to have little interest in who I was beyond some projected status associated with my westernness or white skin. I gained an inkling of what Hollywood stars must face as strangers and paparazzi swarm them for their commodity value, not their unique humanness.

Upon my return to Canada, I shared my complaints with a woman of colour, who responded, "Now you know what it's like to experience racism." My grievances were indeed a product of privilege; for most of my life, my white skin had served as a protective cloak.

While in Khajuraho, as the only visitor at the town's archaeological museum, I soon became the focus of the lone middle-aged male employee, who gave me a free guided tour. Throughout his spiel in English, he stared at my breasts and continuously flicked the fringe of his scarf. He pointed to some of the museum's statues of contorted couples and explained the difference between right-sided and left-sided sex. (I think it had something to do with the woman's leg action.) He suggested that certain positions would be uncomfortable for the female. Why was I listening to this? Wedded at fifteen through an arranged marriage, he lamented his union, yet, invited me to dine at his home and meet his wife. I refused.

"Women in India consider their husband a god," he told me. I laughed. When I mentioned that I taught writing, he seemed pleased. "Teachers are revered as gods in India," he said. I didn't laugh.

While travelling for six months in Latin America, I had encountered similar harassment (grabbed on the street, groped in buses, victim of obscene comments and gestures) but had never faced it as continually and for so long. None of it seemed dangerous, yet its accumulative effect over seven months left me feeling worn and raw. To my shock, a feminist writer told me decades later that I needed to "take responsibility" for my choices in India. She gave an example from her own travels: somewhere in Europe, a man had offered her a boat ride to get to her destination. After she accepted, he assaulted her. Her conclusion: she should not have gotten into that boat alone with him.

I take responsibility for choosing to walk city streets in India and remain in the country for many months. Were my friendly smiles construed as come-ons? Probably. Yet, I'm tired of accepting assaults as a "normal" part of solo travel for single women. Female victims are told to adjust their behaviour; what about demanding that the men who harass and assault change theirs? Even some educated female feminists have implied that these assaults must have been the result of my own actions. One friend suggested that I just laugh off the men's pestering or turn it into a joke. I tried that, but after months of daily harassment, responding to such behaviour brought me frazzled frustration and anger.

In a Facebook post in recent years, a twenty-something, red-headed female described the harassment she endured while travelling solo in India. A number of women responded, implying that because they had not had similar experiences in India, it must have been something she was doing. Incredulous, I immediately posted words to support her, sharing that I had suffered the same treatment. While I was in India, one backpacker had recommended that I dye my red hair black to avoid undue male attention in India. Perhaps the rarity of our hair colour (only four per cent of people in North America are redheads) made us more unwitting victims in India. I would like to hear from other redheads on this subject.

I tried my best to comply with my Lonely Planet guide's advice to women travellers in India: "Keep your upper arms, chest and back covered because these areas are, for some reason, considered erotic." The guide book also stated: "Getting involved in inane conversations with men is also considered a turn-on." There must be far more aroused males in the world than I thought.

While in India, I did not dress suggestively nor seek out one-night stands. Yet, the child part of my brain, which sought my dad's validation, still seemed to equate sex with feeling wanted and loved. This push-pull conflict—find me attractive but don't get too close—kept me separated from the true essence of myself and others. Rejecting this part of me as less than or shameful, I projected these characteristics onto others. My friend David Roche says in *The Church of 80% Sincerity*:

> *I do believe that we each have a place inside of us where fear resides, that fear of being unworthy, a sinner, carrying bad karma, untouchable. Seeing and accepting one's "flawed" condition is a core spiritual experience, an essential step in developing emotional maturity. It is a basic human task, the*

*task of redemption, and it is hard work. There is no turning
aside. If we ignore this soul retrieval work, we remain
fragmented and powerless, vulnerable to fear, addiction and the
metaphor of victimhood. Because that place of fear is where
predators and manipulators of all sorts—sexual, financial,
religious, political, warmongering —come to feed. And that is
where cruelty is born—in fear of not being acceptable, worthy,
valued and loved.*

What joy I denied myself in the moment, preferring to cling to a
preconceived notion of someone or something rather than open up
to all of who they, and I, are or aren't. My either-or thinking brought
life's complexities to a narrow head, threatening to register my responses and beliefs as solid truths, rather than mere possibilities.
Such quick summaries of experience appeared to make events more
manageable, but they created unnecessary distance from others.

I was trying to bring forth aspects of *ahimsa*, a greater Love that
connects me through my heart to all. Nonviolence or *ahimsa*
(Sanskrit "a" for "not" and "himsa" (violence)) encompasses the ab-
sence of violence both in gross forms, such as physical violence,
harsh words or feelings, and in subtle ones, such as violent thoughts.
Yogi Amrit Desai says of *ahimsa*: "It is not something we have to
acquire; it is always present and only needs to be uncovered. When
one practices *ahimsa*, or nonviolence, one refrains from causing distress—in thought, word or deed—to any living creature, including
oneself." Mahatma Gandhi espoused *ahimsa* as a way of life.

Yet, as he preached celibacy, even in marriage, Gandhi slept with
young girls in his sixties and with his nineteen-year-old grand-niece
in his seventies, receiving daily naked massages and shared baths.
He wrote and spoke often of his sexual urges. Did his actions cause
distress or shame for these females? They resulted in emotional and
psychological trauma for the girls and women used in what he called
his "experiments," says Indian activist Rita Banerji, author of *Sex
and Power: Defining History, Shaping Societies*. Her research has revealed that most of these women, in their late teens or early twenties,

became depressed and wept without restraint. Several documents described their mental state as "psychotic" as they appeared to be completely under Gandhi's control. She believes that his so-called celibacy likely focused solely on control of ejaculation, as per the traditional, historic form of Indian celibacy. Otherwise, everything else was permitted. These "experiments" continued at Gandhi's ashram for the last ten years of his life, says Banerji, and led to the departure of some in his closest inner circle.

His associate Nirmal Kumar Bose, for example, wrote a letter to another close Gandhi colleague on March 16, 1947, stating: "I would not tempt myself like that and more than that, my respect for [women] would prevent me from treating her as an instrument in my experiment." R. P. Parasuram, Gandhi's personal secretary and typist, idolized the Mahatma and lived at his spiritual leader's ashram to help with India's freedom movement. But he left after two years of working with Gandhi due to his distress at seeing how his guru behaved with women and girls in the ashram. Parasuram wrote a sixteen-page "letter of indictment" to Gandhi, saying that he could no longer remain silent about this issue. He wrote, in part, "After coming here I must confess to having lost a portion of the respect I had for you. You are the Father of our Nation. You have taken us so far along the path of freedom and independence ... I object to your sleeping in the same bed with members of the opposite sex." Some accused Gandhi of hypocrisy since he demanded celibacy of everyone who lived at his ashram, including his married son, stating that even touching one another was not acceptable.

As happens so frequently with high-profile leaders, such unseemly information does not appear in official biographies, films or school texts. Socially and culturally, we prefer the Hero myth, not wanting to sully an admired man's stature by highlighting his darkness. Did Gandhi tell these women, especially his own grand-niece, that being selected to participate in his experiments was a privileged task? With incest, that's part of what creates such wrenching inner conflict: a victim is made to feel "special" although she (usually, it's a she) is wholly used and objectified. As with my father, my learning of Gandhi's actions and attitudes towards women made him another tarnished hero for me. The Mahatma's views reflected familiar patriarchal outlooks: when some men were caught sexually harassing women at his ashram, the females were accused of tempting the males and he thought they should cut off their long hair as a preventative measure. When it came to rape, Gandhi thought that female victims should consider killing themselves since they no longer held any value.

While in India, I still specialized in severe criticism and rejection, both of myself and others: my own inner form of assault. The term "assault," commonly used in the climbing world to describe an attempt to summit, implies the conquering and subjugation of a mountain, rather than respect and opening into oneness with it—like the difference between rape and making love.

I was still at war with myself. "Every day, at the moment when things get edgy, we can just ask ourselves: 'Am I going to practice peace, or am I going to war?'" noted Tibetan Buddhist teacher Pema Chodron says.

I realize now that *ahimsa* is available in any instant, if I am willing to shift perspective. It's like a reverse negative of an old black-and-white photograph: what's white in reality appears black on an image and vice-versa. In changing perception, I can visually shift white space, like the silhouette drawings used in psychology: one can choose to see either a goblet or two faces, two realities in one. Love or fear. Peace or conflict. Attraction or repulsion. Oneness or separateness. Yet, life has so many gradations and contradictions beyond simple polarities.

Throughout childhood, I had grown accustomed to assuming that men wanted something sexual from me, that their perspective translated to my self-worth. As a kid growing up in Toronto, I had discovered that smiling at a male stranger could be interpreted as flirtation. I learned to avoid eye contact. At school, a male teacher in grade seven looked me up and down and said: "Gee, I wish I was ten years younger." This prompted a blush. Someone admired and appreciated me, I thought.

When I walked home from school as a child along busy Lakeshore Boulevard, cars would sometimes honk or stop. Male drivers would ask me if I wanted a ride. One man pulled up in a sleek convertible, his arm slung across the back of the seat. He invited me to go for a spin. Wanting to deter him, I walked into the yard of the nearest house, as if it was home. But even after I knocked on the door and a woman answered, he did not drive away immediately.

At about age eleven, when I stopped at a gas station to put air in my bicycle tires, a male driver came over and deliberately overinflated one of my tires until it burst. He offered to drive me home. I refused and told the gas station attendant. The man drove off. Around the same time, when a boy at school dragged me down, pulled up my top and exposed my naked chest, smearing it with snow, I felt helpless and violated. When I told my mother, she laughed.

I reminded myself: *You have to save yourself because no one else will.*

Babysitting at thirteen for a conservative, church-going couple in my neighbourhood, I was shocked to find, while looking in a drawer for a pen, a copy of *The Happy Hooker*. Once, while I was dancing with the husband of this couple at a church function, he squeezed me too tightly to his chest and held me there, my still-undecided breasts pushing against him. He frequently winked at me, as if we were sharing a secret code that I had no desire to crack.

As a kid, I told myself: *Don't trust men. Always assume that they have ulterior motives.* But I didn't think of my dad in those terms.

Chapter Six

SHAMED

Shame corrodes the very part of us that believes we are capable of change.
—Brené Brown

I STOOD UNDER the white marble dome inside the Taj Mahal's main antechamber. These white, seventeenth-century walls, inset with flower-shaped, semi-precious stones and carved with bas-relief roses and irises, spoke of Moghul glory and Muslim rulers long gone.

It was the afternoon of a full-moon night in early September 1990. I was with Mukesh, three months after we had first met. I had told him about Michael and let him read my journal. Amazingly, he had accepted this temporary liaison with another man as part of my emotional process.

Mukesh chanted a low, strong tone of Aum (Om). Reverberating inside me, the deep, vibratory note filled the air above us. Its soaring sound brought me tranquil joy, as if a petal, aloft in the sky, was drifting down towards me on a soft pocket of air. The building felt laden with lost voices and distant whispers ready to be heard and released, if only one would listen.

We stood next to the white marble tomb of Moghul emperor Shah Jahan and his "favourite" wife Mumtaz Mahal, who died in childbirth after bearing fourteen children. *I'm surprised she lasted that long,* I thought. This exquisite Taj Mahal, called "a monument to eternal love" by one poet, stands in honour of Mahal; her grieving widower commissioned it in 1632 as her mausoleum.

Mukesh and I walked in slow circles on the marble floor, a sweep of whiteness and shadow. It felt cool to my bare feet. As clumps of tourists surrounded us, their presence felt like hazy wisps that could disappear with a swish of a hand. A male employee, short and fragile-looking, stood by the tomb surrounded by rows of tiny candles. He held out a delicate white lily blossom for me as a silent gift, prompting a minimal donation. Again and again, I inhaled the flower's subtle lemony scent, opening to its sensory caress. Then a crowd of raucous tourists entered. The room's mystique disappeared; it became a mere claustrophobic hall, packed with sightseers.

With my lily blossom in hand, I escaped with Mukesh onto the back terrace that overlooked the Yamuna River, swallowed into a glorious near-sunset of deepening red-orange. We splashed barefoot through puddles from afternoon rain that filled the large array of square tiles in alternating black and white. We laughed and chased each other, king and queen on a giant chessboard in a game with no rules, stepping into wetness, admiring reflections, walking on clouds and patches of sky.

We lay down on the vast checkered floor and lost ourselves in quiet, in whispers and laughter, in the unending stretch of sky, in the emerald green parrots with turquoise tail feathers that swooped and dipped above us. Shadows stretched and splayed around us as pink clouds deepened into red, swelling against the sky's saturated blueness. Reds reflected in the river, drifting into patterns of orange within minutes. The now-wilted blossom in my hand still smelled fresh.

We were experiencing this bliss far removed from Mukesh's family—or so I thought. While in Agra, we met briefly with his aunt and some female cousins, who welcomed me warmly, in English. But neither of his parents had met me. His mother, a traditional Hindu, was horrified that he was travelling unchaperoned with an older, white woman. She sobbed when he told her about me; he was bringing shame to the family. I discovered that his father had called Mukesh's aunt and asked her to track us down in Agra. His dad feared that I was an international heroin smuggler intent on kidnapping his son and luring him to the West, ready to turn him into a junkie; he based this opinion on a British television program he had seen. I could only laugh and shake my head when Mukesh told me this. I felt like Biblical Eve, unjustifiably maligned.

Slated for an arranged marriage, Mukesh wanted to leave his native country and flee his parents' influence and yet, he said: "This is India, honey. In my culture, it is a disgrace to go against your father's wishes. I cannot disobey him. I owe my parents so much." We had talked about marrying once we were in Canada together. I wondered repeatedly how my life would unfold if I stayed in his country, married to an Indian man and living with him and his parents, forever the outsider.

After our visit to the Taj Mahal, Mukesh's male cousin located us in our hotel and talked hurriedly to Mukesh in Hindi. Mukesh said he had to return to Delhi right away. He gave no explanation, other than his family needed him. Dejected, I left to go back to the city by train on my own, on what was meant to be our romantic evening together.

Earlier, when Mukesh and I had tried to get an autorickshaw ride from the Agra train station to the Taj Mahal, the driver had shaken his head "No" with a figure-eight gesture of nodding, a familiar trait across India. He and Mukesh exchanged a barrage of words in Hindi and the driver waved his elbows at us like dried wishbones, ready to snap.

"What's he saying?" I had prodded. Other autorickshaw drivers, hungry for a fare, had paced around us. With clicks of their tongue, they gave me lurid looks as I glared back. Mukesh didn't want to answer, but I insisted.

"He told me, 'I wouldn't fuck her' and then he said he couldn't give us a ride because he'd get in trouble. He's not allowed to give rides to prostitutes." I had stared, dumbfounded, at Mukesh, then at the driver. Shocked, yet not wholly surprised, I felt tainted, like a stinky fish carcass rotting in the sun.

Nevertheless, my visit to the Taj Mahal felt like an indirect path to my dad's heart. When telling me of his first sight of this magnificent structure, he had softened his voice to a church-like whisper.

Without articulating how or why, it had clearly moved him; he kept a miniature replica of it in his den. Now I shared the same reverence. When first seeing the Taj, I felt my eyes get wet and wanted to cry, but didn't know why.

* * *

During a family vacation, my three sisters and I pick wild raspberries somewhere on a country road in the States with steep hills. My parents, seated in the car, drive away.

Still small, I watch the car disappear while sobbing. They're gone for good!

Minutes stretch out for too long. I stare at the road. No car.

Finally, the vehicle returns.

My sister Wendy, who was ten when this happened, tells me now, "Dad said: 'I'm leaving.' He was so mad he made mom get in the car. Mom cried. He wanted to move on, do five hundred miles a day, come hell or high water. They drove off. How cruel and unusual is that? You were four or five, sobbing your eyes out. I thought he had abandoned us. I remember being terrified."

I've always loved to pick raspberries, wild ones as a child and those on droopy branches in my garden today. Tender lush redness. Juicy delight. Fingers stained red.

"Raspberry" is slang for the fart sound someone makes when they put their tongue between lips and blow. This can be done on another's bare skin, usually on a stomach, creating a tickling sensation for the "victim."

My dad liked to tickle my feet and try to tickle my waist. Although giggling and savouring his attention, I did not like his intrusive clothespin pinch. Despite my requests to stop, he continued. Only when my mother asked did he comply.

My dad liked to watch Cher on TV on *The Sonny and Cher Show,* eagerly absorbing her skimpy costumes and exposed flesh. He joked that Ursula Andress's last name was "Undress." He never hesitated to remark on a woman's outfit that he found sexy. Compared to the daring décolletage on television, my mother seemed too wholesome and demure.

I saw what power these visuals held for my father and wanted to dress to have him find me attractive. I learned to judge my worth through sexual allure, never knowing which role my father would seek out with me. Would he pretend I was his mistress, treat me like a daughter or do hidden things with me, like the copy of *The Joy of Sex* he kept reversed on his office shelf, so the title wasn't visible?

When my dad and I, as a teenager, watched Friday late-night "baby blue movies" on television together in Toronto, in which nude or semi-nude adults cavorted in what amounted to soft porn, I wasn't sure how to react. Inclusion in such odd closeness made me feel mature and special, part of cherished intimacy. Yet, I knew that Mom would not approve. I was the only one in the family to share these programs with our so-busy father.

My dad was like an adolescent who wanted to tell bawdy stories and get away with naughty things. His attitudes towards women seemed frozen at puberty. As he had done with me, India had pushed sex underground. However, making sex off-limits in any society raises the stakes of its allure. In a culture that represses instincts, "a mind/body split, and power, avarice, infantilism and lust" dominate, says Robert Stein in *Incest and Human Love*.

When I was six, my mom moved my sister Wendy to the basement, where my sisters Mary Ann and Nancy's bedrooms were; she wanted to use Wendy's bedroom as a guest room. That left me as the only daughter upstairs, just down the hall from my parents' bedroom: an easy reach for my father.

Not until age fifty-one, in the same year my father died, did I access a memory about that guest room. In an exercise as part of a 2010 workshop called *The Journey Within*, I chose to delve into my subconscious to the deepest level I was willing to access. A spontaneous image appeared that I had never seen. My dad and I, a child, were sitting on the edge of the bed in the guest room, a pull-out couch. He was stroking my genitals and saying: "Doesn't that feel good?" I was clothed but not wearing underwear.

Oddly, a sense of love flowed through this visual for me. Later, a therapist said she thought his words were grooming me for more such interactions; my dad was suggesting how I should feel, rather than allowing me my own responses. Sexual predators test their child victims through "grooming," trying to find out what level of bodily contact or intrusion a young one will find acceptable.

At age ten, I liked to lounge around the house in white go-go boots and paisley bell-bottomed pajamas, a gift from my favourite aunt, feeling the embodiment of "cool"—a chic hippy chick. (It was 1969, after all.) Two years later, I was the only daughter living at home.

As a pubescent teen longing for breasts, I remembered poring over my dad's *Playboy* magazines, bug-eyed over the glossy photos of nude, buxom women. Some of the publication's cartoons featured a granny with a droopy, wizened bosom, visible under see-through baby-doll pajamas. These images captivated me like a foreign culture, so distant from the world in which I lived. They held no resemblance to my body. I don't recall feeling envy or disgust—only fascination over an unreal domain that my father visited through these pages.

How did these depictions help determine how he viewed and treated me?

As a kid, I relished the cozy camaraderie shared with my dad. It felt flattering to know that I was his eager listener, not prudish like my mom. During my teen years, a thread of sexual innuendo in his jokes or comments was never far away. He warned me, as a teenager, that drive-ins were "passion pits." He said that paintings by Georgia O'Keeffe, whom I admired, were erotic depictions of female genitalia. Although these tips belied my own perceptions, I trusted that he held more authority in such matters.

My mother had no language or sensibility for sex or anything related to it. During my puberty, she handed me a book called *Love and the Facts of Life,* and said: "Read this." The cover showed a blonde-haired woman with a polka-dotted headband and red finger-nails leaning her head on the shoulder of a preppy-looking man. Her eyes, shrouded in mascara, looked catatonic. That book, with chapters on subjects like "What's the harm in petting?" formed a quirky, clinical foundation to my understanding of the opposite sex.

Today, I keep it on my book shelf as an anachronistic souvenir—without hiding the title on the spine.

* * *

For me, the word "shame," so popular in therapeutic circles, evoked a child in a corner wearing a dunce cap, or A.A. Milne's woe-is-me Eeyore. I did not see myself that way. About three years before arriving in India, I remember declaring to my spiritual mentor, "*I* don't feel any shame." Yet, as a sexualized creature both in India and my father's eyes, how was I to show up, in womanhood, to myself and others?

I found India, in 1990, a nation of simmering sexuality. Despite a *Kama Sutra* heritage of tantra and healthy sensuality, the country's films faced heavy censorship, showing no kisses or physical intimacy between lovers. Instead, male audience members were left to fanta-size over covered, jiggling breasts in simpering dance sequences or the revealing wet sari of a female star, plastered to her pert nipples when she just happened to find herself lounging under a waterfall. Such indirect titillation stunned me. A billboard in Delhi showed the profile of a couple about to kiss; a black censor's band covered the spot where the lips almost touched. (In typical colonialist fash-ion, Christian missionaries during India's early British rule forcibly removed any lingam pendant worn by an Indian attending a Sunday sermon.)

India's official repression of sexual desire made a redhead like me—a rare, freckled "freak"—a blank film screen on which Indian men could project their sexual frustrations and fantasies. In my family, I had served as a private, small-screen option for my dad; in India, I symbolized a Jumbotron of possibilities.

In Indian culture then, "Eve-teasing"—pinching or groping a woman in public—appeared acceptable. (This was well before the Internet and satellite TV invaded the nation with sex-obsessed language and images.) Contraband porn videos and bootlegged copies of books such as Nancy Friday's *My Secret Garden*, a ground-breaking account of women's sexual fantasies published in the early 1970s, also proliferated. This led far too many Indian men to believe that a western woman like me was highly adept at lovemaking, would talk eagerly to any stranger about intimate matters in any public place, and wanted sex anywhere, any time. The sexualized comments directed at me were cruder than my father's words but felt similar. They were getting to me.

Although outside India's caste system, whose roots go back to 1000 and 1500 BCE, I felt like an open, borderless zone. Too often, it seemed as if I was wearing an invisible sign that read: "Please touch me. I'm free and available and anxious to have sex with you." In India then, white skin symbolized both sex and status. "If skin is white, it is love at first sight," is an ancient proverb in the nation, according to Australian author Sarah Macdonald, who lived there. Billboards in Bombay offered "return to fairness" skin-lightening cream while New Delhi newspaper ads, placed by Indian parents seeking a marital partner for a daughter, mentioned her light skin as a bonus feature.

Travelling acquaintances in India told me this story: an African-American friend of theirs from New York had volunteered with Mother Teresa in Calcutta, driven by a desire to tend to the poor and sick. He soon discovered that a number of Indians, including those who had lost all use of their limbs, refused to let him touch them because he was black, and therefore, in their eyes, low caste. They viewed him below a *Dalit*, India's lowest caste, formerly called "an untouchable."

As a privileged westerner, at least I had the resources to leave India, unlike many young girls in this nation enslaved in brothels in Bombay or sold to circuses by their families. Or those innocents blinded or disfigured after having acid splashed on their face as punishment for defying their family. Others were raped, then rejected by their village for bringing shame upon themselves and their family. Pre-pubescent females were forced into marriage with men, even relatives, decades older than themselves.

More than two-thirds of married women in India, between ages fifteen and forty-nine, have been raped, beaten or forced to have sex. In 1990–91, a husband in India could legally rape his wife without penalty if she was fifteen or older. One backpacker told me that a western friend of his, who visited Rishikesh the previous summer with her daughter, was raped twice. Most countries have one-hundred-and-five women for every hundred males; India has less than ninety-three, due to female infanticide and abortion.

Traditionally, girls in India have held little value. The year I visited, 1990, was India's Year of the Girl Child, reaffirming the value of daughters. In India, female infanticide was and remains common practice. Newborn girls are often aborted, undernourished or murdered because the country's dowry system makes daughters an unaffordable financial burden. One custom at birth has been to lay the infant on a table with her head hanging off the edge until she dies; this gets reported as a stillborn.

My father had mentioned his four daughters only occasionally in his short-lived journal, often irritated that because of us, he could not get any work done at home on Saturdays. He complained about having to babysit. At one point, he referred to our house as "the feline den." When, at age seven, I tried to move my dolls and dollhouse into his home office, he wrote: "Typical feminine takeover bids for use without responsibility."

Later, I explored how my experiences with my dad and men in India compared to those of Indian women. One-fifth of marriages in India occurred between uncles and nieces while a third were between first cousins, according to William Saletan, a slate.com science writer, in April 2008. A 1999 report revealed that almost three-quarters of upper- and middle-class women in India were abused by a family member. Seventy-six per cent of respondents to a survey by the Indian foundation RAHI (Recovering and Healing from Incest), said that they had been abused as children; 40 per cent of these incidents were by a family member. Even by 2011, a rape occurred in India every twenty minutes; nearly one in three involved a victim under age eighteen. But by then, young girls in the country were fighting back, taking their dad, grandfather or other perpetrators to court. Laws were changing to protect them. A bold sign of resilience.

Rema Rajeshwari, a female superintendent of police in India's southern state of Telangana, says that it took the much-publicized case of Jyoti Singh, the New Delhi female who died after a brutal gang rape on a bus in 2012, to empower Indian women to speak out about sex crimes. Before that, talking about such crimes, sex or even appearing as a female at a rural Indian police station was taboo, she told Canadian Broadcasting Corporation's *The Current*. In 2017, more Indian women felt brave enough to go to the authorities about such crimes; the number of reported rapes increased by 12.4 per cent, she said.

In fact, after Rajeshwari helped launch "She Teams" in Telangana —groups of specially trained officers who gather evidence to arrest men who are harassing women on the street—they registered 800 cases in their first six months. Eve-teasing was not considered a crime until recently, says Rajeshwari. But enforcement alone isn't good enough, she adds. In her view, it will take a sense of shared social responsibility, including educating boys to respect a female, before slow-to-change sexist attitudes will evolve in India. (I agree. In Chapter Twenty, I address the effectiveness of North America's "Be more than a bystander" approach with programs such as Mentors in Violence Prevention.) Patriarchal views remain entrenched in India and elsewhere. For example, the *Indian Express* reported that National Commission for Women member Chandramukhi Devi said in 2021 that a fatal gang rape of a 50-year-old woman in Uttar Pradesh's Badaun district would not have happened if the victim had not been out unaccompanied at night.

I felt thankful to learn that in May 2012, India's parliament passed the Protection of Children Against Sexual Offences Act, the country's first comprehensive law in this area. This means that a child, no longer treated on par with an adult case, can file a complaint directly. The burden of proof is now on the accused, not the alleged victim. Although these regulations are in response to rampant child trafficking in India, they will hopefully have important repercussions in sexual abuse both within, and beyond, families.

For example, in December 2019, a leading Indian politician, Kuldeep Singh Sengar, was sentenced to life imprisonment for raping a teenager and fined 2.5 million rupees ($35,000 US). Convicted under the Protection of Children Against Sexual Offences bill, he was expelled from the nation's ruling Bharatiya Janata Party. At the time of this writing, he is expected to appeal. Yet, data from India's National Crime Record Bureau revealed a 22-per-cent increase in child sexual abuse cases between 2017 and 2018.

Meanwhile, During the COVID-19 pandemic, child marriages in India increased and related distress calls to a helpline rose 17 per cent from 2019 to 2020, reports the British Broadcasting Corporation. India has the most number of child brides of any nation in the world, according to UNICEF.

I am heartened to learn that one Indian village, at least, has found a healthy way to reinforce the value of females. Piplantri celebrates the birth of every girl in this Rajasthani community by planting one hundred and eleven fruit trees in her honour. Since 2007, they have planted almost a quarter of a million trees. Villagers and each girl's parents pool their money (the rough equivalent of $380 US) to deposit in a bank account created for each newborn female. The parents must sign an affidavit promising that they will not marry off their daughter before the legal age, will send her to school regularly, and tend the trees planted in her name.

CHAPTER SEVEN

FAMILY

If you cannot get rid of the family skeleton, you may as well make it dance.
—**George Bernard Shaw**

UNDER DRAINING SUN, I stood before sandstone tableaux of naked, sculptured bodies, some in coitus, which appeared on long, outdoor panels. They stretched across walls next to erotic sandstone temples in Khajuraho, a UNESCO (United Nations Educational, Scientific and Cultural Organization) World Heritage site in north-central India.

I was travelling alone again. Mukesh was back in Delhi, working. It was almost two-and-a-half months after we had visited the Taj.

These suggestive sandstone images from the ninth and twelfth centuries were not designed for family viewing. In passionate contortions, lithe and graceful celestial maidens, nymphs in solo rapture, and couples (*mithunas*), even foursomes, embrace, one leg lifted or a partner's toes tucked in arched discreetness. Skyward, hands float in fluid stillness or deliver feather touches. These sandstone women have perfect, rotund breasts, sprays of carved jewellery encircling necks, chests, arms or wrists. Some consort with an elephant trunk or play a flute with a chaste smile. To summarize such provocative frivolity, a local museum guide used charming understatement: "The art of Khajuraho represented by the sculptures ... revels in admiring the charms of the human body from the most fascinating angles."

Mukesh had told me these sculptures were meant to reignite

passions after medieval birth rates dipped too low. But any notion of a declining birth rate in India seemed ludicrous to me: the country had 844 million people in 1991.

Beyond their cultural and historic value, I had sought out these beautifully sculpted scenes to tap into some notion of sacred sensuality, something beyond the clamouring of lustful boyfriends, sweaty Indian men, and the urges of my father. This Hindu and Jain art reaffirmed sex as a path to integrated purity, a union with not only another, but a divine whole. Like pop-up pages from a *Kama Sutra* text, the carved scenes and serene female smiles in Khajuraho's temples reminded me that intimacy can be a tantric playground of deep, fulfilling love.

It was challenging to think of my body in tantric terms, as a path to *moksha* (salvation) or the soul's true nature. I saw these sculptured maidens far differently than how my 1987 Lonely Planet guide book described them: "They pout and pose for all the world like Playboy models posing for the camera." Yuck.

While viewing the temples, I ignored remarks from men like "Want to make like statues?" I wondered how my father would have responded to these images. He'd likely have made some chauvinistic wisecrack, perhaps even jokingly caressing one of the figure's breasts with his hands. (Decades later, I discovered that incest was an accepted social norm at the beginning of India's Vedic period, starting c. 1700 BC. Vedic hymns frequently had references to incestuous relationships between siblings while father-daughter unions were allowed.) "The father's sexual privilege over the daughter was regarded as an ordained aspect of the sacred order till quite late in the Vedic age," Rita Banerji says in *Sex and Power*.

"Dad had a very earthy, crude side," my sister Mary Ann says. "Mom was elegant. She had the class. She was the one with her feet on the ground." (That makes me think of some tongue-in-cheek art I saw in Vermont, which said: "Men are from Jersey City, women are from Paris.") My sister Wendy adds: "He had a coarse side that I didn't like. He liked raunchy things, which always surprised and disappointed me. At the dinner table, he'd tell an off-colour joke and there'd be an awkward feeling around the table. He seemed disappointed that we weren't more fun. It got worse when he was drunk."

In my family household, sex was hardly an inspired path. My sister Nancy remembers our mother wearing an old, thick-wool, plaid housecoat around the house. Around age sixteen, Nancy read a magazine article by psychologist Joyce Brothers, which said, as she recalls: "If you wear something like that, you don't care about sex or don't care about him."

Around the same time, my dad told Nancy: "The main reason why men get married is for sex." When Nancy was a teenager and I was about six, he gave our mom some slinky underwear for Christmas: bikini panties and a top in bright-red lace. My mother returned them. "That's not her style at all," Nancy says. "What does that tell her about what he thinks of her? He felt deprived. He's not happy." Was it my mother's job, exhausted from cooking, primary child care, and housekeeping, to play sexpot?

Nancy recalls my dad giving our mom a book with a title like *Real Women*. I'm guessing that it was Marabel Morgan's 1975 best-seller *The Total Woman*, with the subtitle "How to make your marriage come alive." I was sixteen. My father gave me a copy of this book years later, knowing full well that its message would infuriate my feminist sensibilities. Rooted in evangelical Christianity, it re-affirms that the husband is boss, and a wife should follow his leadership. Morgan writes: "It's only when a woman surrenders her life to her husband, reveres and worships him and is willing to serve him, that she becomes really beautiful to him." Nancy says: "That's what he wanted out of the relationship. He didn't want to be challenged." Morgan recommends in the book: Greet your husband in the front door, dressed only in Saran wrap.

My mother preferred to use Saran for sandwiches and felt no need to match my father's daring spirit. As consolation, he tried to live out his desire for adventure with me. Nancy remembers her saying: "I want to stay quietly at home." Equality was not a part of their marriage. "It was a ninety-per-cent/ten-per-cent relationship," Nancy says. "She (our mother) was kind of eclipsed." In the words of Mary

Ann, who's eight years older than me: "She was insecure and passive. Women of that generation couldn't cope with living life on their own terms. You had to put up with almost anything." Wendy, born five years before me, comments: "She was in her own prison."

In Khajuraho, I had difficulty reconciling sculptures of females as beloved, revered souls with India's mistreatment of real-life women. It surprised me that erotic images, including acts of bestiality, were available for public viewing in such a censorship-ridden nation. I struggled to integrate the gulf between India's modern sexual repression and its liberal art history. How did the nation's ancient culture, rooted in sensual sensibilities, which viewed female forms in mystical texts as enlightened *yoginis* (yoga practitioners) and *tantrikas* (followers of *tantra*), as embodiments of the sacred feminine, end up treating women so poorly and emerging with such rigid, gender-defined inhibitions?

My own family bore the same dissonance. How did my father ignore cultural morals and decide to use and demean me for his own needs? In *Born Liars: Why We Can't Live Without Deceit*, Ian Leslie contends that the more accomplished you are, the more you lie to yourself about who you are or aren't. He cites a survey of champion swimmers: those who won the most races were the best at self-deception.

Did my dad's status and privilege make it easier to use his own child for sexual gratification? Like celebrities cocooned by wealth and others' deference, some part of him was used to getting what he wanted. Research shows that people's power and status are key factors in how they accept their own amoral behaviour. Due to their sense of self-aggrandizement, powerful people can justify more easily than others their own straying from a moral or legal code. Such were the results of a 2009 experiment, led by psychologist Adam Galinsky at Northwestern University's Kellogg School of Management. One need only think of Harvey Weinstein and Jeffrey Epstein…

Gene Abel, a psychiatrist who has extensively studied unreported sex offenders, says that such people have a "very disruptive" slice of behaviour, but otherwise can lead stable lives. They appear no different than anyone else, except that they can't control one aspect of their conduct.

Our family certainly mirrored the larger blindness of our culture: Uphold the hero (or celebrity) myth at all costs. Disregard abusive behaviour in favour of applauding and benefiting from someone's talent or success.

Decades after my time in India, a dream fragment came to me: *An infant in sleepers, I stand up in my crib, my small hands clutching the top of its horizontal wooden frame. My father stares at me from less than two metres away. I become him, looking at the child me, thinking his thoughts: Kill her—I don't want her.* I woke up from this, appalled. My dad never intended to kill me literally, but I could understand the sentiment. *Not another daughter.*

Family photo #4: At age seven, I stand against our white picket fence, all a-grin with bangs cut straight and even. I'm posing with my three sisters for our annual family Christmas card photo in the winter of 1966. In the summer, my dad usually posed us in a row on a backyard picnic bench. While my siblings, in blazers, sat with demure smiles and straight backs, skirt-clad knees together, I normally slouched at the edge of the bench, squinting into the sun with a scrunched-up nose, wearing too-big, hand-me-down pants. A mischievous tomboy, I refused to wear a skirt, looking more like some neighborhood misfit who happened to sneak into the shot, teetering away from the trim trio, rather than someone who belonged.

After three daughters, my dad had wanted a son; I was his last hope. For years after my birth, he would say with a tease: "When little Alan (his namesake) comes along …" I remember how strange that made me feel, as if I was a mere consolation prize. My sister Wendy recalls our father joking that his first grandson would inherit everything.

For much of my childhood, I felt like someone burdened with a mistaken identity, like Cary Grant in *North by Northwest*. By age seven, sure that my parents had adopted me, I pestered them to tell me the truth of my origins. Surely, I was not meant to grow up in such a family.

Married at twenty-three and the sole breadwinner for a wife and four kids by age thirty-four, my father would likely have preferred to remain a bachelor much longer. He alluded to his college years as the best of his life. In his diary, which he kept when I believe the incest began, he referred to a Quebec fishing trip with male colleagues as "one of the most wonderful weekends of my whole life."

The few times my dad mentions my mom in the diary, it is mostly to say things like "nagging incessantly" or "harassed by Marian." In February 1964, when I was five, he wrote: "Marian complained bitterly of total lack of attention Friday night and too loud and too high." Clearly, he was not seeking solace with his wife. He told my sister Wendy, when she was a teenager, that he was considering divorce. Wendy believes that my mother did not want more than two children, that she and I, the two youngest, were an effort to give my dad a son.

If marriage and family were such a burden for my father, and his duties at work so overwhelming, I see how he could search for "an outlet," as he later termed it. My role. But many, if not most, dads who feel overtaxed by family and job stress don't end up molesting their children.

* * *

Later, I wound up in the Khajuraho home of Dilip, a poor teen artist and his family: small upstairs rooms in a shared complex of crude bricks and plaster. With a gentle voice, simple English, and light-flash smile, he unrolled watercolour paintings on large sheets of beige silk, some as big as a single bed. With meticulous detail, created with a fine-haired brush and hand-ground colours, the scenes depicted Krishna, the blue, flute-playing Hindu god of love, rows of decorated elephants, and romantic scenes of couples nestling in the woods. I felt in awe of the patience and finesse required to complete these images.

"My father and I do painting together," he explained, indicating the floral frames he painted and the figures that his dad drew. "We like to leave the animals' eyes for last." The specialty of his dad, a jokester with a handlebar moustache, was miniatures. "Will you please check the quality of detail?" Dilip handed me a magnifying glass and I inspected the minute, painstaking brush strokes. He showed me the paintings that took a day to complete, and the huge ones, as big as a double bed, which required a month or more. Before showing me traditional erotic paintings of couples in coitus, he warned me and asked permission; I appreciated this respect. His fee was staggeringly cheap: fifty rupees a day (about three US dollars) for labour and twenty rupees ($1.20) or so for supplies. I wanted to buy several of his paintings, but had mostly travellers' checks with little cash left.

"It's okay," Dilip said, "you send me the money from Delhi." Admiring his trust, I bought a painting of decorated elephants, in profile, marching in a line, and a miniature done by Dilip's father. It showed a naked woman with flowing hair on a riverbank whose outstretched hand reached for a message from a dove. I imagined it as a love letter. Dilip's mother, tall and delicate, stood in the doorway in a stunning pink sari, backlit by the sun, a striking tropical lily. She beckoned me towards a small photo album, poring over photos of smiling travellers who had visited their home.

"You are our friend," Dilip's sister said, beaming at me behind dimples and long, dark hair. "We have many friends in the west. Western people, very, very nice people."

Dilip's mother slipped a toe ring onto each of my feet, onto the toe next to my big toe: a common accessory for married women in India. Was she suggesting something? Yikes. Dilip looked like he was no more than thirteen. She smiled and laughed, then gave me a pair of small, bright earrings, expecting nothing in return.

We ate lunch outside on the stone floor. Dilip's mother squatted and rolled out dough for *chappatis*, lying them as flat circles over a small fire. The deadly-hot curry chili sauce with cauliflower made my eyes water with explosion. Unwilling to mar their hospitality, I tried not to show my discomfort. Dilip's mom gave me a sweet fudge-like dessert to cool the taste.

"You like?" she asked. The whole family watched me, waiting for my answer. When I nodded "yes," their faces popped with smiles. I felt moved by their warmth and generosity, admiring their affection-ate closeness. They laughed frequently, lovingly teasing one another.

I absorbed this easy-going family with tremendous gratitude. At our dinner table, my mother chided anyone who raised a voice. No elbows allowed on the stylish place mats. No slaps on the back or guf-faws. No squirming on the plastic-covered seats. Conversation rare-ly strayed from intellectual topics. Politics leaned to conservatism. We ate everything on a polished walnut table, an heirloom that my mother treated like a one-of-a-kind museum piece. Besides any drops spilled, the worst thing you could do was push a plate across its surface, risking a scratch. Folded napkins and silverware were placed to line up visually with thick maroon glasses. When com-pany visited, we used sterling silver candelabra and fancy cutlery kept in a velvet-lined case. My mother considered it gauche to use your knife to take a slab of butter directly from the butter dish. No, indeed. We had to use the specially appointed silver butter knife. My friend Persephone told me that as a child, she was afraid to eat at our house since she might use the "wrong" fork for a certain course.

Image is everything. Keep smiling and keep quiet.

"I feel honoured to be here with you all," I told Dilip's family, softened by their kindness and spontaneous joy. Later that night, we dined under the stars on the same stone floor. Dilip's sister sifted rice through a wide, circular pan of cross-weaved bamboo, and cut vege-tables. We ate potatoes and rice with cauliflower and sweet *samosas* with a honey-like syrup. I sensed that the family had bought the latter, a splurge for their meagre budget, expressly for me as a treat.

Their heartfelt openness made the term "rich" seem vastly rela-tive. I was raised in privilege, yet, my family implied affection rath-er than directly expressed it. With Dilip's family, I felt part of their caring glow, wholly valued and heard.

Dilip rode me back to my hotel on his bicycle under the stars. I sat on the bike's rear carrier, flopping my legs as we wobbled forward through the night coolness with no head light and no street lamps.

A few cars passed us, head lights off to save battery juice. After months in India, functioning in the dark seemed normal.

The next day, Dilip came to see me off at the bus depot; I was returning to New Delhi to see Mukesh. With Dilip was Nem, a postcard salesboy, bottom-rung-poor, whose generosity had melted me. Without my knowledge, he had bought me a lunch of roadside snacks: potato cakes, beans, and chutney. Those few rupees were undoubtedly at least a day's pay for him.

The boys' unexpected appearance touched me. I had not invited them. Nem seemed truly choked up to say good-bye. It was difficult for me to accept their thoughtfulness at face value. Was my brief acquaintance worth that much to them? They had given me so much with so little. Still, I wondered if these two boys wanted something: a tape cassette of music, a western trinket, money?

"You are good friend," Dilip said, reaching up to squeeze my hand through the bus window. "I will always remember."

"Thank you," Nem said.

Thank *you*. Back in Delhi, I sent him the money I owed for the painting. Two months later, upon my return to Canada, I received a mailing tube; inside was a silk painting done by Dilip and his father. It showed a row of three adult elephants with two young ones at their side. A family. All wore fringed head gear, decorative square covers on their backs, and ornamental anklets.

The generosity of this gesture touched me deeply. I knew the astronomical cost of sending this overseas on their paltry pay. Today, the framed painting hangs on my wall, a reminder that kindness and friendship can begin in the most unexpected forms, true and un-sullied.

At last, I was allowing more love to seep into my heart. A slow realization emerged: I had wasted too many resentful years raging against the lack of emotional nourishment in my family home. Staying defiant and defensive over this only separated me from the essence of others and from any love someone might offer. In my twenties, for instance, I avoided monogamy and revelled in many sexual encounters. My mother admonished me with a scornful, goose-related reminder: "They mate for life." To her, I was defying the laws of nature through promiscuity. Her husband had done the same with me.

Nowadays, I hold the power of geese in awe: the strength of one of their wings can break a human arm. I admire their symmetry in flight, their willingness to aid an injured member of the group to ensure collective progress. Beyond the fluid beauty of their V-formations, they squawk through the sky, announcing their presence with distinctive, throaty honks.

I needed to find this love within myself, to share it in daily encounters with others, life, nature ...

We are all on a journey to find and heal ourselves. May we all revel in who we are and who we can become, as Pulitzer-Prize-winning poet Mary Oliver invites in her poem "Wild Geese" in *Dream Work*:

> *You do not have to be good.*
> *You do not have to walk on your knees*
> *for a hundred miles through the desert, repenting.*
> *You only have to let the soft animal of your body*
>   *love what it loves.*
> *Tell me about despair, yours, and I will tell you mine.*
> *Meanwhile the world goes on.*
> *Meanwhile the sun and the clear pebbles of the rain*
> *are moving across the landscapes,*
> *over the prairies and the deep trees,*
> *the mountains and the rivers.*
> *Meanwhile the wild geese, high in the clean blue air,*
> *are heading home again.*
> *Whoever you are, no matter how lonely,*
> *the world offers itself to your imagination,*
> *calls to you like the wild geese, harsh and exciting—*
> *over and over announcing your place*
> *in the family of things.*

CHAPTER EIGHT

TOUCHED

Touch has a memory.
—**John Keats**

FROM MY TRAIN window in Rajasthan, I saw spindly white egrets, swallowed into green, standing motionless at the edge of ponds as silent feathered forms. Sometimes they rode the backs of water buffalo. Bird tails of turquoise darted in front of the glass, then disappeared. Peacocks swaggered, their blue-green feathers aglow, hovering, horizontal, above the ground.

Many birds in this country were bursting prisms of colour, exotic gifts to the eye. Breathtaking emerald birds, with orange wings and heads, perched on telephone poles as my train clattered past. My reference book, *Collins Handguide to the Birds of the Indian Sub-Continent*, identified them as little green bee-eaters. Tired of writing generic phrases in my journal like "I saw another beautiful blue bird today," I had bought this small handbook to learn the names of these glimmering bodies of flight. The brilliance of landscape and wildlife in this western state stunned my eyes.

It was mid-December 1990. I was heading back to Delhi and Mukesh. Through the window, I watched an old man kiss a baby black-and-white goat on its nose. Rural boys washed their water buffalo, like North Americans soaping down cars. Children rode the backs of these slow, snuffling beasts, lowering them into muddy water with kicks. After whacking them with sticks, they herded them back from a river or waterhole. Often, the only visible sign of the submerged buffalo was a snout and part of its back, like tiny brown stepping stones. At least, I hope that's what they were.

I filled my journal with the scenes before me.

Pink, fuchsia, orange, and yellow saris flutter as women walk within lush fields, sparking the dusk sunlight with brilliant swatches. Hips swaying, they disappear down a wisp of path, balancing bundles of sticks on their heads. Wobbling, a man struggles on an ancient-looking bicycle, crooked tracks through bamboo thickets. Dabs of yellow rapeseed—a horrible name for such vibrancy—wave in the twilight wind across hilltops. From my headphones, Pachelbel's Canon *flows, putting me at ease.*

Desert dust clung to me as I stretched, alone, across my upper train bunk in a four-berth compartment. Exhausted, I squeezed inside my mummy bag, unnecessary in this 42°C heat. Its sweaty, puffy layers gave me an odd sense of protection. My wallet and passport lay against my stomach, my hiking boots tucked against my head. Like a silent partner, my backpack curled next to me: a solo backpacker's precautions against theft.

Gratefully cocooned in the semi-darkness, I allowed exhaustion to engulf me. With my back turned away from the other bunks, sounds held only a muffled presence: syncopated drum beats of wheels on track and the faint hint of voices. With little awareness of the four or so others who occupied this stuffy, dusty room, I just wanted to sleep.

Within drowsy minutes, someone grabbed my back.

Did I imagine it? *Leave me alone. I want to sleep.*

Moments later, I felt it again. Someone's hands had grabbed my lower back, then let go.

How dare they! Who was it? After six months of harassment and attempted fondling from Indian men, I had to do something. Still wrapped within my sleeping bag, I gave one hard kick. My feet hit what felt like someone's stomach on the berth across from me.

Whoever it was did not retaliate. I felt victorious. No more grabs. Too groggy to investigate further, I fell asleep.

The next morning, I wanted to dismiss those nighttime jabs as imaginary, just as I had done with my dad's touches.

Legs dangling inside my sleeping bag, I sat up on my berth and studied the other occupants. In the lower berth across from me, a sixtyish Indian woman patted down her waist-length, black-gray hair. Clusters of thin bracelets jangled on her wrist. She straightened and smoothed out her sari. In the berth above her, a young man in his twenties in tailored pants and a well-pressed shirt smirked at me. Assuming that he was the guilty party, I glared at him. He turned away.

I had to confront him. Stuffing my sleeping bag into its nylon sack, I surveyed my crumpled shirt and cotton pants; they would survive another day without a wash. Now everyone in the compartment sat facing each other. The old woman opened a round tiffin, a three-tier stack of stainless-steel food containers, and offered me a red-orange, curried vegetable dish. I declined, marvelling at the common practice in India of sharing food with fellow passengers.

The young man avoided eye contact with me. From his middle-class appearance, I assumed that he spoke English.

I looked straight at him.

"You know what you did. You had no right to touch me."

Straightening his back and lifting his chin, he denied knowing or doing anything wrong. "I am the son of—"

"I don't care who you are. You should respect women—all women."

The old Indian woman nodded her head in agreement. Bolstered by her silent support, I looked out the window.

Ten minutes later, the young man's dark eyes found mine.

"Sorry, sorry," he said. Astounded, I smiled in gratitude. *Ah, triumph.*

It would take me more than a decade to confront my father.

* * *

I experienced more badgering and sexual offers in Rajasthan than anywhere else in India. By the time I had arrived there in early December 1990, after six months in India, my tolerance had snapped. I had witnessed this condition in other solo western female travellers in that country. On arrival, they eagerly and repeatedly gave money to throngs of child beggars, tried to listen attentively to male comments, and sought a sense of open discovery with each encounter. However, after months of provocations and poking, warding off pestering hustlers from age five to fifty, and feeling treated like a stripper at a drunken frat party, even gentle souls usually lost their cool and shrieked, swore, or elbowed men away. I could no longer slough off the impact of frequent assaults. I had even learned the Hindi word for "asshole," *ghandu*, which sounded incongruously close to "Gandhi."

Elsewhere in India, I had seen squealing animals butchered in sacrifice, human bodies burning with a sweet, acrid odor beside the Ganges River, human feces floating as one with laundry and dirty dishes, and male genitalia bobbing in the breeze during public defecation. The full sensory wallop of it all had become too much. I wanted to go home.

Yet, I was not ready to say good-bye to Mukesh. About a week before arriving in Rajasthan, I had applied in New Delhi to extend my six-month tourist visa, the maximum time limit, for another month. Behind a counter at the Foreigners' Registration Office, a uniformed sub-inspector in a beard and turban had asked why I wanted to stay longer. I gushed about wanting to spend more time with my Indian boyfriend and how we hoped to travel together to southern India. I praised India's beauty and spiritual depth, showing him my postcards and manhandled copy of *Autobiography of a Yogi* by Paramahansa Yogananda.

The official gave me long, lurking glances.

"Where does your boyfriend live?"

I told him.

"And where do you live?"

I told him.

"How often do you see each other? Where do you sleep at night? What do his parents think about this?"

Geeze, I'm almost thirty-two years old.

"What are you doing today? I'd like to see you again." He gazed up and down at me with a sly smile. I wondered what this visa extension was going to cost me.

"May I keep one of your passport photos?" He rubbed his fingers against my black-and-white image, taken in India. Soft focus and cut crooked, it showed a white gash, a printing glitch, between my eyebrows. This made me look like I was wearing a *bindi,* a decorative dot that symbolizes protection of the esoteric third eye of consciousness.

My stomach made a fist. The official feigned putting the photo in his pocket. The inspector beside him made a few comments, presumably in Punjabi. They both looked at me, then laughed.

"I'd like to see you again," he said, looking into my eyes. "We could go for dinner, then to a movie …"

I refused politely. He offered me tea, seemingly intent on delaying the process. After more than an hour, I received my visa extension.

Someone might well ask: Why didn't you leave India sooner? My attraction to Mukesh and our plans to have him immigrate to Canada kept me rooted in his country. Beyond the trash and brashness of India's cities, its formidable natural landscapes still beckoned to me.

In December 1990, I walked alone or rode a rented bicycle through Keoladeo National Park, a 2,832-hectare bird sanctuary near Bharatpur, about 200 kilometres south of New Delhi. Here, among large clusters of mimosa trees sprinkled with yellow blossoms, black cormorants weighed down branches, their outstretched wings drying as if pegged to a clothesline. On top branches, farther away, storks and cranes perched, their whiteness the flush of starched laundry. Siberian white cranes, also known as snow cranes, winter in this wetlands park, which became a World Heritage Site five years before my arrival. These elegant birds, with long, spindle legs of scarlet and a dash of red on half their face, are critically endangered.

At that time, in 1990, only one hundred and fifty remained on the planet. This park had twelve; six had arrived the previous day.

Tall and serene within acres of wild marsh, these rare winged beings provided a gift of silent grace. What stillness they brought beyond the brash, fluttered green of parakeets, the shrieking alarm call of a peacock (India's national bird), and the frenetic dips and darts of kingfishers shimmering in iridescent feathers of turquoise and copper. I spent several afternoons walking around the park until dusk. A munching cow ignored me while what looked like two wild boars dashed across the road. Several others sprang away into thick greenery. Two blue bull antelopes, resembling spotted deer, stared at me, then darted away, their tall racks a poise of points. I heard the haunting howl of a jackal and saw two on the road about five metres away as I cycled past. They, too, stared at me. I had expected them to look like hyenas, but they seemed more a mix of fox and dog or mini-wolf. At dusk, the sky swam with pink light, dipping clouds onto the marsh water. Before the three-quarter moon appeared like a fingertip, silhouettes of storks floated on trees, bobbing against pale blue.

Away from probing male eyes, I relaxed, lost in the discovery of wildlife. What joy to see wild animals at ease, with no attack stances. Here, among these park animals, I had no concern about lustful stares, exploring hands or leering grins. I was not prey.

* * *

Back in my room at a tourist bungalow in Bharatpur, I noted a red *bindi* stuck on the wall. In my imagination, it symbolized the start of a collection of conquests, like notches on a bedpost.

While taking a shower or undressing throughout India, I had discovered a quirky feature in some tourist bungalows: apparent cracks or decayed areas in the walls functioned as peep holes, either by default or intent. After noticing an eyeball observing me at previous accommodations, I had quickly learned upon arrival in any overnight room to survey the walls for tell-tale holes and cover them up.

My first such wall surprise occurred in Canada in my teens at the local movie house in my old Toronto neighbourhood. In a dark upstairs room, about to wriggle into my snack bar attendant's uniform with a young female co-worker, I stood shivering in my bra. We noticed a tiny blip of light on the wall. Peering closer, we realized that an eyeball was spying on us through a hole. It was the projectionist.

His audacity horrified me. I can't remember if we even told our boss about this Peeping Tom. If we had, would it have made any difference?

I remember, at age nine, feeling frightened when boys at school stood at the bottom of the stairs and looked up my skirt when I walked up to the second floor. Wearing shorts felt safer, less revealing. As protection, I wore the same top-and-shorts outfit every day for a week.

When I was nine or ten, my father did not let me go about topless. When my sisters were teenagers and I was a pre-teen, my mom said that he didn't like us coming down to the dinner table wearing only a shirt and half-slip. I can't even remember if my sisters and I complained about such directives. Did the sight of us partially dressed arouse him? We definitely obeyed.

Once, while I was a teenager, my dad entered my bedroom in the daytime. Naked, I hurriedly hid behind my open closet door. My father, in housecoat and pajamas, walked up and peered behind it. "Oh, you're like that," he said. He stood there and looked at me for what seemed like a minute, not trying to move or look away. I remember cowering, cold and hunched over, trying to cover myself with my hands. I wanted him to go away, but he didn't.

During my childhood, a painting of an elegant Edwardian woman graced our dining room wall over the polished walnut sideboard, which housed silverware and candelabra. Inside a scalloped gilded frame, this slender woman gazed down a long, aquiline nose, her shoulder-length hair powdered white, ending in tasteful curls. She wore a light blue dress with a white ruffled collar and a bow at the bodice, revealing china-white skin and a peek at the top of her bosom. A white-and-blue hat sat angled on her head, a wide ribbon draped down the back of her hair. To me, she embodied my mother's implied advice: Let elegance and family privilege trump any nastiness in life.

"Follow her eyes," my father would say. "Wherever you stand in the room, she's looking at you." He would demonstrate, crouching down by our walnut dining room table to look at her. Her gaze met his through magnetic quiet.

"This shows that it's a good painting," he said. "It's like *trompe l'oeil.*"

My friends and I would challenge this theory from every corner, even standing parallel to the painting, flat against the wall. No matter where we were in the room, her eyes reached ours, spooky and enchanting.

The face of this woman resembled that of *The Honourable Mrs. Graham*, a portrait by eighteenth-century artist Thomas Gainsborough and one of my dad's favourite paintings. He wished that he had reveled in aristocratic grace in Edwardian England. To him, Mrs. Graham—tall and slender, bedecked in satin, feathers, and jewels with piled hair—seemed to personify perfect womanhood, an exotic bird of paradise. My father kept a framed picture of her in his home office. I wondered how my mother, sisters, and I stacked up against this feminine ideal of his.

CHAPTER NINE

MOLE

The truth is rarely pure and never simple.
—**Oscar Wilde**

MUKESH AND I were in Goa, a casual, offbeat enclave of beaches on India's southwest coast, in late December 1990. It was his first holiday away from his family. For the first time in his country, we felt free to express our affection publicly. In the laid-back spirit of this former Portuguese colony, locals treated me like just another human being. No more male stares, lingering like silent grabs. Relief at last.

At an open-air deck at a beach restaurant on Christmas Eve, we picked out pieces of soft, white lobster flesh, and fed them, on a fork, into each other's mouths. I ate garlic calamari, vegetable curry, and rice—a decadent meal for a backpacker. Around our wicker chairs a cat scrounged food scraps while a stout, middle-aged German man, who'd been drinking with a table of Indians, wobbled as he tried to stand, drunk and alone. He began to sing Christmas carols in operatic style, conducting an unseen orchestra with grand sweeps of his arms. Lilting through the night, his songs disappeared into the blackness. From nearby tables, westerners and locals watched and laughed, as if he was the featured entertainment. After several minutes, he could no longer stand and fell against a table.

After midnight, I called my family in Canada from a beach pay phone. For about fifteen minutes, I talked to my three sisters, brothers-in-law, and parents gathered at my sister Wendy's then-home in

Montreal. Our words hung in superficial chit-chat, as if with ac-quaintances: no "I miss you's" or emotional expression. My father, sounding business-like, wanted to know what time it was in Goa. I imagined him yanked him away from a Christmas-season football playoff game, one of those holiday bowls he liked so much. I felt glad that Mukesh was with me.

"We've never said, 'I love you' to each other," I told him, about my family. "Can you believe that?" He shook his head. The idea was inconceivable to him.

Even after three decades, the dispassionate stance of my family stunned me. Similarly, my incest memories still hovered with no built-in feelings; the child within them reflected no anguish or fear. It was as if these images hung suspended, emotionally dead, in a cryo-genics chamber, waiting to be brought to life by a technology not yet available to me.

Rather than feelings, I focused on the realm that gives me com-fort and control: words. I deconstructed the word "molestation" to tame it: a station for a mole. This description works for an abuser. A near-blind creature, adapted to life underground, works in the dark yet can be seen by others aboveground. A double agent, he inhabits two worlds. No one suspects his true identity.

By the new year, I was back in New Delhi. On January 17, 1991, the headline of the city's *Indian Express* newspaper announced with stark simplicity: THE GULF WAR IS ON. Men crowded around the *Hindustani Times* building downtown to read the flashing news captions about Operation Desert Storm on a giant digital display board, like a stock-market readout. The city's revitalized atmosphere repulsed me; war had amped up humdrum routines.

About a hundred people thronged outside American Center, part of the U.S. Embassy that housed a library of English books and art exhibitions, where Mukesh and I had met seven months earlier. They shoved and yelled, trying to get through the gate to watch television news coverage of the Gulf War. Security was ridiculous: a hastily erected fence about 1.5 metres high, several gun-toting secur-ity guards, and two police with long *lathis* or sticks. At the American

Express office, a man with a metal detector frisked me; I had to walk through a security archway to receive my *poste restante* mail. Now symbols of war-mongering, Delhi's U.S. businesses and buildings were presumed targets for bombs or violence. In this pre-9/11 world before Al Qaeda and ISIS, strangers warned me of potential danger, saying my white skin personified "America." Already accustomed to feeling like a target, I wasn't too concerned. Besides, I was leaving soon.

Three days after the war broke out, Mukesh and I stayed at the three-star Hotel Janpath to celebrate my thirty-second birthday. No more cockroaches, flaking plaster, and leaky taps from my usual guest-house fare. He spoiled me with a lush-smelling bouquet of roses, lilies, and daffodils, a surprise butterscotch cake, and a matching necklace and bracelet of white-and-gold cloisonné. While he stood behind me to put on my necklace, Madonna pranced provocatively on TV in a tight, black merry widow. Suddenly, the screen image froze. Mukesh assured me that Doordarshan, the censorship-driven government station, had undoubtedly stopped the broadcast. I envisioned some terrified civil servant, minutes before his termination, madly jabbing at control buttons, wondering: *How the hell did that get through?*

On the night of my birthday, I dreamt that my dad was trying to hold me around my neck and I wouldn't let him, not trusting him. The following night, while in bed with Mukesh, I awoke in the dark early hours. Although we were in an ideal romantic setting, I did not feel like making love.

The next morning, Mukesh and I left for the airport at 4:30 a.m. in a checkered cab, a cavernous sedan. Still dark, the city felt serene, with few cars and no one on the streets. Upon arrival, I discovered that the airline wanted to fine me 770 rupees ($43) for overweight luggage. I had almost no cash left and they would not take credit cards. Nor would they accept my day pack as hand luggage because it wasn't "regulation type." If I did not come up with the money, they would not let me on the plane. Determined to obey every rule, the officious young male airline employee ignored my pleadings and wheedling.

"You'll have to take another flight," he said.

Already upset about leaving, I ran out to Mukesh, who wasn't allowed in the airport due to India's rule of "passengers only" inside. We commandeered a security guard, who accompanied both of us into the building. I stood, astonished, at how easily Mukesh, a perfect diplomat, waived regulations; he was gifted at melting away red tape and dissipating anger, often mine. With smooth conviction, he talked assuredly with the airline official in Hindi. I had no idea what they were saying. The official let me go through without any fine. I was amazed.

During pre-boarding, another airline employee wanted me and dozens of passengers to line up in single file. Ignoring his order, everyone continued to mill about. A middle-aged western woman next to me said: "I've never seen a civilized, organized queue anywhere in India. Why start one now, when we're leaving?"

Mukesh and I stood alone, embracing. He looked on the verge of tears. I felt sad but surprisingly calm. As if in a cliché film moment, I imagined a movie camera panning across, then zooming in to capture the scene: two lovers melded in a hug, the bustle around them a soft-focus blur. Freeze frame. Fade out.

Oddly, I felt excited about returning home, off to Bangkok for a week to hit a remote Thai beach, then back to Vancouver. Although this meant good-bye, Mukesh and I planned to reunite in Canada, assuming that he could get a visa and clearance for immigration. With me helping from Canada, we felt determined to beat bureaucracy and get him out of India.

* * *

While in India, I had this dream: Watching people lift an open coffin over the heads of a crowd, I am shocked to discover that the corpse inside is me.

I could extol the moments of love and grace that people of all ages shared with me in India, but that is for a different story. The soulful culture of this ancient nation touched me more profoundly than any other. I met kindness from *saddhus*, respectful elderly men, aged women, and curious children. These connections of quiet elegance, framed by daily meditations, allowed me to savour India beyond the caustic intrusions, like my father's favoured qualities beyond his unwelcome remarks and actions.

The profane side of some of the country's men brought me, ironically, closer to my own sacredness. To question and reject their version of me, I had to reaffirm to myself who I truly was. Responding to many of them forced me to defend myself, to gain more authority over my body. Like my dad, they were my indirect teachers, wielding disrespect, rather than an honouring hug. Through Michael and Mukesh, I realized that I was still looking to see and define myself through men, including my dad, rather than wholly embracing my own being. I needed to reclaim this lost piece of myself.

Like a too-large slice of mirror, my seven months in India reflected back my glinting anger, self-doubt, and brokenness. I was using sex not just to feel loved, but to validate that I mattered. My relationships with Mukesh and Michael and sexual abuse from lustful Indian males helped shake out sharp fragments of my past. These links seemed unrelated to my dad and me at the time; I did not fully realize their significance until my return to Canada. Exploring the extremes of India was like experiencing the conflicting facets of my dad. I was immersed in an overpowering presence that combined tenderness with bawdiness, soul with assault, and loving kindness and generosity with objectification.

At a tactile level, the nation's market stalls provided sensory pleasures and delicious discoveries from startling piles of dye, powdered and royal-blue, and dark orange spices to the scent of fresh cardamom and curry and mounds of tearfully hot peppers. Melodic, repeat cries of *Chai, Chai, Chai* from tea sellers at train stations became an urban background mantra for my travels.

The rigour of India's mountains and terrain, and its sentient extremes helped to open my body while the remarkable beauty of its land and creatures widened my heart. To not acknowledge the stillness and sacred power that one can find in India, even amidst tremendous turmoil and overcrowding, would be to remain inured to its gifts. As with my father's shortcomings, it seemed too easy, while in India, to focus solely on the nation's negative traits.

I thought that a solo spiritual quest would bring me closer to myself in India. It did. But through relationships, I learned far more. In seeking a new form of identity, some "felt" sense that I mattered, two disparate men and my inner and outer worlds, melding and colliding, brought me into a dance with sex and Source, a divine essence, that catapulted me into jarring new awareness. My blind mole self was spending more time in the daylight.

Upon my return to Canada, an excruciating healing process would begin.

PART TWO

HEALING AT HOME
(1991–2011)

*You can look at all the parts of a terrible thing until you
see that they're assemblies of smaller parts, all of which you
can name, and some of which you can heal or alter, and finally
the terror that seemed unbearable becomes manageable.*
—Barbara Kingsolver, *Small Wonder*

CHAPTER TEN

RATS

The truth about our childhood is stored up in our body, and although we can repress it, we can never alter it. Our intellect can be deceived, our feelings manipulated, and conceptions confused, and our body tricked with medication. But some day our body will present its bill, for it is as incorruptible as a child, who, still whole in spirit, will accept no compromises or excuses, and it will not stop tormenting us until we stop evading the truth.
—Psychoanalyst **Alice Miller**, *For Your Own Good*

I RETURNED HOME to Vancouver, on Canada's west coast, exhausted and with little money in late January 1991. The country was in a deep recession. For months, I could find no suitable full-time editorial work. Résumés and phone calls prompted rejection after rejection and no interviews. Physically, I felt compromised. My right knee, injured while trekking in Nepal, made walking painful; it eventually resulted in arthroscopic surgery to remove a bone chip.

I had hoped that my spiritual mentor would help me re-integrate into my own culture but he and his wife had recently fled the city. The mother of a young woman in his spiritual community had accused him of sexually assaulting her daughter. Some people were calling him a sociopath. Others felt that he had started a cult. With this news of yet another fallen male role model, my trust buckled, sensing betrayal. Yet, as with my father, conflict remained. This man had emphasized the importance of inner peace; the seeds of his vision remain with me today.

The stress of rising debt and unsuccessful job-seeking, combined with culture shock, triggered high anxiety. With each rejected job application and increased expense, I grew more reactive and fearful. North America felt like an alien island of glitz and glibness. Chat about who-was-seeing-who or what bauble or accessory somebody "needed" seemed banal. After India's tin-roofed shops, dust-village life, and cow-dung fires, my first re-entry into a deluxe supermarket provoked jarring shock. The towering long shelves of glistening goods and plastic containers under brash fluorescent lighting re-pulsed me. Vancouver's well-heeled shoppers, décor, shops, too-big cars and homes screamed needless excess.

I kept thinking of the stark room in New Delhi where Gandhi spent the last three months of his life with only a small spinning wheel, thin mattress on the floor, and four white walls. I held that bareness, a blatant contrast to his rich contribution to the world, as an ideal. (Later, a therapist told me he thought Gandhi's ascetic life meant he was out of balance, but I disagree. Anyone who spurns materialism and focuses, instead, on an independence movement that empowers society's underdogs deserves praise. Buddha himself rejected wealth and privilege to help the masses. This was many decades before I learned of how Gandhi had treated women at his ashram.)

By then, at age thirty-two, it was growing increasingly difficult to manage daily reality and not face what had happened between my father and me. Oddly, it felt reassuring to learn that survivors of incest and sexual abuse often begin to recover memories in their early thirties.

I turned down an invitation to spend a vacation with my family in Prince Edward Island, feeling disloyal. "Your mother hasn't seen you in three years," my dad said on the phone. Still in turmoil over his alcoholism, I explained in a letter that this was my main reason for not wanting to accompany them; incest wasn't yet part of our conversation. I feared my parents might disown me. "You won't endear yourself to people by pointing out their shortcomings," my mother wrote in response.

I continued to struggle along on meagre freelance writing and editing assignments, emotionally marooned on a sinking ship from which the rats had fled. As my heart pulled me underwater, my mother's chiding words returned: *When are you going to get serious about your life?*

My parents had difficulty understanding anyone who had not etched out a solid, singular job path. For years, I had inwardly seethed at them for not applauding my life choices. My mom had told me several years earlier: "If someone doesn't know what they want to do by the time they're thirty, there's something wrong." She had asked me: "Do you want to be living out of a suitcase when you're forty?"

My father always seemed to view situations in comparative terms, deciding who had done better, even if it was just us working together on a crossword puzzle. When I told him of a friend's blossoming career as a musician and performer, he said, "And what do *you* do?" as if my years of teaching and professional writing held no value. He was someone who believed in the saying: "Those who can, do. Those who can't, teach."

* * *

Following my return to Canada in 1991, Mukesh was denied a visa to leave India. After struggling to maintain a long-distance relationship for more than six months, I chose to end it. In anguish amidst the stress of debt, unemployment, knee surgery, and trying to face incest, I found our separation and uncertain future too overwhelming. I knew that my love for Mukesh was not deep enough to make me want to move in with him and his family in New Delhi. But perhaps I had just kept my heart closed too tightly ...

With this decision went Mukesh's dream of leaving India and finding happiness with a westerner, as his friend had done with an Australian woman. Mukesh said he could not defy his parents. He went ahead with the arranged marriage they had planned; they had already selected his mate while he and I were involved.

Since I left India almost three decades ago, Mukesh and I have not seen each other. Still continents apart, we remain in each other's lives via occasional emails, Facebook, cards, and the rare phone call. Mukesh has two kids and runs a travel agency in New Delhi. I asked him once, over the phone, if he was happy. Pausing, he replied in a wistful voice: "This is India, honey."

Michael and I met once in Vancouver, not long after our time together in India. We went for dinner at Granville Island joined by a local friend of his who brought along a group of young male outdoor enthusiasts. I guessed that they had heard of Michael's mountaineering exploits and expected to be enthralled by non-stop anecdotes but they left early, seemingly disappointed. Michael remained reserved. Later, we fumbled with each other on a futon on the floor of my apartment.

We have had no contact since. I heard that in recent years, he was living in Nepal. I discovered online that Michael, in his sixties, had been involved with a woman about forty years younger. This news did not surprise me.

* * *

In that first year back in Canada, I borrowed money to attend a week-long yoga retreat in June 1991. (On the advice of a friend, I had started hatha yoga after my return.) I joined about forty others at a resort in Tofino on Vancouver Island, part of Canada's Pacific Northwest coast. In this stunning ruggedness, impressive forests of cedar and Douglas fir surround long, wind-beaten beaches that curve into charged ocean waves. A walk along the region's many beaches put me hand-in-hand with the hardy elements: pounding waves and wind, a slippery maze of washed-up giant logs, and large, circular root clusters that rose like sunflower faces without stems.

Nature's wild freedom flowed through me. Splayed across the sand, tangles of yellow-brown bull kelp formed long tendrils of patterns intertwined. Like forlorn scarecrows, orange-brown arbutus trees extended gnarled, misshapen arms from cliffs and hilltops, their growth stunted and shaped by fierce storms, their peeling bark a patched garb. My spirit relished the area's vigour of water and wind, each barefoot step in sand an intimate rub of nature's belly. Now homeless on a beach, shells, driftwood, a sand dollar, broken crab shells, bones, pieces of rotten dock, a soused running shoe, foam cooler parts—such seeds of life, organic and otherwise, lay torn from their source.

Indoors, in a large hall with high ceilings, the emotional flotsam and jetsam of my shipwrecked life streamed out during yoga sessions. The youthful spirit of Sandra, our lithe, black-haired teacher in her fifties, gave me inspiration. She urged us to breathe deeply and to release vocally any feelings locked inside our bodies. My mind fought the need to let go physically; I did not want to submit to some unknown realm within myself. But my body prevailed, releasing long, low tones, guttural cries, and animal-like wails that seemed to have no connection to my conscious self. They emerged spontaneously, a sustained minor chord of disembodied voices. Scarcely willing to believe that they came from me, I found their unflinching fervency terrifying.

In the squalls of a colicky infant, my voice shrieked like some otherworldly entity. After I stopped fighting the sounds, sobs wretched up between strafing cries. The more deeply I inhaled, the more this deliberate voice hollered. The process grew so intense that no one else released at all—just me in a continuous long series of sound. Sandra held me up and intoned close to my right ear to give me an accompanying voice. Just wanting to let the pain out, I no longer felt any self-consciousness.

Afterward, two women in the group came over and rubbed my back. My sobs welled up without restraint. My body was no longer just a mechanistic shell of muscles and aches that furthered or foiled personal goals, but a fluid energetic force. How indescribably free to be so emotionally unclogged.

Hours after my raucous roars, my voice was still hoarse and raw, yet, I felt far lighter. One of the men in the group later told me my sounds had evoked, for him, a maternity ward. Sandra told us that a student in a past yoga class, a Vietnam war veteran, had had to leave the room when similar burning cries had emerged because it had reminded him too much of combat.

I had arrived at the yoga retreat in Tofino, BC depressed and vulnerable, wary of what I might discover within me. Yet, Sandra's warmth and grace, combined with her open heart and decades of spiritual exploration, created a cushioning nest. Besides yoga postures, we practised *pranayama*, controlled breathing techniques that access deep, belly breathing and can tap into physical areas of repressed energy. Patanjali, the ancient Indian scholar and attributed author of the *Yoga Sutras* text, believed that breath control enables a person to achieve a higher state of awareness or *samadhi*, a blissful form of unity and concentrated meditation.

At first, expanding my belly in a series of breath holds and inhalations or holding an alternate nostril and breathing through one at a time felt bizarre. But months later, after I attended a regular yoga class, it became easier and almost automatic at times. Helping to release attachment to thoughts, fears or worries, this process allowed me to dispel stress and anxiety.

At the retreat, during meditations and guided visualizations, my energy flow or *chi* felt like electric impulses, a sensory liquid movement within my limbs and veins. With eyes closed, I saw starbursts of white light, intricate geometric patterns, images shifting and transforming in seconds like video images in blues, silver, and sparkly swirls. Seated in the half-lotus position, my body motionless, I felt my hands, feet, and sacral area grow dramatically hot, as if fuelled by a blazing fire. I had never experienced such heat from within.

Each day, in a circle, our group chanted Om or Aum as a collective hum. In a multitude of tonal ranges and voices, our combined sounds evoked a glorious choir. My tears flowed. I felt utterly reassured by, and linked to, others in the room, part of a beautiful non-song without words.

At the end of the retreat, we each had the chance to express ourselves to the group, seated on the floor in a circle.

"I was thinking about the word home and that it contains 'OM,'" I said. "That makes me think of the expression 'Home is where the heart is.'" Hardly a revelation, yet, I began to sob uncontrollably. My childhood home had rarely felt open hearted.

A woman held my hand and rubbed my back.

"Thank you for providing a safe place for me to grieve," I said, squeezing out only a few words at a time between sobs. This lack of control embarrassed me profoundly. I talked of the lack of emotional support in my family. Later, at least half a dozen women gave me a hug and shared their story. They all said how much they had connected with my words. Their acceptance brought me the validation I needed. *You have a right to feel the way you do. There's no reason to be ashamed.*

* * *

Back in Vancouver after the yoga retreat, I sought a teaching job and continued freelance writing, supplemented by temporary secretarial duties at a rehabilitative centre for people with brain and spinal cord injuries. Although feeling ashamed about not finding a job that required journalistic and editorial skills, I was still too vulnerable to subject myself to the stressful rigours of a daily deadline position. Interacting with the centre's patients—paraplegics, quadriplegics, and others grappling to learn to walk or speak again—put my own invisible toils into clearer perspective.

I went through my family photo album, created by my mother, as if to get reacquainted with my child self.

Family photo #5: A pudgy two-year-old clutches and munches on a long *baguette*.

Family photo #6. A grinning child queen mugs in a too-huge vintage dress, her skinny arms extended at opposite sides in an exaggerated model pose.

Family photo #7. A pony-tailed imp poses by the backyard swing set with her beloved German Shepherd named Whiskey.

Family photo #8: My mother, snuggling the infant me in her arms, beams at me with unrestrained love. My heart could not let in this alien image. Since I had rarely experienced physical love that way with her or my family, it seemed a lie.

* * *

In March 1992, almost a year after the yoga retreat, I garnered enough resolve to explore further the memory of my out-of-body experience as a child, of floating near the ceiling over my bed. After visiting Pat, a hypnotherapist in Vancouver, for several months, I booked an appointment for a session of childhood regression. I felt safe and comfortable with her, ready for hypnosis that would take me back to age five, when I believed the out-of-body experience, related to incest, had occurred. (The mean age of victims when incest begins with a biological father is 5.2 years, according to one research sample of 196 "paternal caretakers.")

Before the session began, my stomach tightened. My chest felt crushed over an aching heart.

Eyes closed, I relax into my chair, breathing deeply, my feet flat on the floor. Pat's reassuring voice puts me into a trance-like state, aware and open.

"What are you feeling?"

My stomach quivers. The area around my heart is painfully sore, yet, my genitals feel aroused. I don't want my body to respond this way.

I see a man's head and sense that he is stimulating me orally. My arousal continues as moderate, constant pleasure. I can feel fingers inside my vagina, some sense of penetration, but it feels pleasant. A heavy body pushes on my chest, but I can't see a face. Somehow, I sense that I am lying down and the man is standing up.

"What else do you see?"

My closed eyes flutter repeatedly beyond my conscious control. This occurs several times. I say nothing. Where are these visions and sensations coming from? My adult brain rapidly tries to form an explanation: I must be conjuring suggestive material because I'm in a vulnerable state. I'm subconsciously trying to please my therapist. Maybe a stranger or neighbour molested me, although I can't remember ever being alone with anyone like that. This can't be Dad.

Any previous sense of who I was and how I had grown up—sedate family in a lakefront mansion—was gone. No metaphor or descriptor, from "nightmare" to "repulsion," seemed adequate. Rats had led me to a dank and clammy room. My body and mind felt besieged by them, hungry and mean, gnawing through my stomach. Soiled and sick, they had built messy nests inside my hidden spaces, tugging at my flesh, crawling towards my heart.

I could not rid myself of these pests, not dismiss this tactile truth, not deny the sensations felt or the images seen. But this event was impossible.

I left the session in numb distress, never seeing Pat again. Unable to face any further probing into my past, I struggled to integrate what my body had shown me.

CHAPTER ELEVEN

HEALING

The wound is the place where the Light enters you.
—Rumi

THE WORD "SHAME" was always sticky to me. I didn't want to acknowledge it, yet so many of my words and actions came from not feeling good enough, not measuring up to external markers of success. I wanted to reclaim this part of myself and believe inherently that yes, I was enough just being me. I wanted to gain more trust in how life unfolds, to let go of my need for certainty and control.

To heal meant releasing my anger, but I had no idea how much debilitating grief lay beneath it. I figured that getting more in touch with my emotional self would help me function more fully in life and open me up to give and receive greater love. But my wounded child self was stomping her feet, preventing me from integrating love and abuse within myself. Rather than feel compassion for this little tyke and hug her more closely, I felt determined to purge any remnants of incest from my body.

I felt like Kafka's beleaguered salesman Gregor in *Metamorphosis*, who finds himself transformed into "a monstrous vermin." Like an overturned cockroach flailing legs in an attempt to right itself, alienated from his insect body, he strives to bring sense to his newfound condition. When he tries to call out, no one can hear him. His father tells him to forget about the past once and for all. Scuttling to hide under furniture, Gregor refuses food and perishes. Like him, I wanted to sever myself from my family forever.

I decided to immerse myself in solo healing, away from regular life. In April and May 1992, I rented a funky, two-storey rural home on a forested acre on Cortes Island, between British Columbia's mainland and Vancouver Island. Located in the Salish Sea, this idyllic haven, like much of BC's Gulf Islands, is home to many counter-culture enthusiasts who seek retreat and a back-to-the-land lifestyle.

Settled into a cozy, wooden house on Cortes, built by a friend of a friend with materials and appliances retrieved from demolished urban homes, I did not speak to another person for at least a week. My first human communication was a male voice: a wrong number. This sudden connection with a stranger heartened me, a reminder of the outside world.

Wholly alone at age thirty-three, I relished solitude, spending hours each day beginning to write a manuscript of my India travels. I wrote in my journal, meditated, and gloried in nature's presence. Chittering rufous hummingbirds dive-bombed the feeder on the front porch. A pileated woodpecker tapped on a tree trunk. Deer foraged in the front grass. I surrendered to the timelessness of days, my schedule determined by when I chose to rise and retire. This two-month visit fortified my desire to live in the country, away from city routines.

But underneath this sanctuary, that pack of rats, my stain of pain, often took over. On too many days, I found myself sobbing without prompt. Grief poured me into the fetal position, leaving me huddled and weeping on the floor. I sometimes keened with long, low cries spilling from my belly, gasping and wailing until my breath subsided to whimpers. I could barely read a paragraph in a book as benign as *The Wind in the Willows* without exploding into wrenching cries. I remember wondering if I would ever again be able to read an entire book without agonizing spasms of tears.

I had never experienced such unbearable anguish. Feeling powerless to this crawling presence, I felt unsure of what "I" existed, even if that "I" wanted to exist. It seemed simpler to die and discover what lay beyond this flawed realm.

I could not yet share my incest story with any friend or relative.

From a childhood defined by the Protestant work ethic, I felt like a failure for not keeping this smear of emotion under submission. Thoughts of suicide became my fantasy of control and containment. Swallowing pills would be my salvation, a way to rid myself of the rats. Perhaps I could stick my head in the oven, Sylvia Plath style. Yet, compassion for another eventually stopped me: I thought it horrendously unfair that my friend, the home's unsuspecting owner, would have to suffer after finding my corpse.

Distraught, I reached out to a friend by phone, to another in Vancouver who had visited for a weekend. I picked up a stranger hitchhiking, a doctor's aide visiting from Oregon. He had arrived via sailboat with a disagreeable couple and decided to ditch them. As with Michael and Mukesh, I fell into banter about bohemian lifestyles, arts and culture, life philosophies, and spiritual outlooks. But my spreading darkness overrode any sense of mutual enjoyment. Unable to hide my depression and sensing his openness, I confessed: "I've been feeling suicidal."

"I can't leave you in this condition," he said. "That's part of my training. You have to reassure me that you will call somebody before attempting suicide." He stared at me, concerned as I drove.

Initially, I could not make the agreement. He returned with me to my rental home and we talked for several hours. Only then, did I consent to call someone if necessary. We spent subsequent days of heartfelt talk and meals, which helped my floundering self regain some perspective.

Days before I was to begin an editing contract for a specialty publication, my client-to-be cancelled, then reneged on payments owed. I had already turned down other work to make way for this project. How would I pay next month's rent? After I left a message with a friend of hers requesting payment, the woman phoned, called me "a fucking bitch," and promised: "You'll never get a cent out of me," then hung up. Her reaction floored me. An Easter phone call from my mother, thousands of kilometres away in Toronto, seemed abstract and foreign, a distant line to a parallel world long lost. She wrote me later in a letter: "You sounded subdued on the phone." I had only half-hidden my overriding gloom.

One night, while lying in the upstairs bed of the house on Cortes, I heard a female voice say distinctly: "I was raped by my father." It sounded as if it had emerged from about three metres away, from someone standing beyond the foot of my bed. I wasn't sleep deprived and had taken no drugs or alcohol. My mind tried to convince me this was my own projection, a strange form of wish fulfillment to quell my quest for truth. The writer and editor in me felt annoyed by the passive tense of the phrase, rather than the much-preferred active version: "My father raped me."

I have never experienced any phenomenon like this before or since. For weeks, the emphatic certainty of that external voice haunted me. Even though I was reading books about incest and recovery, it felt as if I was doing it on behalf of someone else. I learned that victims of incest and sexual abuse rarely make up stories and exaggerate them. Instead, they more commonly minimize, deny or withhold anything from their inner life that relates to hurts and traumas.

After my stay on Cortes, when my parents phoned me in Vancouver before Christmas, I shared some of my trials regarding work and money. My mom told me: "Your life sounds horrible" and added later in the conversation: "Your life sounds as if it's always in crisis." She reminded me that she came from five generations of farmers who lived secure, traditional lives, implying that my behaviour broke that pattern of solidity. My father, to his credit, told me to call collect if I felt in need.

Today, my heart appreciates that male stranger from the US who appeared, listened, and provided support when I most needed it. A few years later, another man would come to me this way—and remain in a similar role for much longer.

* * *

As I awoke to my body memories, they were difficult to explain logically. They emerged as involuntary reactions: a gag reflex, dry heaves, tonal cries, unexplained sensory déjà vu. Once, in my thirties, when a friend asked me what had happened between my dad and me, I began to hyperventilate and gag, feeling as if I had no control over these bodily reactions. I learned to accept that such odd occurrences and my memory fragments lived in a realm beyond my thinking self.

I believe now that both the childhood regression session and yoga tapped into what some call cellular, somatic or body memory. Sexual abuse or any trauma is said to remain encoded and stored in a victim's neural and sensory circuits, distinct from the mind. Hence, the body "knows" what someone does not, or perhaps cannot bear to, grasp consciously. Charles Whitfield, a doctor who helps survivors of childhood trauma, says: "The body stores and re-enacts traumatic memories in gross and subtle ways."

"Memory resides nowhere, and in every cell," Saul Schanberg, Duke University professor of pharmacology and biological psychiatry, says. "It's about two thousand times more complicated than we ever imagined." One study of young girls who were treated in an emergency ward for proven sexual abuse is revealing. When contacted as adult women seventeen years later, forty per cent of these victims did not recall or else denied outright the event. However, their memory for other incidents in their lives was found to be intact.

Even years after my initial therapy session, while visiting a different therapist in her home, I insisted that she close the door to our room so that it would feel safer. There seemed no logical explanation for this, yet, I felt adamant about it. Was this in response to some long-forgotten memory?

When Christine Blasey Ford gave Senate testimony in the fall of 2018 regarding her alleged teenage sexual assault by then-Supreme Court nominee Brett Kavanaugh, I totally understood when she said that decades later, while remodelling her home, she needed two doors built on her house, so she'd have one for escape. I had felt just as adamant about wanting and needing my therapist's door shut for safety. Yet, I grasp that anyone who hasn't had such an experience would find this odd and perhaps not credible.

Still distrusting my perceptions, I wanted to seek out the viewpoint of someone who works professionally with people's bodies. Marlena Blavin, a British Columbia massage practitioner who provides a variety of body-focused therapeutic techniques, frequently unlocks childhood blocks that lie buried in someone's muscles and tendons. "The body doesn't lie," she says, likening the physical impact of abuse to scar tissue. Even if the response to the original event is subtle, the victim's reactive body takes on a certain shape, perhaps as muscle memory, and remains in what she calls "frozen time." In Blavin's view, even if an adult with a child just thinks of violating her but never does, a sensitive child can pick up that intention through a look in the man's eyes or a tone of voice. "We're such imprinting machines," she says. "We do have that place in us that knows (what happened)."

To heal, I had to re-integrate this displaced, shut-down child part of me with my adult self.

CHAPTER TWELVE

VALIDATION

Just like children, emotions heal when they are heard and validated.
—Jill Bolte Taylor

THREE YEARS AFTER my return from India, in 1994, I had the following dream:

My family—mom, dad, and three older sisters—are sitting at our dining room table. I am an adult of unknown age. My father shows us a card, which he has kept all of his life. It is a picture of eight bodies of young children, dead, lying on a frozen lake. They look asleep. There is no blood. I turn over the card and see the name of the card company printed in the bottom corner: INCEST.

I begin with a quivering voice, in tears: "There is something I have wanted to say for two years—"

"What?" my sister Wendy asks, sounding angry and accusatory. I am not sure if I feel safe to continue.

"I don't know where to start—"

Wendy gets up to leave, but I ask her to return to the table, which she does. Before I can explain what has happened, my dad sheepishly says that he has called the press. He will be on the six o'clock television news in an hour.

"Why?" Shocked, I feel sadness and compassion for him. He doesn't reply. He mumbles something about a fourteen-year-old robbed of the best years of her life.

I awakened from that dream at four a.m., sweaty and disturbed. My heart felt tiny, stretched tight. The night before this dream, I had had the same eerie sense of déjà vu during fellatio with a lover in Canada as I had had with Michael while in Ladakh.

That same year, I was startled to read in Sylvia Fraser's *The Book of Strange* how she had discovered a partial self she called Wendy; this teenage self was the one who knew about incest with her dad and acted as a "sexual drudge" for her father. She says of her Other Self, the child one who did "scary and repellent things" in her father's bedroom:

> *She was my inner shadow, whose presence I felt but whose face I couldn't see, like the light in a closet which illuminates only when you're inside with the door closed. Dreams were like the pages of her secret diary, which she left around for me to find, often appearing in them as a young savage, or a mute, or a retarded creature with bad skin and scraggly hair … [T]he 'I' who operated outside of my father's bedroom identified with an achieving head, while the birth child was left with an abused body and a grieving heart.*

This passage absorbed me like a heartfelt hug; someone else had experienced the same kind of disorienting dream images. Fraser had believed that incest with her dad stopped at age five but later discovered it continued through her teens. Did abuse continue past age five and into my teens? Had it begun even earlier? Later, I learned that the average duration of incest is four years.

To people who have not experienced incest or sexual abuse, it is difficult to convey how essential and affirming it is to find external sources—books, other survivors, therapists, and trauma experts—that provide words and explanations to name and validate a jarring personal issue previously experienced in a vacuum. For me, the vital formative books were Sylvia Fraser's *My Father's House* and *The Book of Strange: A Journey* and Ellen Bass's *The Courage to Heal*. Admitting the reality of incest to oneself is only the first layer; finding an external framework that brings meaning to it is another.

* * *

About a year after my return to Canada, I started dating Brian (not his real name), whom I had met in a screenwriting course before leaving for India. Reluctant at age thirty-three to plunge into any dealings with the opposite sex, I did not initially return his call. When he phoned again, I decided to join him for a short mountain-bike ride on forested trails on Vancouver's west side. As we continued to meet, I found his warmth and understanding, combined with a sharp mind and humour, a remarkable salve and invitation to open to love. He had done spiritual exploration through meditation, and the readings and group work associated with the mystic-philosopher Gurdjieff.

When I told him about the incest, he listened with a supportive heart; he was the first partner with whom I shared this piece of my healing journey. I finally felt trusting enough, and safely vulnerable, to break my silence; it would still take years before I would share this information with my family.

During the early, vulnerable stages of my healing process, Brian's mother casually hands me a newspaper article about False Memory Syndrome. She implies that incest never happened to me. Aghast at her insensitivity, I tell her: "You giving me this would be like me giving you Holocaust denial literature." Her Jewish relations died in Nazi death camps.

This would be the first of many instances in which people would minimize or question my experience.

Within a year, Brian and I were living together; our relationship continued for four years until the fall of 1996. Despite her response to my incest revelation, his mother's directness and his parents' leftist views were a refreshing contrast to my parents' conservatism. Brian and I talked easily with his parents about politics, art, and current issues. His mother doted on me as if I were her daughter, painting personalized cards for me, sharing books and newspaper articles, and inviting us for weekly dinners. As Brian endured stressful work conditions, I bolstered his confidence and listened to tirades about opponents he faced. Together, we repainted and revamped several rooms in an old Victorian home he had bought on Vancouver's east side. At that time, our union marked my longest and healthiest relationship ever with a man.

Brian was instrumental in helping me heal. He cooked me nutritious meals, rather than the cheap on-the-go microwavable dishes I had eaten too often when living alone. Knowledgeable about alternative medicine, he introduced me to vitamin supplements and traditional Chinese medicine. When I had to book appointments with allopathic doctors, as required by my employer's insurance company, he found reputable ones who were sympathetic to sufferers of chronic fatigue syndrome and fibromyalgia like me. These medical allies made a tremendous difference in helping me feel supported when dealing with insurance reps who, initially, sounded skeptical of my condition.

Today, I feel tremendous gratitude for Brian's attentive caregiving. Acting as a much-needed advocate and informal healing coach, he demonstrated the power of selfless love. At the same time, he pushed me to express myself more emotionally, saying, "We're not robots"—the same phrase I had used with my mom.

CHAPTER THIRTEEN

ANGER

Where there is anger, there is always pain underneath.
—Eckhart Tolle

MY MOTHER FIERCELY followed the maxim: "If you can't say anything nice, don't say anything at all." But as someone who, since early childhood, has always spoken her mind, I found no space in my family for anger. By my mom's definition, my anger was not "nice." Although I could express myself more openly with my father, he, too, was mostly shut down when it came to feelings. As I was growing up and throughout my twenties, my parents' refusal to acknowledge any emotions became a focal point for my anger.

At age forty, seven years after my regression session with a therapist, I free-wrote the following note in December 1999:

> *Dear Dad:*
>   *I don't want to be part of your self-absorbed talk. Leave me out of it.*
>   *I don't want to be part of your jealousy.*
>   *Everything is comparison and competition with you. You judge everyone and everything.*
>   *I do not need your praise and recognition.*
>   *Your love for me was always conditional.*
>   *Don't share your sexist comments with me.*
>   *Forget about viewing me as a sex object.*

I don't want to hear any of your dirty jokes or inappropriate comments.

Stop interrupting me.

You didn't consider my needs or interests. You never asked. Everything was You, You, You.

I don't want to be your ego-chaser.

I don't want to make you the centre of attention.

How dare you abuse me sexually!

GO AWAY AND LIVE YOUR OWN LIFE.

I never intended to send my father this note, the voice of my shadow self, and never did. It was just an exercise to help me connect, wholly, with my buried anger. On the reverse side of the paper, I wrote: *"Dad, I am my own person. I love you. I am not letting you control my life anymore. I am living my life the way that I want."*

* * *

How do you let go of an emotion as natural and easy as breathing? I was never one of those women who had to learn to give herself permission to express anger. With me, it was blast now, think later. Now I wanted to transform that energetic urge into something that would serve me and others better.

However, reaching that goal was still years away. I continued to rage on the page against my dad, slamming him for narcissism and exploitation, lack of self-control, his inability to love me with honour, and his resentment, at times, of my successes and travel adventures that he never had. I spilled my angst, questions, goals, and dreams, plus others' inspirational quotes, onto journal pages, half-filling a closet shelf with them. Countless long creative threads—therapy, art, photography, and Inner Child work—helped me release anger and pulled me closer towards loving myself. I opened up to healing in a multitude of forms, from anger workshops to collage, twelve-step gatherings, dream work, Jungian symbolism, and venting on paper with "hate letters" never sent. In my mid-forties, I partnered with a friend for one session of a day-long yoga workshop. She told me later that I had whispered "Help" in her ear in a child's voice. I had no conscious awareness of this at all. Such utterances unnerved me.

Incest survivor Eve Ensler, author of *The Vagina Monologues*, writes that she was "always inexplicably angry," having suffered physical and sexual abuse from her father. "Anger is a poison you mix for a friend but drink yourself," her mother told her, in response to her daughter's unfettered rage.

Zen master Thich Nhat Hanh says that anger is the wounded child in us. He reaffirms the need to smile at and embrace it tenderly, rather than resist and fight it with our ego. Through mindful breathing and walking, he says we can recognize that anger is within us, look more deeply at it, gain insight, and transform and liberate ourselves from it.

Anger in my body, festering in my bones, remained an obstacle. Miriam, an Inner Child therapist, recommended smashing pillows or a tennis racquet on the bed to vent my rage. This seemed silly and ineffective at first, and I barely thwacked the covers. But once I allowed myself uncensored release, it felt truly freeing. (Decades later, I discovered that some Buddhists, such as Thich Nhat Hanh, believe that if you repeatedly hit a pillow in anger, you're actually rehearsing and strengthening your anger, making it habitual, rather than releasing it.)

In my late twenties, before even acknowledging my incest history, I had attended a therapeutic workshop in Vancouver, BC to address my anger. I thrashed a tall cylinder of two rolled-up newspapers so fiendishly against the floor that it shredded in tatters, leaving me winded and utterly absorbed in this physical act. Seemingly alarmed at this intense activity, the rest of the participants had stopped and stared. Only one other woman had attacked her newspapers with equal fervour: she had been sexually abused. If only I could commit myself as completely to love, I thought.

Getting in touch with my anger in such a hands-on, visceral way was essential to release the fury stored for too long. I could have easily focused on knee-jerk rage, reinforcing the same hostile groove in my neural pathways rather than releasing it. But my desire to find love for myself and forgive my father was stronger.

Many years of meditation, hatha yoga, and body work have helped me peel away embedded layers of pain and anger. Anger is still comfortable and familiar for me, but it now has less bite and disappears more quickly. I believe that its healthy expression is essential. If expressed with respect, it is an empowering way to show that I feel maligned, taken for granted, or abused.

Slowly, I have learned to speak more kindly to myself, letting go of habitual attack thoughts. Mindfulness has helped me grow more aware of how emotions dictate responses, which has brought me more empathy and compassion. I have learned not to lash out as frequently from reactive habits. Instead of mindlessly raging at someone, for instance, I can choose not to get angry, or "see" myself getting mad and take immediate responsibility for the impact of my words and actions. When expressing dissatisfaction or frustration with a salesclerk on the phone, for instance, my tone of voice can usually stay calmer and at normal volume. A stream of oaths no longer splashes forth during an upset. Slowly, I was developing a stronger version of what meditators call the Witness Self.

Like my father, I can be ambitious, angry, distant, self-absorbed, compartmentalized, abusive (in my case, verbally and inwardly) *and* kind, warm, caring, generous, loving. But I chose not to be *how* he was—that how or Tao, the Middle Way, makes all the difference to me: learning to live in harmony with one's inner being, with others, and with Nature's rhythms.

Still, while discussing the Harvey Weinstein rape and sexual assault allegations with friends, I reacted with instant rage when a male friend commented, "I feel compassion for Harvey." I lashed out, shaped my hand like an imaginary gun, held it to his head, and feigned pulling the trigger. For someone like me who abhors violence and has served as an anti-violence mentor for high school students, this spontaneous physical response horrified me.

I immediately apologized and later continued an email dialogue with this friend, trying to understand and challenge his perspective.

I had not reacted in such an extreme way for many years. Through this incident, I realized how, even with years of conscious effort, fear and anger can remain deeply embedded. Some observers, such as trauma expert Gabor Maté, believe that the brain neurocircuitry in those who have endured childhood abuse can predispose someone to a lifelong habit of over-reactivity in stressful situations. Although I was enduring prolonged high stress at the time, I don't want to use that as an excuse for my behaviour.

Rather than resist and reject the undesirable bits of me, I try to understand, then release them. I strive to acknowledge my own and others' faults and wonders, without judgment, as a small way of recognizing our common humanness. Trying to learn self-compassion is part of my mindfulness journey. I wobble in and out of the blessed state of presence: extend, then retreat, judge and scorn, then welcome and thank.

Forward, back. Forward, back.

CHAPTER FOURTEEN

FATIGUE

I feel occasionally my skull will crack, fatigue is continuous—I only go from less exhausted to more exhausted & back again.
—Sylvia Plath

COMMITTED TO HEALING from chronic fatigue, I switched from full-time to part-time work at a government agency and moved to the country in 2000. My parents, both aged seventy-five, drove across the country with a U-Haul to bring me some of their antique furniture. While helping me move into my newly purchased rural home, they seemed like iron-pumping weightlifters compared to me. While they unloaded and carried heavy pieces, I had to keep stopping to lie down and rest. Now *that* was hard to accept. Grateful for their selfless assistance, I still struggled to integrate their generosity with our silence around incest.

Newly ensconced amidst forest and quiet, I gave more credence to intuition, the spark of my spiritual self that leads me to books, events, and people that reach and connect beyond my achiever persona. The more I slowed down and awoke to the grace of a moment or day—listening to bird song, crouching to peer into a flower, smiling at the sun—the less weight the allure of accolades and a conventional career held.

Ultimately, a core belief in being part of Source or Spirit, an indefinable, ever-present force far grander than my tiny self, helped sustain me through grief and healing. Every time I felt worthless or depressed, I would remind myself to tap into that Source. For flickers of time through meditation, stillness in nature, intuition, and contemplative readings, I could reaffirm this union, connected to All That Is.

In my rural backyard, I watched a garter snake rise up next to my chair and look at me. A friend's dog seemed to appear exactly when I most needed comfort. An astounding iridescent dragonfly landed on the lid of my garbage can.

Laurie, a therapist friend, says that incest shatters any sense of living in a benevolent realm or having a spiritual guardian. Psychoanalyst Leonard Shengold has called incest and other forms of child abuse "soul murder." U.S. memoirist Mark Matousek considers incest survivors "spiritual orphans." But in my usual contrarian style, such pronouncements made me all the more determined to prove them wrong. I wanted to believe that Source energy, as shared power, could help me co-create life in new ways. Over many years, I learned to trust that this connection, which often felt like a dubious thread at best, would see me through times of greatest pain and doubt. Thich Nhat Hanh calls this deep interconnectedness and interdependence between all beings "inter-being."

* * *

A framed pen-and-ink collage of familiar famous rock star faces—Mick Jagger, Bob Dylan, and others—hangs in a medical office in Vancouver that I visit in 2000. At age forty-one, I stare at these faces, struggling to name them, unable to identify a single one, even though I know who they are. Nothing. Minutes, hours, days later, the names still won't come. Supremely rattled, I think: *This must be what stroke victims feel like.* Previously, people always tapped me to remember a name, which usually came readily. This cognitive gap is more than the result of aging. What has happened to my memory? I learn that this is a condition of chronic fatigue syndrome.

During my job as corporate communications manager at a government agency, I remember my first day back after a vacation, feeling relaxed and replenished. By noon, after a scramble to catch up, take phone calls, and fulfill demands, I was a pile of depleted jelly. A senior executive, who had requested the immediate launch of multiple new initiatives, wanted to see a schedule of related events. When he commented, in jest, to a colleague, "We don't want Heather to burn out," I replied, "I'm already burnt out."

Due to chronic fatigue and related depression, I ended up on medical leave. Weak, burnt out, and blue, I felt embarrassed to have the company send me to a psychiatrist. To test my memory, he gave me a verbal list of five simple words. Within ten minutes, he asked me to repeat them. Even with strong hints, I could remember only the first word. This left me deflated and forlorn. What was wrong with me?

A doctor tapped my right knee to check my reflexes. My knee flung up so fast it seemed like it might kick him in the crotch. "Wow," he said. "You're pretty high strung, like a thoroughbred racehorse." I didn't know that my startle response was extreme; hyperarousal and hypervigilance are common amongst unhealed sexual abuse and incest survivors.

I learned that memories of danger and threat are stored in the amygdala, the almond-shaped part of the brain that plays a vital role in how we link stress and anxiety to overwhelming events and inter-actions. After a trauma, it keeps churning out stress hormones, says post-traumatic-stress clinician Bessel A. van der Kolk. As these hor-mones continue flowing, they can create an adrenaline overload, like a car draining its battery while trying to race the engine with no-where to go. The doctor used that drained battery metaphor with me; he said that due to my chronic fatigue, my energy levels would never fully recover. I felt determined to prove him wrong.

Since my regular doctor was on holiday, I visited her young fe-male replacement, describing my months of insomnia, tension head-aches, aching elbows and hip joints, swollen neck glands, and limbs that felt wholly drained of any strength or energy. Even after rare extended hours of sleep, I never felt rested. Always exhausted. Standing up for more than a few minutes, I felt as if my knees would buckle. "Maybe you have yuppie flu," my sister Nancy said. On the outside, I looked fine.

Would I ever know again what it was like to have eight hours of consecutive sleep? The glands in the side of my neck, sore and enlarged, felt like golf balls. The replacement doctor put her hands on them and pressed.

"Ouch," I said.

"I don't feel anything," she said curtly. She asked me repeatedly: "Are you sure you don't have AIDS?" No! I wasn't sexually active at the time and had had several HIV tests, all negative. Yet, she kept pushing AIDS as a likely diagnosis. She handed me a brochure with a list of HIV-positive symptoms. Appalled, I left the office.

Chronic fatigue syndrome (CFS) is a condition with a list of symptoms ranging from memory loss to severe joint pain. Some people call it Epstein-Barr virus or myalgic encephalomyelitis (ME). Limited information about this auto-immune illness, similar to fibromyalgia, was available in the 1990s. Until fibromyalgia became prevalent, many people in the medical field considered it and CFS psychosomatic. Their only treatment: Take anti-depressants. Stress, anxiety, and depression are common aspects of these conditions.

Today, some doctors, such as Ric Arseneau, a clinician at University of British Columbia's Complex Chronic Diseases Program, believe that genetics and childhood abuse can predispose someone to a condition like CFS. Viral infections and trauma are known triggers. My mother had mononucleosis in third-year university: did she pass down a susceptibility to me? Yet, none of my sisters has had CFS. This unexplained condition increased my sense of alienation within our family.

Feeling severely depleted with CFS, I knew my immune system was shot. Many weeks of intense grief, sobbing, and depression had helped over-activate my adrenal glands. Like a semi-invalid, I lay in bed or on the couch off and on for months, barely able to sleep or be active. To some, it could look like malingering or desperate attention-seeking. To an active doer like me, it was daily torment.

It is difficult to convey the challenge of looking fine on the outside but feeling wholly spent on the inside, as if stuck with a flu that lasts for years. As with incest, it is easier for people to feel empathic if they can see something tangible like physical scars. Even after minimal tasks, I tired easily. Highly sensitive to noise, I cherished silence, yet at my rented condo, construction workers, with a blaring radio, began work at 7 a.m. on a balcony only centimetres from my bed. Every interaction, from a brief phone call to a personal encounter, seemed too taxing. To cope, I began to break each day into increments of energy: Do I have enough energy to make a phone call, have lunch with someone, read a book? The answer was usually no.

It felt demoralizing to admit my body's limitations. As a child, I was the Brownie who, while at a weekend camp sleepover, with lights out and everyone in their sleeping bags, stood up on a bed and yelled, "On with the show," ready for a fun night of more songs and jokes when everyone else was trying to sleep.

* * *

Slowly, I allowed the truth of my memories to give me a fuller sense of self. No more wasting so much energy resisting and rejecting my past. I continued to open more to encounters in nature and sought out its healing presence. A coyote peered up at me outside the window of a trailer I rented for several months in BC's Slocan Valley. Later, the owner told me it was rare to see one on that property.

With the same determination to heal from incest, I shifted my focus to CFS recovery, immersing myself in a potpourri of attempted antidotes, from massage and chiropractic care to vitamins and supplements. Strict diets, sometimes little more than a flax-bread-and-water regime, helped eliminate allergic reactions and heighten nutrition. This gave me a small boost in energy. After a brief stint of using anti-depressants to a year of therapeutic mixtures from a trained herbalist, I felt motivated to become strong and healthy again.

I felt hugely grateful for my company's medical and financial support while off work and trying to get better. Later, they accommodated me by providing part-time employment that was less stressful.

Slowly, over several years, my body began to feel hardier. I tested myself gradually: a short vacation with a friend started with a day of rest but produced no relapse. I went on a hike and didn't collapse. These seemingly new abilities seemed miraculous.

By the fall of 2001, I was laid off, along with other managers and several executive staff. Through my entire process of healing from chronic fatigue, neither my parents nor my sisters ever asked how I was doing. This didn't surprise me; I knew our family's silent rule: *If you don't talk about something, it never happened.*

What astounded me most during months of extreme fatigue was discovering, for the first time, that I was lovable even when not achieving anything. My friends didn't care if I wasn't working or publishing. They wanted to spend time with me purely for who I was. After a lifetime of pushing myself to feel valued through achievement—a sentiment nurtured fiercely in my family—this new awareness felt like a "Hallelujah" moment.

Having regained some physical sense of the old me, I felt more determined than ever to prove to myself that incest would not limit who I was to become.

CHAPTER FIFTEEN

SHOES

I believe every woman should own at least one pair of red shoes.
—Terry Tempest Williams

WE HUMANS TRY to understand the world through story and create meaning from our experiences. As trauma therapist Barbara Allyn says, "If you don't make meaning (around) an event—of why it happened to you—then you hold on to that event." In her view, if something disrupts a person's ability to fold an experience into their personal narrative, this can disrupt their ability to function in an orderly way.

Hallelujah. She summed up in a few sentences what I've been trying to explain for many years. In a writing workshop I attended decades ago with author Deena Metzger, she encouraged us to find a Larger Story, a fairy tale or other archetypal saga that illuminated our individual life with deeper meaning. I chose Hans Christian Andersen's story *The Red Shoes*. Even now, it resonates.

After a self-absorbed young girl receives a pair of coveted red shoes, she spurns opportunities to help and serve others. As if in punishment, she discovers that the shoes have a willfulness of their own, forcing her to dance endlessly beyond her control into deep forest on a dark night. Desperate with exhaustion, she begs a woodsman to lop off her feet; he does, replacing them with plain, wooden ones. This transformation brings her new humility: she chooses to serve others from a foundation of selflessness and spiritual peace.

Incest might have metaphorically hacked off my feet, but, ultimately, it made me stronger. Only now can I see the gift inherent in
this wounding. My willfulness, shame, and approach of "Never
good enough, push to succeed" were the feet that needed to be
lopped off. The symbolic axe that removed my feet slowed me down
enough to accept the term "trauma" to describe my experience. My
own healing could help me feel greater compassion for the pain of
others.

*Around age seven, I covet a child's pair of red velvet shoes. They are
hand-me-downs, rarely worn. Their hint of black heel and thin strap
across my ankles make me feel like a princess, a fancy pants, someone
able to make magic real. But my stern mother tells me I can wear them
only on special occasions. I sulk and complain. Why can't I feel special
every day? Subverting my mother's plan, I stash the shoes in a hall closet
just outside our back door. That way, I can wear my everyday shoes out
the door, take them off, put on the velvet shoes, and wear them to school,
leaving my regular ones hidden in the closet. Returning from school, I
simply reverse my morning process to complete the ritual.*

I don't remember how long this ruse continued before my mother
discovered it. "You're a disgrace!" she said, implying that I was revealing some latent criminal gene in our otherwise Puritan family. "That
shows how deceptive you were," she said, decades later.

As a child, I scribbled in *Ring-a-ling*, a large, hard-cover collection of verses adapted from folk songs. It is one of a few books from
childhood that remain in my household. The wonderful coloured
drawings by a Czech illustrator portray animals and insects cavorting
like humans, doing chores in nature with mischief and pleasure. A
few pages still bear my frenzy of orange parallel lines, small orange
circles, and geometric shapes. Angry at this act of defilement, my
mother warned the young me that I would be in trouble when my
father got home. Instead, he said: "At least it shows she's creative."

Creativity was my solace for loneliness in childhood: drawing
and making figures in clay or fabric and tapping out stories on my

mother's typewriter. When I wasn't making mini-newspapers or concocting overwrought fantasies, my spirit flew into the adventure lands of *Treasure Island* and *White Fang* and the drama of Helen Keller's *The Story of My Life.*

Although my mother introduced me to the world of literature, she seemed bent on moulding me into some version of Victorian-era propriety. She encouraged my creativity as long as it wasn't rowdy. I sensed that ideally, she wanted me to sit quietly in a rocking chair doing needlepoint; forget any games that could prove too boisterous. From her own childhood on a dairy farm during the Depression, she lived and shared the message that life is work and discipline and getting things done. If you weren't out of bed by six, you were a sloth. If you followed your own desires, you were selfish.

My mom told my sister Wendy in the summer of 1980 that if she put her eldest daughter, then an infant, into daycare, her child would likely wind up a juvenile delinquent. Similarly, she criticized Wendy for breastfeeding rather than using a bottle as she had. My mother told me that feminists destroy the nuclear family. Recently, I learned that she told Wendy: "Women who are raped deserve it." Hardly an advocate for a child who would accuse her father of incest!

Despite our relative wealth, the spectre of doing without always hung over our household. If you didn't work hard enough, a Depression might descend and then you'd know what it's like to suffer. In the meantime, keep your voice down, don't sit on that furniture, you might break it, don't be saucy, don't interrupt, don't, don't, don't.

As the spoiled youngest child, I usually got what I wanted, whether a talking doll with a pull-string or a red Jaguar XKE (not the real thing, but a Dinky toy). I never had any lack of playthings, clothes or food. But our museum-like home stifled my rambunctious nature. There was the antique pine church pew too uncomfortable to sit on; the shelves of historic glass goblets that we weren't supposed to touch; the elegant Queen Anne armless chairs that we couldn't lean back on; the bubbles that we couldn't blow because they might stain the wallpaper; every *National Geographic* that we were never, ever to cut up. Our home was not somewhere to have fun—you had to go outside for that.

* * *

I adopted red shoes as a symbol of rebellion. In my early twenties, I wore red high-top Converse sneakers. At the Burning Man festival in 2006, I wore red, knee-high, lace-up canvas boots, fancy versions of sneakers. Several years ago, I ordered through a catalogue velvety red shoes with a simple strap much like the ones I was forbidden to wear as a child.

Red shoes now represent moxie and ingenuity to me. I associate them with passion, adventure, a leftist bent, brashness beyond practical life, and danger colliding with daring whimsy. They are beacons of what I overcame and have become.

Today, the child in me finds cheer in Dorothy's sparkly red shoes in *The Wizard of Oz*, the ones that whisked her away to fantasy and illusion, to the glowing yellow brick road, and the befuddled old man behind the curtain who created the facades. Dorothy's journey provided her with great insight into what is important in life. She discovered and survived fear, assault, and her own weaknesses, learning the power of love, friendship, and finding a sense of home within.

Red shoes, velvet and new. A child's delight, fingers lost in softness. Velvet shoes on my feet, so special, no scuffs. I'm dancing beyond puddles on the path to surprises, pride tucked between my toes. New dreams arise for a young heart.

* * *

For years, I struggled to write this book. Over decades, I had urged writing students to get down on paper their most difficult and unexpressed personal issues. "Bring a voice to what lies hidden," I told them. They had awed me with the courage of their true tales, ranging from surviving rape or mental illness and institutionalization to coping with a lover's death or domestic violence. Yet, other than in a few short writing exercises I had shared in class, my incest story still lurked in silence. I felt like a hypocrite.

After returning from India, I began a manuscript about my travels, planning to write a light-hearted version of survival tales for female solo adventurers. That topic felt safe enough. I pored through my journals, added Post-it notes with headings to many pages and started a box of research files. Everything felt contained and under control. But incest was still not part of my public story.

The more I opened up to the darkness within me, the more I wondered: As a writer, how can I not put this crucial story arc into a memoir? My silence would only perpetuate an illusion of who my father was and wasn't. To both myself and others, I needed to validate my own experience through story.

Like my healing process, the decision to write an incest memoir evolved slowly. There was no pivotal scene or "aha" moment. The pages about my India travels, begun so long ago with a different intent, formed the early framework of this book.

I decided not to complete this memoir until after my father had died. Didn't want to face fallout from him over revealing our secret. More containment and control.

Ironically, the more I've written and talked about the impact of sexual assault and incest, the more challenging it seems to try and make people who haven't experienced it understand what it does to your identity. As I shared my manuscript with others, many people couldn't seem to get the connection between my assaults in India, and the incest. To me, the links couldn't be more obvious, yet clearly, I wasn't conveying their interrelationship adequately enough.

"No one cares about incest," one male agent in the U.S. told me. "Write about your Indian travels." A male agent in Toronto urged me to rewrite the whole book like a novel. The rejections piled up. A rep at a feminist publishing house said that she found my prolonged years of exploration and treatment "discouraging." She concluded that my memoir contained nothing useful for a survivor. Ouch.

But I persevered, determined not to whitewash my experience nor jump from jarring childhood incidents to an adult life of "Everything's fine now," as many incest memoirs do. To me, as with any story, the most interesting part is the messy middle, the conflict and complications, the pain of healing. Why gloss over that?

Many times, I put the manuscript away, only to hire yet another editor who would contradict what a previous one said. Many classmates from my master's program, even one who said she wrote very slowly, had their books published while mine still lay dormant. Wading through draft after draft, seemingly without progress, felt like trying to plod upwards with feet wedged into concrete runners.

Often, I questioned whether it was helpful to regurgitate my past. Maybe, instead, I was supposed to let go of my history and move on. Multiple times, I considered shelving the entire project. But two factors kept me going: if I could bring hope to even just one woman and help her through the morass of her healing, this process would be worth it. And I needed to do it for both the writer and survivor in me. Remaining silent never stayed an acceptable, long-term option.

Healing from childhood incest demands putting tiny feet into huge shoes, ready to get lost and stomped on but willing to grow into new forms that mould to the unique shape of your feet, like a cherished pair of soft, comfy Birkenstock sandals.

* * *

Therapeutic literature for incest survivors emphasizes the importance of reconnecting to the body to regain sensation, lost memory, and feelings. Yet, such sources don't mention how frightening it is to open fully to memory and allow a distressing past to seep, literally, through today's skin. Who wants to re-experience sexual abuse?

How gratifying to discover the term "felt sense" and how it applied to me. I knew that the abused child part of me had become frozen in my body, creating a split-off self. I had no "felt sense" of what made an action inappropriate. I had learned to shut down or ignore any body cues, like a simple knot in my stomach. Dissociation blocked my ability to trust and believe in myself implicitly, to grieve, heal, and let love into my bone marrow. (What irony that this is where my dad's cancer struck.)

Without healing this disconnection within me, I was still conditioned as an adult to freeze, rather than act, when I felt my boundaries had been violated, even if it was something as simple as a person cutting in line ahead of me. Or I would yell in fury at anything that felt like a violation of boundaries, from a stranger's ball falling into my lap by accident to a vehicle boxing me in on the road. (Mental health professionals call such overreaction, common among traumatized individuals, "an inability to regulate affect.")

A therapist told me that sexual abuse survivors commonly have a "freeze" state beyond the usual "fight or flight" response. While experiencing the abuse, we go numb. To our body, this feels as if we're dying, says Peter Levine in *Waking the Tiger*. The same stress hormones and annihilating fear can result. Therefore, rather than open up to something we believe will kill us, we shut down.

When most people feel threatened or at risk, it's normal to run, hit, or push away. But for a child in a sexual abuse situation, this choice often does not feel possible or safe. As child victims, we don't want to ask for help because we aren't sure if something is wrong and also fear we might not be believed. This was the recurring theme in my childhood dreams. Some victims might be told or threatened not to tell. So, we act out, which can bring punishment and a further sense of feeling "bad." My instinctive self, conditioned to override my natural emotional response, got confused over the choice and control I had as an adult versus when the incest happened.

It helped me significantly to hear from an outside professional that while a kid in a sexualized situation with a parent, I was conditioned to trust and honour my dad's requests and viewpoints more than my own sense that something felt strange. Children in a sexual abuse or incest situation, particularly with someone who is otherwise kind and loving, learn to doubt and discredit their own responses in situations with anyone, sexual or non-sexual.

In my forties, lying under a blanket on the floor during a relaxing and nurturing meditation class, I am back in the body of my five-year-old self. For only a few seconds, I am fully embodied as her again, looking out with her eyes. This unprompted return to childhood, after so many years of healing, leaves me unsettled and confused. When will this end?

Living inside an unhealed traumatized body demands constant juggling between the mind and body, rational and irrational ideas, thoughts and feelings, and wellness and illness, as incest survivor Tanya Lewis describes in her book *Living Beside*. These contradictions can prompt an inherent ambivalence toward incest. I don't want to be defined by it, yet it fundamentally altered my life. I want to tell readers how incest affects people, yet it's not a topic shared in social gatherings. I want to recreate my experiences, yet not trigger trauma for other survivors. Too many people still believe, or imply, that the victim is at fault.

It has been tough to accept that I'm a victim of trauma, according to therapeutic literature on incest. For most of my life, I have associated that word with war, terrorism, and catastrophe. A traumatic experience is supposed to be an intense or overwhelming event that someone's psyche can't wholly contain or explain. Some call it a threat to one's dignity. To therapist Gudrun Zomerland, it's "the shaking of a soul." My trauma hardly compares to the impact of a tsunami, deadly explosion, terrorist attack, devastating accident, fire, or survival from a grisly attempted murder. Yet, today we know that lack of emotional support and expression in childhood alone can traumatize us, thanks to the work of Vancouver expert Dr. Gabor Maté.

If my father had beaten or tortured me, made me the victim of a sadistic cult or pushed me into group adult sex or pornography, traumatization would be easier to recognize.

He never threatened to kill me if I told anyone. He didn't force his penis inside me. He didn't rape me with a Coke bottle or broom handle. He didn't abuse me repeatedly for years.

But he stole my personhood, my heart and loyalty, my inherent sense of identity and safety in my body. My autonomy. My trust and openness to love. What entitlement he showed in capturing me as his voiceless companion, there solely to serve his needs. I have since learned of psychotherapist Francis Weller's concept of "slow trauma," which refers to "subtle omissions of attention and care," the childhood moments when we needed to be held or soothed but such support never came. By that definition, almost every individual is likely emotionally traumatized at some level, despite what cynics might think. Only twenty years after my time in India, while writing this book and suffering what my then-therapist called post-traumatic stress, did I consider "trauma" a label that bore any relevance to me. The triggering I experienced while writing was indeed real: anxiety, insomnia, flashbacks, and despondency.

Childhood victims of covert incest like me can feel privileged and pampered, not abused. That makes it harder to understand and believe that incest was indeed abuse, let alone trauma. My former therapist explained, to my surprise, that incest and sexual abuse are among the hardest types of trauma to heal. A natural disaster, fire, or war might be horrific, but if people who survive these have an intact sense of self, the trauma remains only an event, she said. Because they don't need to heal a core part of their psyche, these survivors can benefit from therapy more easily and quickly than a sexual abuse victim, she said.

In contrast, incest and sexual abuse reinforce that someone's innate being or identity is like rotten food that needs to be thrown out. This self-assessment, which manifests as shame in countless ways, is the invisible enemy that I struggled with for years. People like me are deemed to have suffered a double whammy of trauma: not only were we betrayed and mistreated by the person who was supposed to protect our well-being, but this same person injured our fundamental sense of self.

I wanted to build a new equation. Heck, I wanted adventure, contentment, joy, success—let me invite it all in and savour it. Learning to accept and access all my feelings, in whatever form they came, was my entryway to healing and wholeness. But although I knew this intellectually, my body was still programmed to resist and dissociate in subtle ways around unpleasant people or experiences.

It's challenging, as Lewis points out in *Living Beside*, to try to find a language for the experience of trauma, particularly for an adult trying to grasp something that occurred to her child's body and mind. For me, it has been like asking a timid three-year-old with amnesia to blurt out her story to a critical judge, threatening prosecutor, and frowning jury, forced to use their complex words, which she doesn't understand.

* * *

I am not a woman who fills her closet with shoes, who can never have enough pairs. No rows of flashy stilettos for me. Metaphorically, shoes have kept me grounded. In recent years, Joanne Harris's evocative story "The Scarlet Slippers" from her book *Honeycomb* has brought me renewed validation for my life choices. In the tale, she describes a young man in a desert world who falls in love with a veiled woman whose face he cannot see. She wears "slippers of scarlet silk." If she will become his queen, he promises her everything from protection to fine wines.

The woman agrees to be his forever on one condition: he must take her to the sea, where she has never walked on a beach or heard waves.

After three nights of camel riding, they arrive at a wild stretch of beach. The woman stands on the shore in her red slippers, gazing out to sea, where mermaids are said to lure men to their death. "This is where I shall take off my veil, stand barefoot on the sand, and be yours," she says. She tells him to wait on the cliff, which he does, as she climbs down to the beach.

After waiting a long time, he climbs down to the beach but there is no sign of the woman—only her slippers neatly arranged at the shore. They form part of "a long line of women's shoes that stretched right across the little beach and disappeared around the base of the cliffs." Hundreds of bare footprints lead to the water's edge but none lead back from the sea because "mermaids have no need of embroidered slippers—or of silken veils, or even men."

The young man, sitting by the water's edge, weeps. "I would have kept you safe," he said. "I would have watched over you day and night. I would have made sure no other man ever came anywhere near you."

Far in the distance, he hears the sound of laughing mermaids.

I had no idea how differently this story would end for me.

CHAPTER SIXTEEN

LOVE

*I'm selfish, impatient and a little insecure. I make mistakes, I
am out of control and at times hard to handle. But if you can't
handle me at my worst, then you sure as hell don't deserve me
at my best.*
—Marilyn Monroe

FAMILY PHOTO #9. For my father's eightieth birthday, in May 2005,
our family and dozens of relatives and friends gather for a weekend
at my parents' favourite retreat, a lakefront resort in Muskoka, Ont.
We all pose outdoors in a group shot with three rows of people, ten
across. In the front row, each of my parents sits on a separate, bright-
ly painted Adirondack chair, my mom's youngest sister in a yellow
chair beside them. I sit between my parents, balanced on the arm-
rests of their chairs, one arm stretched over the back of each of them.
Everyone is smiling.

In the resulting photo, I look happy. That day, I loved my parents and appreciated the sense of family this event gave me. My dad
had generously covered everyone's expenses for the weekend. The
previous night, in front of the entire group, he had screened a short
film that I co-wrote, which featured two violinists duelling music-
ally for a woman's attention. When more people arrived later that
evening, he screened it again. *How strange this is,* I thought. *Dad and
I still haven't talked about the incest.*

Even by this time, at age forty-six, I still wanted to half-believe
that I had imagined it all. I had heard or read accounts of how other

incest survivors had confronted their perpetrators. One woman had distributed notices at her brother's wedding reception, accusing him of molesting her in childhood. This approach felt too jarring and vengeful to me.

I still didn't know how to respond to the issue within my family. Part of me acted like I had forgotten about it. Some therapists use the label "betrayal trauma" to describe how a child forgets abuse by a loved one because she depends on him for protection. Some people view incest and sexual abuse as a form of identity theft. To remember the abuse would threaten her survival instinct. Jim Hopper, a therapist and psychology instructor at Harvard Medical School, says that at least 10 percent of those who are sexually abused in childhood will completely forget their abuse for certain periods, then have "delayed recall." Some clinical studies have reported a forgetting rate between 19 and 77 percent among childhood sexual abuse victims.

If we don't feel safe or feel unloved as children, we have no alternative but to stay close to the abuser within the family. This sustains an illusion of love. Call it Stockholm Syndrome Meets Pippi Longstocking. This disorienting "trauma bond," which feels like love and caring to a kid like me, becomes even stronger than the connection to the healthy parent who remains loving all the time. Yet, the victim has no bruises or physical scars to hide, no proof of what's happening to her.

There are millions of women like me. Our stories don't make headlines. Our fathers rarely get caught. Few people tell.

Thankfully, therapy in middle age allowed me to reprocess the encounters with my dad with an adaptive or adult understanding. With more awareness and tools of support, I was moving closer to a willingness and ability to truly forgive him. Over many years, forgiveness and compassion have formed the cornerstones of my eclectic spiritual practice, a blend of Buddhism, Taoism, hatha and yin yoga, meditation, and Nature-based transcendentalism. I wanted these two touchstones of shared humanity to be more than just theoretical goals. I needed to live and embody them.

I like what Pema Chodron says: "Compassion is not a relationship between the healer and the wounded. It's a relationship between equals. Only when we know our own darkness well can we be present with the darkness of others."

* * *

That spring, I began to correspond by email with my second cousin Frank, who lived in Massachusetts. (He was adopted; we have no blood relation.) Soon after his father died, I emailed him and his brother my condolences. By then, Frank had been separated from his wife for about four-and-a-half years.

During my childhood, our families spent Christmas and holidays together, visiting between each other's respective homes in Ontario and New York state. Frank's adoptive mother Marge, a loving dynamo and my favourite "aunt," died of cancer when he was twenty-two and I was seventeen; she was my dad's first cousin and they were close.

Although Frank and I had had little contact in twenty years, we began daily emails rich in revelation and humour. Our messages revealed many shared interests, including a passion for the sea, history, film, the environment, activism, and the arts. His tender heart and kindness readily appeared through an obvious love of children and animals. I admired his innate desire to readily help others and serve his community as a volunteer. Frank said he remembered, at age five, holding the infant me in his arms for the first time. An overwhelming sense of precious love for me enveloped him then, he said, and has remained ever since.

Frank valued independent thought and freedom of expression far more than status, ego strokes, and wealth. Maintaining an image meant little to him: he preferred rumpled, paint-stained clothes to crisp leisure wear. Through his one-man law firm, he always put his clients' interests first. I admired his willingness to advocate so fervently for others and to speak out against injustice, greed, and corruption, whether at the civic, state or federal level.

All summer, we continued our online conversation, eventually graduating to the telephone. Our first call, in August 2005, lasted two hours. Frank's laughter, offered in frequent belly roars throughout our chat, stayed with me.

A month later, he came to visit for a week. When we made supper together, it was as if we had been doing it our whole lives; I had never felt so at ease with any man. Two months later, I flew to New York state to help Frank clean out the home of his late father, a doctor like mine. In his later years, his dad had become a hoarder. Amidst the mess, Frank had cleared space on a long table, found candles, and made a delicious salad for lunch. *He's a keeper*, I thought.

Despite our rapport, it took me months to share my incest story with Frank. He had thought highly of my father; my disclosure dissembled that view. Other than Frank's intellect, curiosity, and interest in cars—and his sneeze, eerily identical to my dad's—he appeared to hold little in common with my father. We both grappled with integrating acceptance of my dad's admirable traits *and* his abuse.

By the time Frank and I were together, my self-love had grown markedly, thanks to a year of visits to an Inner Child therapist. Repeatedly, I had drawn and given voice to the pain inside me. In one picture, done hastily with a felt pen during a therapy session, a young girl, crying, hugs herself inside a closet full of empty hangers. At a workshop of somatic experience, I drew a tall tree and wrote: *People want to destroy me.* My conscious self was shocked at such imagery and expression, which sprang from me spontaneously, but I trusted that my subconscious bore messages that needed to be heard and released.

My therapist had encouraged me to make time for the playful activities relished as a child: painting, drawing, finding fun toys, and so on. At her request, I wrote a poignant love letter to myself, which she suggested marketing and distributing as a template for others, which I never did. Once our professional visits stopped, we became friends, and she helped me focus more on daily gratitude. Her outlook allowed me to appreciate more the miracle of nature in a moment, and to embrace vulnerability as a strength and gift to others, rather than a liability.

Addressing the woundedness of my child self became an instrumental turning point in my healing. That young being no longer sabotaged as frequently my efforts at intimacy. Instead, I could remain wholly present to witness another's pain. When Frank sobbed spontaneously over the memory of the sudden death of two close childhood friends in a fire, for instance, I could hold and comfort him unreservedly, soothing and urging him to release his grief without any desire to retreat.

Easygoing and thoughtful, Frank rarely got angry, which freed me to feel open to speak as candidly as possible with him. I wondered sometimes: What if we had gotten together sooner? He would have made an excellent father. But I don't think things would have worked out at an earlier time. Too much anger and resentment would have prevented me from opening, and staying open, to Frank's love. I needed to feel worthy enough to accept unconditional love.

On February 14, 2006, we became engaged. One friend, who disparaged marriage, thought I had been culturally brainwashed to want to take on this tradition for the first time, at age forty-seven. Another thought I was rushing things. Although fearful about losing long-cherished freedom, I knew this move felt right. Ironically, both Frank and I had decided separately, before getting involved, that we would remain single for the rest of our lives.

* * *

The labyrinth is safe territory for many who feel they are unraveling at the seams; it is a place to order chaos and calm the frightened heart.
—**Lauren Artress**, *Walking a Sacred Path*

Clutching a bouquet of wild flowers, with a band of freesias and other blossoms pinned across my head, I stood in the centre of a circular forest labyrinth of smooth white stones. After three days of nervous anxiety and little sleep, I felt amazed at my peacefulness. A sheer, gauze shawl hung across my sleeveless shoulders. A floor-length taupe skirt of beads and embroidered floral swirls, swishing like a vintage gown, hid my beige slippers, their ribbons crisscrossed and tied at my ankles like a ballerina's toe shoes. Thankfully, I was not yet sweating under my top of lace-like net.

On this August afternoon in 2006, my husband-to-be, Frank, stood beside me in a light-olive suit and pale blue shirt, under sun filtered through tall cedars, Douglas firs, hemlock, and alder. Before us stood an altar-like table draped in garlands of cedar boughs and wild flowers, bearing rune stones, incense, a candle, fresh red rose, and two gold wedding rings of carved Coast Salish images. About ninety guests surrounded us in a circle on the outer row of the eleven-circuit labyrinth, a replica of the medieval one in France's Chartres Cathedral. We were in the backyard of a friend, who had created the labyrinth on his .6-hectare rural property. Our Circle of Life wedding ceremony was underway.

Frank and I stood in the centre of the labyrinth's rosette pattern. During our Celtic hand-fasting ritual, we joined hands, a double-looped cord draped around our wrists as a figure eight, bearing knots we had each made prior to the event. We viewed this symbol of infinity as an unbroken sacred circle, representing unity and time with no beginning or end.

As we faced each other, Frank told me: "With you, I have begun to understand, to see beyond, to experience the true meaning of emotion, of love. You are the ocean and the sky, light and lens, a portal looking into humanity."

I told Frank: "You lift my heart, body and soul into blissful flight. You are my wings, my sky, my earth, my partner in the infinite potential of love and life. May we soar aloft together. Love, fly on."

My parents attended the wedding, but I did not include them in the ceremony.

Later, at the reception on a boat, my father eyed one of my female friends wearing a long trench coat and quipped in front of her: "I'd like to see what she has on underneath that." Jarred, I did not let his comment mar the festivities.

Decades earlier, integrating my abused self with a healthful life had seemed impossible. Any form of union with a man, let alone a lifetime act of committed love, seemed inconceivable. My willingness to risk love with Frank, and open myself to the pains and gifts of intimacy with his loving, positive soul, felt like my greatest triumph over incest. I had relearned a healthy way to become vulnerable.

Less than a year before our wedding, when Frank had visited me for a week, we had discussed marriage amidst a remarkable level of effortless comfort. With anyone else, I would have considered this unimaginable and too-fast insanity. It seemed clear to us both that we wanted to spend our lives together. As I told Frank in my wedding vow: "It felt as if we had been together all of our lives. I have never felt so at ease with anyone, so loved by any man. I have never laughed so much and so often with any man." I even created a comical name for our union: Frankenheather. As Walt Whitman wrote: "We have circled and circled till we have arrived home again, we two."

* * *

Getting married inside a labyrinth seemed the perfect culmination of my healing journey. A labyrinth is said to represent intuitive energy, to help a walker replace traditional, dualistic thinking with the more inclusive "both/and" thinking. Carl Jung called labyrinths, with their spiral of concentric circles based on sacred geometry, a blend of form and the Unknown, an archetype of transformation and the sacred Self.

For decades, I have been drawn to these ancient pathways, which people have created and used around the globe for more than four thousand years. Perhaps each walk in a labyrinth was helping me make whole the tiny shards of self lost through my father. Or maybe these steps merely helped to open me more deeply to a wiser Self.

For many years, I had raged at men and my dad, stuck in blame. I've always disliked the label "passive" for so-called feminine energy. It makes me want to challenge somebody with the words: "*I'll* show you what passive looks like." I dismissed traditional femininity as the pink fluffy slippers of life. From about age three on, I threw a tantrum if my mom wanted me to wear a dress. No frills or high heels for me: I'd rather take steel-toed boots any day. But for too many years, I stomped on myself and others, disdaining anything or anyone related to domesticity, the stereotypical female domain. Ever since reading adventure tales as a child, I longed for traditional male lives of freedom and exploration. As a kid, I found Nancy Drew books too boring; the Hardy Boys seemed to have far more fun. Since then, I have learned the value and power of stillness and vulnerability, often aligned with supposed feminine or yin traits. In current times, I am grateful that we are moving beyond limited gender definitions.

Walking the circular forms of labyrinths can help us grow aware of our suffering, says Virginia Westbury in *Labyrinths: Ancient Paths of Wisdom and Peace.* With each step and each day, I was seeking to grow more open to forgiveness and compassion, willing to see into others' suffering hearts and find greater acceptance of them and myself.

* * *

In India, much worship and attention has focused on the *lingam* as a sacred symbol of maleness. I wanted to acknowledge the power of its counterpart: the *yoni* or divine feminine energy. A Sanskrit word for the vagina or vulva, *yoni* represents sacred space. Symbolized as a circle, it embodies creation and destruction, life and death. For me, the *yoni* represents the steel part of the term "steel magnolias," the invisible circle of love and compassion that we share with one who is dying, when we face death unafraid and in truth, naming it when others pretend that its grasp is far away.

For me, the *yoni* symbolizes what happens when the ego lies down and says: "I can't do it all by myself. In fact, I don't know if I can do it at all." The *yoni* offers the arms that hug doubt and tender hurt and say: "There, there. It's alright. You'll be fine." The *yoni* is so much more than female genitalia, than some helpless receptacle, than just a platform for the almighty *lingam*. It is divine love and caring and surrender and the healing wisdom that emerge from suffering and survival. It is that small inner voice that nabs my attention and offers a new idea or possibility when I've stopped long enough to forget my ambitious plans and time lines.

The *yoni* can represent a sacred womb or temple, a channel for universal *chi* energy, but I prefer to think of it as supreme creativity made manifest, the soul and the spirit of life, sex, birth, procreation—whatever is real and raw and respectful to all. Devotion, not desecration. It is found in the love and compassion I felt increasingly for Frank, friends, family, and myself: the circle made complete, the union of being and doing. It is the uncovering of *ahimsa*.

Beyond mere genes, my family remains with me, an inward and outward presence. On my fingers, I wear circles of love, symbols of my ancestry. Besides my wedding and engagement bands, I wear Frank's mother's wedding ring, a thin silver band of tiny diamonds, on the middle finger of my left hand. On the other hand, my third finger bears the plain gold wedding band of Frank's grandmother. When talking about the vibrant and heartful woman who raised him, Frank and I speculate how pleased she must be to know that we are together. I like to think that our marriage embodies her legacy of love, which we both shared and relished so long ago. Her tender spirit soars between us, beyond time.

CHAPTER SEVENTEEN

COURAGE

The tension between what is said and what is not said ... this is the dilemma of the human family. It takes courage to tell our stories. It takes belief that our stories will be received and held in respect.
  —Christina Baldwin, *Storycatcher*

Inside a quaint New England bungalow, an intense professor grips the arms of his adoring bride, facing her with fevered eyes. Glancing up at him, she looks bewildered and afraid. He is about to make a confession, one that will shatter her view of reality forever. She holds on, uncertain if she wants to hear his response to her question: "You killed him?"

I NEVER THOUGHT that a TV thriller would become a pivotal part of my healing process. In the 1946 film noir *The Stranger*, ingenuous bride Mary Longstreet, played by Loretta Young, struggles to reject any truth regarding the allegedly brutal past of her new husband, a menacing Orson Welles. He is a well-respected academic in her wholesome Connecticut town, yet no one knows anything of his true past. Flush with love, his wife wants to believe only in his goodness. Clutching her in a key scene, he confesses that he has killed a man with "the same hands that have held you close to me." A single murder is the least of his crimes; his true identity is Franz Kindler, a former Nazi mastermind of the Final Solution. Only after he kills a Nazi associate, who has arrived to appeal to Kindler to turn himself in (only in Hollywood!) and buries him in the park, does his cover start to unravel.

When I first saw this melodrama, which bears the marketing tagline "the most deceitful man a woman ever loved," in June 2007, I found myself reacting with visceral anger and didn't know why. Even though the murder-genocide story bore no semblance to my life, its themes of duplicity, denial, and a secret past resonated profoundly.

The film seemed to tug at my desire for truth, jabbing me in the shoulders with reminders: "You are living a lie" and "Your father is not who he appears to be." I wanted to challenge his respectability and confront him about incest and the truth of our relationship. Above all, I wanted him to admit what he had done to me and apologize. The movie made me realize that my silence had sheltered my dad for years, enabling him to maintain honour and well-being while I harboured our secret at my own emotional expense.

Yet, I wanted to follow the advice of my former therapist: "Your parents aren't going to be here forever. Why not make the most of your relationship with them while they're still around?" She had encouraged me to let go of recriminations and make peace with my parents, particularly my dad, who was then eighty-two. That didn't mean condoning his actions; it simply acknowledged that our father-daughter connection encompassed far more than just incestuous incidents. Why did our secret past have to define our relationship?

I wanted to rise above past rage at my dad for not being who I wanted him to be. I still admired his wit and humour, probing mind, intellectual curiosity, love of books, history, and travel; we shared these traits as much as our genetic code. To ignore and disdain these parts of him meant rejecting them in me. Yet, I still wasn't clear on how to love and accept my father's qualities without appearing to dismiss or minimize what he had done to me.

By the time I watched Welles' unsettling film, I was maintaining contact with my folks, exchanging letters, emails, and phone calls. My husband and I had stayed at their home, thousands of kilometres away; I even revised parts of this book there, although never mentioned to my parents what I was working on. Everything on the surface of our relationship seemed normal and harmonious.

However, I had wondered about my supposed integration of love and incest. After what he had done, how could I so casually converse with my dad and send him loving cards? Since early 2005, I had thought about confronting him by email. This felt safer than a phone call; besides, our family rarely phoned each other unless for significant news.

Frank thought that I had missed an essential step in the healing process: the act of bearing witness. My father and I had never discussed the incest issue, nor had he heard from me what anguish it had caused in my life. Never having shared anything like a victim-impact statement with him, I realized that my burgeoning sense of forgiveness was more a theoretical exercise than an act that wholly engaged my heart.

In the broadest sense, I heartily endorse police surveillance and stings to catch sexual predators who prey on children through the Internet and in public spaces. And I applaud the efforts of people like Oprah Winfrey and Ghana's investigative journalist Anas Aremeyaw Anas who have sought out pedophiles and rapists for arrest and prosecution. But I didn't want to apply a nab-that-bastard approach with my father.

I believed that he was an opportunistic offender (one who had chances within the family to abuse and took them), rather than a predatory one who seeks ways to abuse through teaching or coaching, etc. He did not scout out schools or neighbourhoods, lying in wait to approach children with some deceptive ploy. Officially, he'd be classified as a regressed abuser: someone with otherwise "normal" sexual interests who might turn to sexual contact with a child as a way to cope or as a substitute for an appropriate partner during periods of extended stress. Two forensic psychology experts, M.E. Rice and G.T. Harris, have stated that incest offenders do not molest children outside their families. If I thought that my father represented a threat to other children, I would have reported him.

An adoptee friend of mine did not choose to contact her birth parents until she felt she could handle any reaction from them. I decided not to confront my father until I had reached that point. I had watched a variety of documentaries in which sexual abuse survivors confronted their abusers; the perpetrators displayed an astounding lack of empathy and compassion. Even with an admission or apology, they generally downplayed or ignored any detrimental impact that their actions might have had on the victim. One handshake, a quick "I'm sorry," and the matter seemed over for them.

I wonder now: Did my dad suffer from post-traumatic stress after decades of seeing infants and young children die and having to tell parents that their child didn't make it? I never saw my father cry over any of his patients' situations. Alcohol helped him repress any related sadness. Even if he did suffer from PTSD, that does not excuse what he did to me.

I could not send my dad another breezy, loving card without sharing my newfound sentiments. As Father's Day approached in 2007, I sent him a card containing a handwritten letter, which included an ultimatum. If he would not admit to me what he had done and apologize for it, I would not agree to see him when my parents visited British Columbia in August, two months later.

I heard nothing for about six weeks, then received a one-paragraph email, which began with "Thank you for your nice Father's Day card." Reading on, I learned that he had tried to write an answer but admitted that "with a faulty memory and the passage of time, any rational discussion is impossible for me." He continued: "I was not brought up to 'let it all hang out'—quite the reverse! I want to apologise for any wrong that may have occurred and ask your forgiveness but would prefer to do so in a face-to-face meeting." His subsequent words took me aback:

I have had my own trials and tribulations unknown to you, so can understand the anguish revealed in the letter. Perhaps when we meet again, just you and I, we can seek solace together and comfort each other. With sincere affection,
   Love, Dad

What was he alluding to? Not for the first time, I wondered if his father, a military man I knew little about who had died before my birth, who looked stiff and remote in uniform in family photos, had abused his son.

My dad's written apology gave me a remarkable sense of validation. He had not denied anything, nor told me that I had conjured a lie. Frank interpreted his response as a confession and more. Begrudgingly, I acknowledged my father's courage in finally responding and making an apology. Strangely, I looked forward to meeting with him.

* * *

August 2007. My father, eighty-two, in a navy cardigan, and I, forty-eight, in a light jacket, leaned back on a wooden park bench. The seat was still wet from rain that morning and a downpour the day before. Under a blue sky, sumptuous sun. We were in Cardero Park, a narrow sliver of green in Coal Harbour, an upscale enclave of downtown Vancouver. The area's yachts and expensive high-rises perpetuate the lie of glossy lifestyle magazines: Doesn't everyone live this way? Around us lay a marina metaphorically made of floating money, home to the gleaming yacht of resident billionaire Jimmy Pattison and those who would like to be like him. We were on the water side of the Westin Bayshore, the hotel where Howard Hughes spent five-and-a-half months of seclusion in a blacked-out penthouse in the spring and summer of 1972. Past that, along the white-railed concrete walkway to the left, lay the Royal Vancouver Yacht Club. To our right, about a block away, gargantuan sea beasts picked up and disgorged the buffet-and-beach set at the city's downtown cruise ship terminal.

We gazed out at the row of boathouse roofs in the harbour ahead of us, sailboats and small craft bobbing in the lapping water. These pleasure-based surroundings seemed weirdly out of sync with the severity of subject matter that my dad and I were about to share. Our small patch of park grass felt like a tethered raft, dwarfed on shore by the Coast Mountains, whose snowy heads hover over the West Vancouver skyline across the harbour. Two SeaBus commuter catamarans traversed the inlet to our right. Sailboats and kayakers passed as noisy float planes landed and took off like crazed dragonflies.

My dad looked out to the ocean, his bald head exposed to the sun, his white sideburns cut short. Through clear-framed glasses, he analyzed a pilot's technique as a plane landed. Seated to his right, I felt as if insects were biting inside my stomach.

My father had tried to avoid this conversation when Frank pulled up near the Bayshore hotel in our old white Honda Accord to take my mom to the art gallery. While she got into the front seat, my dad started to get into the back. My mom looked through the windshield at me, concerned, as if to say: "What's he doing?" After I called to him, he reluctantly got out of the back seat. In awkward partnership, we walked towards the park, trying to decide where to sit. We chose a bench that faced the ocean.

It took a year for me to see how oddly appropriate this waterfront setting was for both of us. We each grew up in Toronto on the shores of Lake Ontario, admiring the sailboats that cruised past our property, the smack and spray of waves, and our backyard's clay-cliffed wildness. The house where I grew up was only blocks away from where my dad had spent his childhood. As a kid, I savoured dips in the cold lake, skipping stones, and cradling the odd crayfish that fluttered near shore. On weekend mornings, from the roof of our long-abandoned concrete pump house at the water's edge, I peered down at carp in the shallow waters below me, early sun converting them to silver dashes. At the pump house, friends and I played cards and games, read books, burned candles, and huddled inside when it rained; it felt like a secret club house. In the sun, we sprawled on its flat, hard roof, waving at boaters who cruised by, and watched mallard ducks and occasional swans bob past.

My father loved the water, sea, and boats and longed for a sailboat of his own. Many years after his kids had moved away, he created an impersonal, pristine breakwater at my childhood home, defined by vertical posts with park-like chain draped in between, and a white-and-red lifesaver. His taming and containment of my former rugged play area, where large boulders heaped against a cliff of exposed tree roots, felt like a desecration. For me, this transformation symbolized how separate the worlds that he and I inhabited had become, just as when he remarked upon seeing my current home, an old board-and-batten cottage in the country: "Maybe you'll get something more upscale in a few years." My father never bought a boat, nor did one ever dock at his new structure. Upon retirement, he passed a sailing exam to become a captain, but remained one without a vessel. When I encouraged him to join sailing expeditions, he would say: "It's too late." Or: "I'm too old."

I still remain fiercely drawn to the sea. Past a delightfully unkempt forest close to home, I launch my kayak at the mouth of a creek that empties into the Pacific Ocean. Chaos tucked within control, the wild and tamed live on in my life.

From Vancouver's harbour, I asked my dad what he meant in his email by the "trials and tribulations" he had endured unbeknownst to me. He began to tell me a long story about his early medical career. His hospital in Toronto made him chief of anesthesia in 1960 when he was only thirty-five; I was one. Apparently, an older man in the department, who believed that the hospital owed him the job, had launched a smear campaign against my father. He spread false rumours that my dad was anti-Semitic, that he would initiate a mass firing of employees, and other lies, according to my dad. A special board meeting and an internal investigation ensued. The hospital even hired a private investigator. All of the evidence seemed to point to the disgruntled employee who felt bitter over losing out this position to my father. My dad maintained the job until he became director of the hospital's intensive care unit in 1971. I wondered if he was telling me the whole story.

My father continued to look straight ahead towards the water. "It must have been the stress and alcohol," he said. "I must have misbehaved, but that's no excuse." Still gazing out over the water, he turned and looked at me.

"I'm sorry. I don't remember. I must have buried it or blanked it out." He added: "I would never consciously do something like that. It's untenable."

I was surprised how perfunctory our discussion seemed, as if we were swapping gardening tips or deciding who would take out the trash. A city-wide garbage strike had been underway for weeks; here, with a sea breeze, there was no related smell. A middle-aged man, wearing one of those orange fluorescent vests with a giant X, appeared to the left of our bench, stabbing at litter in the nearby grass with a long poker.

"I can understand what stress you must have been under," I replied to my dad, "but to go after your own child?"

People strolled by on the waterfront boardwalk. Ahead of us, a sleek, seventy-five-foot ketch motored by, its sails down. Several men on deck were checking the rigging.

My father did not respond. He began to explain that during the ordeal with his jealous colleague, my mother was a stable influence, but he had "no outlets." At times when he needed support, she was hypercritical, he said. My dad acknowledged that he had turned to booze in crises and admitted: "Maybe I am an alcoholic." He spoke of doctors he had worked with who had died of cirrhosis of the liver.

"It was a common outlet in my day," he said. "People kept everything bottled inside. I have spent three or four decades of pure, blameless life." He paused. "You have the power to destroy me."

"I know," I said, crying, "but I've been protecting you for years. Who protected me?"

"I'm sorry. You've been through a lot."

He talked about how some people, such as tragic singer Billie Holiday, used the emotional injuries of trauma to augment and transform their art.

"But look at what cost," I said, my stomach tensing. "She was an addict. She suffered a lot." Did he know that she was raped repeatedly as a teenager?

When I recounted some of our incestuous incidents—fingers in my vagina, a wet spot on the bed, playing doctor—my dad's eyes widened and flickered, then regained their straight-ahead gaze. He said nothing. He did not deny any of it. Repeatedly, he said: "It must have been alcohol. I would never do anything to hurt you."

Through tears, I told him how remembering the incest had shattered my identity and sense of reality, how it had affected my intimate relationships. He seemed genuinely concerned and caring.

Leaving to meet my mom and husband for lunch, we stood and hugged. My father gave me a slobbery kiss on the lips. In silence, we followed a waterfront sidewalk to Cardero's, a glossy restaurant and pub on pilings in the marina. Its corrugated steel and shingled walls evoke a fancy, urban cannery, without the unseemly smell of fish guts.

The four of us sat on the outdoor patio, water drifting around us. We drank chardonnay, ordered by my father, as I picked at a seafood wok dish of prawns and scallops with rice. My mother and husband spoke enthusiastically of the permanent Emily Carr exhibit they had just seen at the art gallery.

Was incest now wiped off our family agenda with a quick checkmark?

I believed that my father could not remember what had happened between us, although my husband didn't. Even if some part of my dad could recall what had transpired but did not want to, I understood. Denial is an overpowering master.

After Frank and I saw my parents off at the train station, we returned home by early evening. I fell directly into bed and slept straight through until the next morning. Days later, while trying to deconstruct the encounter with my dad, anger invaded. How could he equate a career vendetta with incest? And what did he mean by his "three or four decades of pure, blameless life"? Forty years earlier would have been 1967, when I was eight. That's around the time my best friend said she noticed a shift in me; I became more withdrawn, less exuberant.

At least I had cracked the incest silence between us. At last.

CHAPTER EIGHTEEN

SEXSOMNIA

Spirituality means the ability to find peace and happiness in
an imperfect world, and to feel that one's own personality is
imperfect but acceptable. From this peaceful state of mind come
both the creativity and the ability to love unselfishly, which go
hand in hand.
—Bernie Siegel, *Love, Medicine and Miracles*

ABOUT FOUR MONTHS after the confrontation with my father, Frank
and I spent Christmas at my parents' comfortable house in their
gated community in southern Ontario. We settled into the cozy
bedroom in the basement, thousands of kilometres from our west-
coast home. Our spacious room had plush white bathrobes in the *en*
suite bathroom, thick broadloom, a welcoming queen-sized bed, and
antique furniture laden with lamps, coffee-table books, and framed
family photos.

Family photo #10: My dad at age five or six stands on a wagon.
He holds its long handle in both hands, dressed in a white sailor's
suit with white ankle socks, and open, strapped shoes. His straight
bangs look brushed across, conveying obedience and order. As if
viewing the photographer's unseen waving hand, he glances off-
camera. *Watch the birdie.* Embodying a life still unfurled, he offers
only the faint suggestion of a smile, a hint of curiosity.

An acquaintance, a psychotherapist and incest survivor who
works with victims of sexual abuse, has said of abusers: "Think of
them as three-year-old children. That helps." I think of all adults,

including me, as frustrated five-year-olds, scrambling to get their emotional needs met in a myriad of ways.

Since our meeting in Vancouver, my father and I had not mentioned the confrontation or anything related to it. In our family's typical style, we resumed life as if it had never happened. But several days after arriving at my parents' home, I found a vertical brown envelope, 5 7/8 x 9 ½ inches, on our guest room bed. Business-like, it bore a single, underlined word in all caps, written by my father: CONFIDENTIAL. I did not open it immediately, allowing instead the possibilities of its contents to settle inside me.

Opening the envelope while still at my parents' home, I found inside a full broadsheet page cut from the *National Post*. It was dated Oct. 19, 2007, about two months earlier. An article on page A2 bore the headline "Sexsomnia: fast asleep and having sex." The subtitle read: "Disorder studied." My dad had stapled a piece of scratch paper to it, on which he had written and underlined: "A Possible Explanation."

Incredulous, I skimmed over the two-column article, which addressed a "recently discovered phenomenon" in which people have sex while asleep. I had never heard of such a condition. According to Canadian researchers, some of the 219 subjects studied had wound up in trouble with the law because their acts of sex-while-sleep-walking had involved children. The article reported that a man in Ontario was acquitted of sexual assault in 2005 due to sexsomnia— he had been asleep at the time. Supposedly, this sleep disorder, first officially reported in 1986, is more common than experts previously thought, according to a spokesperson from a Toronto sleep and alertness clinic quoted in the article. It is believed to affect roughly three out of every one hundred people.

Conveniently, those who suffer from this condition do not remember anything about their actions. Research suggested that fatigue and stress were major triggers for this condition, although the survey identified contact with a partner's body in bed as the primary cause. About half of those studied had reported episodes including intercourse, oral sex, or "sexualized vocalizations," said the article.

I did not read the feature in full until just before writing these words. My dad was suggesting that he had walked down the hallway from his own bedroom into mine, had lain on top of me, ejaculated onto the sheet and put his fingers in my vagina, all while he was asleep. (Only four months earlier, when we had met in Vancouver, he had blamed his actions on alcohol.) What about at other times, when we had "played doctor" in the guest room, for instance, and I had felt his erection through his pants while on his bed? My memory puts most of our incidents in the daytime, with him fully awake, sober, and aware. Was he dismissing all of these as unconscious acts? No memory, no responsibility.

I am willing to concede that a possible booze blackout could have had an influence. That, plus fatigue, can lower one's inhibitions. Yet, sexual assaults tend to be planned in advance, says therapist Judith Herman, who has worked extensively with incest perpetrators and victims. In *Father-Daughter Incest*, she reveals that sexual offenders often admit they drink to get the courage to make an approach.

When first glancing through the sexsomnia piece, I remember feeling only shocked dismay and disappointment. In the past, I would have raged and roared, wanting to cut off all contact with my father. Part of me wanted to take the article off my desk, fold it back into a square, and tuck it out of sight. Yet, I refused to accept my dad's packaged explanation. Instead, I added it as a new title—My Father's Rationalization—on the shelf of my mental incest library.

During our visit, my dad reached out to me with warmth and generosity as a gracious host. He bantered with Frank, laughing frequently. My father's playful spirit drew me in, but I wanted to resist it. I struggled to match his effusive manner with his "possible explanation" of sexsomnia. His stance took me to a minor family event of the past, to another time when his accountability came only halfway.

At about age ten, I join my family in the backyard on a sunny summer night, eating dinner at our picnic table. Panda, our English sheepdog, watches from behind a black iron gate, separated from us. She barks constantly, annoying my father, who doesn't want our meal disrupted. He strides towards her as I follow. Opening the gate, he gruffly grabs her behind the head and lifts her vertically into the air, a shaggy, mid-sized heft. She yelps in pain, still hanging off the ground, as he carries her away.

Aghast, I cry out: "Leave that goddamn dog alone!"

"Don't talk to me like that." Wham. His arm swings out like a push-button lever and hits me in the nose, which starts to bleed. Defiant, I stand with my hands cupped under my nose to catch the dripping blood. I go into the house and don't come out again all evening. The rest of my family continues dinner as if nothing happened. Later, no one mentions what transpired.

The next day, my dad comes into my bedroom, putting his hand on my shoulder. He says: "We both lost our temper." No apology.

I don't remember apologizing to him either.

* * *

Sleep is a welcome invitation, offering a brief dip into timelessness à la Rip Van Winkle. The word connotes serenity—beauty sleep, lullabies, sleepy head, sleep tight, sleeping potion—but also the frozen passivity of Sleeping Beauty. Innocent childhood sleep often follows soothing words read aloud by a parent. My young dreams came from bedtimes stories and poems like *The Owl and the Pussycat* or *The Land of Nod*, my mother's voice a sanctuary before her good-night peck.

Yet, I wonder now what might have occurred while I slept as a child. For most of my life, except through my years of CFS, I've been a deep sleeper. Even when construction drills bore through walls at a hotel, when somebody pounded their fist on my hotel door at night, when my bed bounced off the floor in an earthquake in Guatemala City, and fire trucks near my Vancouver, BC apartment backed up outside my bedroom window, sirens roaring, I never woke up. Besides my waking memories, could my father have molested me while I slept?

The shadow side of sleep and a travesty of trust, sexsomnia makes me think of hungry zombies invading the darkness.

* * *

"Life's work is to wake up, to let the things that enter into the circle wake you up rather than put you to sleep," Buddhist master Pema Chodron says. Feeling discomfort is part of being human, said the Buddha. Because we do not recognize that we are impermanent, we suffer. "Traditionally it's said that the cause of suffering is clinging to our narrow view, which is to say, we are addicted to ME," Chodron says. "We resist that we change and flow like the weather, that we have the same energy as all living things. When we resist, we dig in our heels. We make ourselves really solid. Resistance is what's called ego."

Although I still resist the label "incest survivor," I can see my father, at last, as a soul connected to me, not someone to rage against. I feel grateful that my spiritual beliefs have enabled me to release long-held anger and soften my heart. I will never condone what my dad did, which defied his Hippocratic oath. He deserves condemnation. My rage was justified. But choosing to hold onto this for the rest of my life, with entrenched rancour, would only damage me further.

Chapter Nineteen

WITNESSED

So what can we really do for each other except—just love each other and be each other's witness?
—James Baldwin

As a child and teen at the dinner table, I eagerly share offbeat ideas or suggestions with my conservative father. "I believe in telepathy." "Why can't I go to an alternative school?" He pauses briefly, sometimes nods, then continues his monologue.

Around age nine, I am proud to ride a 10-speed bicycle for the first time. From my next-door neighbour's yard, I call to my mom to watch me. She's in the kitchen, but only watches from the window for a few seconds, then disappears. She couldn't seem less interested.

I WANTED DESPERATELY to feel valued and seen by the people important to me. The term "to bear witness" implies something more substantial: an important formal procedure that requires at least one pair of independent eyes and probably an official stamp to prove an action true. But what if there were no witnesses to incest beyond the two people involved? I did not have the courage to ask my mother about this again. Instead, I took control of my own story, creating this book as my witness.

None of my sisters knew about the incest until I was in my late forties. It took me that long to feel bold enough to reveal it. Mary Ann was the first sister I told, in a letter. It took her weeks before she responded, by phone; she waited until the end of the conversation before she mentioned it. But she believed me!

All three sisters believed and supported me, for which I am immensely grateful. Nancy cried when she heard the news from my middle sister, Wendy. I had delayed telling Nancy because she was closest to my parents. Soon afterwards, she wrote me a letter of love and appreciation, expressing her dismay that I had endured this alone. She had always considered our family a version of *Leave it to Beaver*, she said. Now, she saw us more like characters from Eugene O'Neill.

Mary Ann recalled our dad's inappropriate remarks aimed at her, which I had never known. Beyond our father's dirty jokes and sexualized comments, none of my sisters recalls any physical incest with him or between him and me.

This made me feel like an outcast. Again, I questioned my status, but learned that sometimes a parent will choose the most vulnerable child for incest. It can indeed be limited to one perpetrator and one victim, says counselling psychologist Christine Courtois in *Healing the Incest Wound*. Regardless of our physical interactions, if my dad's sexual innuendoes, jokes, and suggestions had occurred in a workplace, rather than our home, the law would have considered them sexual harassment.

"Bearing witness is the willingness to hear with your heart another's experience of pain and suffering," says psychotherapist Laurie Kahn, co-director of The Trauma Consultation Training Institute in Chicago. "It is the willingness to be disturbed by someone's life experience."

About a decade before I confronted my father on that park bench, my parents came to visit me in Vancouver. Then in my late thirties, I asked them if they had seen the movie *Secrets and Lies*. Both of them lowered their heads and avoided my eyes, not answering the question. During the same conversation, my father asked: "If a girl at the age of three was left in a forest by herself, would that have a long-term impact on her?"

"Of course it would," I replied, surprised by this odd question.

Was this oblique reference an attempt to minimize his actions and appease his conscience?

In Canada, making sexual comments to a child is considered sexual abuse. Sexual assault can happen whether there is penetration or not, and whether there is contact with genital organs or not. Under Canada's Criminal Code, I believe that my father was guilty of sexual interference, sexual assault, and sexual exploitation. (Section 155 of the code defines incest solely as "sexual intercourse" between two people who share a blood relationship, identifying "parent, child, brother, sister, grandparent or grandchild, as the case may be.") To me, that's too narrow a definition; covert incest can be equally damaging. As Judith Herman says in *Father-Daughter Incest*: "[F]rom a psychological point of view, especially from the child's point of view, the sexual motivation of the contact, and the fact that it must be kept secret, are far more significant than the exact nature of the act itself."

Most importantly, in the skewed power dynamic of child-adult incest, especially with a parent, informed consent is not possible.

If a perpetrator is dead, if there is no weapon or forensic evidence, and no one knows that the event occurred except the remaining victim, does that mean that a crime never happened? Of course not.

Frequently, children who dare to speak up about sexual abuse by a family member face shaming, shunning, and punishment. Some receive threats to remain silent while others are accused of lying or behaving suggestively. The offending parent or a spouse might minimize the adult's actions: "Daddy was just trying to be friendly" or "He wants you to know that he loves you."

Based on his female patients' stories of incest and other forms of child sexual abuse, Sigmund Freud suggested in his seduction theory that these women's emotional disturbances were caused by sexual contact with their father. But the horrified reaction by Victorian society and Freud's own deep discomfort around this revelation caused him to abandon this belief and replace it with the Oedipus theory. This switch helped ensure, as Courtois points out, that any subsequent complaints of incest were dismissed as fantasy. Hence, an adult perpetrator could be easily exonerated. Society's denial could continue. For far too long, this approach has officially sanctioned our prevalent blame-the-victim culture.

Through family or social denunciation, how does any victim maintain integrity and self-respect? I struggled for years from harbouring a lie with silence. Do the victim and abuser tell the same version of the story if they tell it at all? How does the story change if left untold or when one or both parties recount it? An unspoken incest story melds both people into a bond of mutual recognition, whether or not they ever dare give voice to it. When the victim speaks and the abuser listens without condemnation, the previously fused relationship loosens. Denial can no longer be maintained. The gap of separation between the acts themselves and the lie that they never occurred is gone forever. The man behind the curtain in the land of Oz is revealed.

Thankfully, I no longer harbour an idealized notion of my father. Eve Ensler, author of *The Vagina Monologues*, has said of her dad, a battering sex abuser: "Let the mythical daddy die."

Bearing witness to anyone's suffering, our own or others', whether in public or private, demands tremendous bravery. I feel kinship with those who publicly decry betrayal, hypocrisy, and injustice, particularly the sexual-abuse survivors who have openly named the priests who molested them. Some seek recognition of the crimes from the Roman Catholic Church, which has fostered and protected perpetrators even at the Vatican level. Individuals, institutions, and nations are slow to bear witness publicly to any travesty, if they acknowledge it at all.

Most abusers remain unchallenged and unpunished. Incest is rarely reported and when it is, it is difficult to prove. Only two per cent of childhood incest cases are reported to police. Conviction in the United States has resulted in only 0.5 per cent of incest cases. Around the world, we still have the so-called "Lolita defense," with judges ruling that children from ages four to sixteen have "seduced" their adult sex partner. It's no surprise that the overall reporting rate of sexual assault, including adult victims, is alarmingly low.

Statistics Canada reports that in 2014, only five per cent of sexual assaults that year were reported to police. In the U.S., it is believed that only 15.8 to 35 per cent of all sexual assaults in the U.S. are reported to police, based on Bureau of Justice statistics from 1994 to 2013.

* * *

The term "False Memory Syndrome" was coined by Peter Freyd in the early 1990s, even though neither the medical or psychological fields had produced any such diagnosis. Freyd's adult daughter accused him and his wife, Pamela, of sexually abusing her as a child. This "syndrome" refers to a condition in which someone fiercely believes in a memory of traumatic experience that never happened. As a result, this person focuses his or her identity, personality, lifestyle, and interpersonal relationships around a non-fact, refusing to confront any contrary evidence.

I recognize how much our female-as-victim culture, embedded in media stories, television shows, literature, and films, affects attitudes and perceptions about sexual behaviour. It was shocking to discover that even some educated women, whom I considered progressive, aware, and feminist, implied that the sexual assaults I suffered in India must have been the result of my own actions. We're so conditioned to let a perpetrator off the hook and discount a victim's accusations. As a society, we expect women to change their behaviour to avoid, or respond to, possible attacks, rather than challenge the predatory acts themselves. From date rape to serial killing and incest, why do so few men face accountability and consequences for their actions? Why do so few change their attitudes and actions?

Unless we bear witness to, and speak out against, any act of disrespect or objectification as the #MeToo movement has, such behaviour gains silent sanction. Some survivors who publicly name their predator, especially a high-profile, powerful one, can face smear campaigns, bullying, threats and intimidation, either on social media or in person. Despite concerns and conflicts about sharing my story publicly, my desire to break the silence and help inspire or empower others won out.

After bearing witness, with my father, to the incest, I later wanted to reconcile with him. Vietnamese Buddhist master Thich Nhat Hanh says, "The practice of peace and reconciliation is one of the most vital and artistic of human actions." But I needed to create a private form of reconciliation that worked for me. In a public forum, recognition of abuse does not always further healing. In South Africa, the government established its Truth and Reconciliation Commission in 1994 to investigate "gross violations" of human rights committed during the apartheid regime. However, former perpetrators of torture, beatings, rape, and other travesties could receive amnesty from prosecution on the witness box by saying that the government or a political organization caused or fuelled their actions. This often left victims without any formal apology; their reconciliation came at little or no cost to the ones who did horrible wrongs, as author Ellis Cose points out in *Bone to Pick*.

Although I did not endure torture, I understood this sense of injustice, of feeling unrecognized and cheated of the opportunity to receive an apology. Reconciliation, in Cose's view, and I agree, requires a willingness of those estranged to form some kind of alliance, friendship or involvement "in a psychologically complex and intimate way." In other words, forgiveness can occur in a vacuum. Reconciliation can't.

I listened to the wrenching, painful stories of some of Canada's residential school survivors, many of whom were beaten and/or sexually and emotionally abused, at Truth and Reconciliation Commission (TRC) hearings in Vancouver, BC in October 2013. It seemed important to me to bear witness to the truth of their experiences. Canada's former prime minister Stephen Harper apologized in 2008, on behalf of the federal government, for its role in these travesties. But many felt his words were hollow, rooted in hypocrisy, as his government continued to cut funds to Indigenous communities, dismantled environmental laws that protected their salmon fisheries and traditional territories, and ignored or defied treaties. TRC chair Justice Murray Sinclair stated, "Reconciliation is about forging and maintaining respectful relationships. There are no short-cuts." True reconciliation requires bearing witness to unacceptable acts, not just paying lip service.

For me, wanting to choose forgiveness was a first step in bearing witness to my incest. I believe that my flawed father genuinely tried to atone for his acts by offering me a trip to Asia and giving me un-characteristic recognition in his later years. Although I had pub-lished in dozens of publications over several decades, he waited until 2002 and 2009 before choosing to frame and hang up newspaper articles I had written.

I appreciate the compassionate approach used by the Babema tribe in South Africa when a community member has done some-thing that destroys the "delicate social net." The entire village stops all work. In her book *Storycatcher*, Christina Baldwin describes their response:

> The people gather around the "offender," and one by one they begin to recite everything he has done right in his life: every good deed, thoughtful behaviour, act of social responsibility. These things have to be true about the person, and spoken honestly, but the time-honoured consequence of misbehaviour is to appreciate that person back into the better part of himself. The person is given the chance to remember who he is and why he is important to the life of the village.

This wouldn't work with a sociopath or psychopath, but at least it acknowledges the potential for good in someone. Although denoun-cing my dad's actions, I don't have to hate or obliterate him. It's too easy to label an abuser "evil." Condemning someone as "other" pre-vents any opportunity for understanding. Rather than demonize my father, I tried not to blind myself to the insights and opportunities he provided. Beyond his selfish conquering and despicable betrayal, I chose to maintain a relationship with him and acknowledge his goodness. Although I will never dismiss what he did to me, I can still choose to forgive him for it.

CHAPTER TWENTY

FORGIVENESS

Life has no other discipline to impose, if we would but realize it, than to accept life unquestioningly. Everything we shut our eyes to, everything we run away from, everything we deny, denigrate or despise, serves to defeat us in the end. What seems nasty, painful, evil, can become a source of beauty, joy and strength, if faced with an open mind. Every moment is a golden one for him [or her] who has the vision to recognize it as such.

—Henry Miller

My father shows me, as a child, a miniature clipper ship inside a sealed glass bottle with a short neck, only several centimetres long. Fascinated, I take in the carefully shaped sails and thin wooden masts mounted on a string. A brown hull rises from blue swirls atop a plasticine sea.

He challenges me to guess how the ship got into the bottle. Intrigued, I stare at this dilemma. Does the bottle have a false bottom? No. Did the artist build the bottle around the ship? No.

I grow restless, wanting to know the answer. My dad explains: If you pull the string, the masts collapse, rendering them low enough to push through the neck of the bottle. Once the ship is inside, the model-builder re-adjusts the string, pulling it tight to raise the sails, perhaps with the help of tweezers.

As a kid, I admired this feat of creating a tiny, contained universe. My father held the secret of how to access it. As an adult, I had to find my own truth and access to our incest secret.

When my husband Frank and I returned to the west coast from my parents' sixtieth anniversary event, in September 2008, we each carried a different thick red book in our luggage. The heavy tome in my husband's bag (I had made him carry it) was the Canadian *Who's Who*, a copy of which my father had rush-ordered for all four daughters. We were meant to read his listing, of course, and maintain it as a keepsake of his success. I picked up the 6.3-centimetre-thick volume and found his 9.5-centimetre-long write-up. After his name appeared that familiar acronym I had seen on his stationery since childhood: FRCP (C). (These initials, etched on his gravestone, stand for Fellow of the Royal College of Physicians of Canada.) His summary listed the proverbial family connections and education, military reserve service, his gold medal awards in medicine, memberships in private associations and several clubs. His political allegiance: Progressive Conservative.

I wasn't sure how to react to this gift, his early epitaph delivered little more than two years before his death. At the anniversary event, he had told our assembled group of sixty-five guests: "The pearly gates are not far away." Why did he feel compelled to prove his worth in print, pay for its inclusion, then buy a book for all four daughters? He could have simply photocopied or scanned the page and sent it to us. One of my sisters thought this present the height of self-absorption; within days, she indignantly gave her copy away to the local library.

I carried the other red book, 3.8 centimetres thick, in my luggage. This one was Nancy's genealogical study of our mother's side of the family entitled *From the Scottish Borders to Upper Canada: the Hart and Hotson Families*. It was her fourth volume that delved into our family tree, rooting out burial sites, church records, correspondence, and photos from previous centuries and several continents. On page two, I was intrigued to learn that a Scottish peasant in the 1500s, said to be our ancestor, had saved the life of King James when the ruler was attacked by gypsies (now called Romani) while crossing a bridge near Edinburgh in disguise. Impressed by the depth of Nancy's research, I began to leaf through the section on my mother's parents, who had died before my birth. My grandfather perished in a head-on car accident, my grandmother of cancer when my mother, age twenty-one, was at university.

In the book, Nancy summarizes an interview with Isobel, my mother's younger sister, talking about their strict upbringing on a dairy farm in Woodstock, Ontario. She writes: "Theirs was a religious household, very Victorian, with Bible reading on one's knees every breakfast and Sunday ... Truth, honour and fair play were emphasized, with smoking and liquor frowned upon. My mother's mother used to comment: 'You're a Hart—they don't do things like lie, cheat, and have children out of wedlock.'"

My sister Mary Ann remembers my father as "scrupulously honest." She says: "Not once did he tell a lie. He always had a high moral ground of integrity." But how did this perception relate to him and me, especially when he was drunk? Once, when I had returned to my childhood home in my twenties, my mom found red wine spilled across the table in their kitchen nook. My dad had been drinking. When she asked me if I had done it, I said no. When she asked my father, he said no. She seemed horrified that he might have lied to her.

The two red books I brought home represented two primary family values that have shaped me: virtue (Always be good, look good, speak of good, exude good) on my mother's side, and achievement (I'll tell you what I've done and what I know and will ask little about you) on my father's. Incest is the errata list stuck between these pages.

Forgiveness is the new gleaming cover, beckoning someone inside. Some people don't understand my desire to forgive my father, which serves to help me, not anyone else. One reader wrote in the margins of my manuscript: "Does it matter, forgiveness? And what is it—really?" It matters hugely to me. Like a mother who still loves her murderous child, forgiveness is the unconditional embrace that can hold caring, horror, disgust, betrayal, and acceptance in the same tender grasp.

The late feminist author Bell Hooks said that forgiveness and compassion were always linked for her. She asked: "How do we hold people accountable for wrongdoing and yet at the same time remain in touch with their humanity enough to believe in their capacity to be transformed?" Could I forgive someone who showed little empathy for a relative who was a victim of violence?

While still at my parents' home following their anniversary celebrations, Frank and I pored over some family photo albums with my dad at the kitchen table. One image prompted a discussion of Frank's grandmother, whom I called Aunt Mildred and whose wedding ring I wear. She was someone whom I had always known as frail and quiet with a gentle spirit.

"She was unemployable," my father said. "She couldn't hold onto a job anywhere." This summation surprised me. He suggested that family connections had propped Mildred up in various office positions yet she had never risen to shine within these supposed sinecures.

I did not know the truth about Mildred, long dead, until I married Frank and he told me. Her husband had physically abused her and their three children. She also lost her youngest daughter, who died suddenly at age seven following an asthma attack or scarlet fever or choking on chicken bones or a poisonous Brazil nut, depending on which family version you heard. (The obituary used the chicken-bones story, probably because that generation, and my parents,' abhorred acknowledging any medical condition. They likened it to a personality flaw that must remain hidden. The true cause of death, according to her sister, Frank's mother, was asthma.)

"Maybe she was distraught over the loss of her child," Frank surmised later about Mildred's lack of job prowess. But my father's version of events stood as unofficial truth.

My family has prided itself on what good historians we are, how well we communicate on the page. Yet, the language of secrets, the hidden gaps of family life and what we do not say, interest me far more than pasty-faced ancestors, righteous and God-fearing, toiling in the fields. Trying to deconstruct and make sense of that tiny ship in a bottle, I want the unseemly truth of my bloodline.

For years, I wanted to shake the truth out of my mother, to get an admission. What did she know? After my father died, she burned all of the letters they had shared. I can only wonder if some of them discussed incest.

My dad's words have stayed with me: "You have the power to destroy me." In our triangle, my mother's view of events formed one side, my father's, the other. The bottom side, exposed, lay unfinished. Now I am creating some semblance of a complete form. The structure had to come first, before I could overlay it with forgiveness.

* * *

To settle into my heart and belly, and exist beyond an intellectual exercise, forgiveness needed to surpass all previous obstacles: outrage, self-righteousness, resentment, disdain—even pity. For me, there was no "aha" moment of finding forgiveness. Gradually, it emerged after exploring many healing techniques including different modes of therapy and body awareness, meditation, contemplative readings about love, reconciliation, and compassion, and attending Adult Children of Alcoholics meetings.

Learning the process of SoulCollage®, and later gaining training in it as a facilitator, was particularly helpful. The late Seena Frost launched this fun, intuitive process of self-discovery, personal empowerment, and self-acceptance, which involves creating 5 × 8 collage cards of symbols, people, and archetypes that have particular meaning and significance for each individual. Through SoulCollage®, each person discovers how their own life story connects to a collective Larger Story.

I learned of Ho'oponopono, the Hawaiian practice of reconciliation and forgiveness, during a SoulCollage® Zoom workshop in the fall of 2021. The term roughly translates to "being right with both ourself and others" or "to cause things to move back in balance." Today, it can involve a simple prayer of "I'm sorry. Please forgive me. Thank you. I love you." Someone can say these words inwardly, chant them as a mantra, or focus on them in meditation, directing them at someone else or to an aspect of oneself. Traditionally, this process of accountability has taken varied forms: two people can speak their truths face to face on their own, or with a family member as facilitator.

All of these methods have helped me to reorient my perspective of judge, blame, and attack into something milder or more accepting. For someone goal-oriented like me, forgiveness gave me something to strive for. Yet, I still took to heart the advice of author and abuse survivor Mary Jane Williams: "Never fool yourself into thinking that it is more important to forgive the perpetrator than it is to rescue your own inner wounded child."

For me, forgiveness and compassion go hand in hand. Oddly, it seemed easier to seek compassion for my father than find it for myself. I continued to beat myself up inwardly about any and everything—but at least with a much smaller hammer. I continue to learn to question my assumptions and try to listen more deeply to people, and express gratitude and appreciation to myself and others as often as I can.

To open up to self-compassion, psychotherapist Francis Weller says we all need to make three moves: shift to seeing ourselves as wounded rather than worthless, view ourselves with "budding compassion" instead of contempt, and share our vulnerable truth with people we trust, rather than remain silent.

Former Catholic nun Karen Armstrong, who helped launch a global Charter for Compassion, offers twelve steps for a compassionate life, including empathy, mindfulness, action, and compassion for yourself. The writings of Thich Nhat Hanh, who promotes peace and compassion, remain an ongoing inspiration for me. He inspired Martin Luther King Jr. to speak out against the Vietnam War when such statements by a high-profile figure were deplored.

* * *

By the spring of 2010, almost five years after my parents' sixtieth wedding anniversary, my dad went in and out of the hospital three times following blackouts and anemia. During my visit in May that year, I accompanied him on a short, slow amble. Using a walker, he told me "Slow down!", collapsing to rest only minutes after we had begun. My dad chided himself for his lack of energy.

A gaping distance of unexpressed feelings still lay between us. Adult loneliness in my parents' house at that time revived sad memories of similar feelings in my childhood home. My father's repetition of the same story within minutes and hours and over days, plus his dwindling abilities, left me feeling bereft, grieving the loss of who he once was.

My dad sneaked liquor from the basement and snapped at a physiotherapist or anyone who tried to help him. Like my mom, he insisted that he was fine to drive. Two months earlier, he had lain in a hospital for days of tests to find out why he had suffered recent blackouts. A few months before my dad turned eighty-five, a doctor was talking about palliative care. My father had always said: "If you can't be good, be lucky." At that time, we heard no explanation for his condition.

Quiet and sullen, my dad sat with a book in his lap in his favourite wing chair, long since reupholstered from my teen years. Home from the hospital for ten days, he had remained in bed for most of that time. He didn't go outside. "He has little energy or appetite," my mother reported. "His spirits are low." He had lost fifty pounds. My sister Nancy, who visited with him for an hour, said she was surprised to see him sitting in the living room with a lap blanket and cane, like his elderly mother had before him.

The hospital said that he had had an infarction (mild heart attack), but my mother refused to acknowledge the news. Later, doctors determined that he had suffered a mini-stroke; again, my mom would not accept this diagnosis. His taste buds had changed, he said: a drink of Scotch now tasted like turpentine. Finally, we heard a diagnosis: multiple myeloma, a highly painful cancer that strikes the bone marrow. "I'll be dead in three months," he kept saying. It took four.

While my dad was dying and in too much pain to get out of bed, my mother blamed it on arthritis in his back—not the bone cancer that was slowly damaging his spine. When we spoke on the phone, she would say "myeloma" but not "cancer." She had always used cheer to cover sadness: Why would she change now?

My father's sadness reached me through silence. He had returned home in a gurney with two attendants. My concern for his future and quality of life replaced any contempt for his past misconduct. I had never seen my dad so vulnerable and helpless. Caring for him made finding empathy easy. Forgiveness seemed almost an afterthought.

Hallucinating and deluded from heavy medication, my father thinks he's on a battlefield.

"I'm worried about you," he tells me. "They're heading this way. I don't know if it's one of us or one of them. I think we need to take 'em out."

Embarrassed and nonplussed, my mother ignores his comments. I play along.

"Why would we take him out if he could be one of ours?" My dad gives no response.

Another time, sitting up in bed, he re-enacts one of his many slide show presentations, made at medical conferences around the world. In a formal voice, he announces, "I am sorry, but I am unable to give a speech at this time. Instead, I will pass you over to my daughter Heather." To an invisible audience, I explain that I am not able to give the presentation. My mother looks mortified.

All incest survivors must decide how, or if, they want to remain in contact with their abusing parent. By no means do I condone attempts at reconciliation with all abusers. For some, it could mean continued abuse, which is unacceptable. For others, it might mean trying to span a rift too vast for comfort or survival. Maintaining no contact with an abuser can certainly be wise self-protection.

Forgiveness is a personal choice. How easily could I forgive a pedophile who kidnaps, rapes, and murders an infant or teen? Or who peddles child pornography? Or who takes sadistic pleasure in molesting and torturing a child? Or who lures underage children with lies on the Internet? I can't imagine how long that process would take.

Thich Nhat Hanh wrote a poem after receiving a letter about a twelve-year-old refugee girl raped on a small boat by a Thai pirate. After the attack, she jumps into the ocean, drowning herself. Here is an excerpt from his poem *Call Me By My True Names*:

> ... *I am the twelve-year-old girl,*
> *refugee on a small boat.*
> *who throws herself into the ocean*
> *after being raped by a sea pirate.*
> *And I am the pirate,*
> *my heart not yet capable*
> *of seeing and loving...*
>
> *Please call me my by true names,*
> *so I can hear all my cries and laughs at*
> *once,*
> *so I can see that my joy and pain are one.*
>
> *Please call me by my true names,*
> *so I can wake up,*
> *and the door of my heart*
> *could be left open,*
> *the door of compassion.*

I could pretend that my father's admirable qualities did not exist. I could choose not to see or talk to him, which I did for brief periods. But it takes energy to act as if a loved one no longer exists. He and I shared a half-century of moments that link a parent and child, from simple lessons of how to use tools to lending favourite books and buying novelty gifts that he knew would make me laugh. His gift of diplomacy, a stance of "Agree to disagree," is one that I appreciate and still find challenging to adopt. In learning to love and accept his whole essence and my own, I can now see him as a total being. For me, forgiveness could not come without that.

Family photo #11: Less than two weeks before he died, my dad sits upright in his bed, wheeled onto the balcony of a hospice. He's staring at the camera, for a photo taken by a close friend and former medical colleague. He looks thin, solemn, and bewildered, without a smile. Wearing a red T-shirt with the word "CANADA" and a maple leaf on the front, he's gripping the arm rests of the bed, as if to hold himself up. My beaming mother stands beside his bed, leaning towards him with her arm around his back. Their opposing expressions seem to convey that they must be at two different events.

When I saw my dad two weeks earlier, he was joking and playing with the hospice puppy on his lap. But in this photo, he looked like someone who didn't want his picture taken, or perhaps didn't understand what was happening. When I look at this photo now, I want to know: What were you thinking? Were you unhappy? I know that he wanted to die. Perhaps he wanted us to see him as a whole self, not just a fading body and mind in a bed. In the same way, throughout my life, I wanted him to see all of who I was.

Years later, at age ninety-one, my mother, barely spoke. At times, she struggled to find the right word or phrase. Previously, she wobbled when she walked; as her knees weakened and her balance worsened, she fell frequently. Initially refusing to use a cane, she grew dependent on a walker, then wound up in a wheelchair.

It was too late to seek corroboration of my incest memories from her; due to dementia, she remembered almost nothing of the previous day and few incidents, even mundane ones, from my youth. I accept now that I could never find out how much my mother knew about my dad and me. Losing this chance for validation leaves me sad.

While visiting her home in 2010, I sat with her on the guest bed, discussing family issues. When I mentioned, again, that dad had sexually abused me, she made a face and said: "I don't know anything about that." I reminded her that when I had first confided in her about this years ago, she didn't believe me. This time, my mother put her hand on mine to offer comfort, but clearly did not want to discuss the matter further.

Part of me found her silence and lack of action around incest incomprehensible. Yet, given her repressed upbringing and non-confrontational style, it was understandable.

My mom's desire to retreat was too familiar. Perhaps her lifelong denial was not much different than my own attempt to filter and suppress the truth. Her reluctance to emote, combined with her overwhelming need to maintain appearances at all costs, made her an unlikely champion of a sexually abused child.

I could forgive her for her silence.

It took far too many years to release my anger at both parents for their inability to accept, save, and protect me and to give me the emotional nurturing and intimacy that I craved. Often operating as a single mom while my dad was away lecturing, my mother ran a household with four demanding kids as best she could. I rarely saw her confront my dad about anything except when I visited as an adult. Only then, while making me her ally, did she dare to challenge him in the open. Once, after she had raked outside the house and swept the patio, my dad cleaned out the eaves, leaving piles of mucky leaves strewn across the same areas she had just cleared. She forcefully shared her anger at him, with me as witness.

Through her dementia, I could still see and feel my mother's essence, yet, I mourned what was no longer there. Her critical, punitive tone was gone. She laughed frequently, likely due to Alzheimer's, yet still responded with the same facial expressions—a raised eyebrow or gaze of dismay—that she once did. Whether she was attempting to lift a foam noodle in a wheelchair-bound fitness class or full of angst because two sets of blinds in her room were not raised evenly, I strived to allow myself to open to the sacred grace of a moment with her.

Once, unexpectedly in her dementia, my mom reached up to cup my chin in her hands and struggled to say: "I'm grateful you're here." As she once did for me when I was a child, I fed her and read her picture books. Our relationship had come full circle, a fluid line of giving and receiving. After decades of raging against her, I could see, at last, her goodness. Hearing a song sparrow, whose call she identified for me in childhood, still makes me think of her. So do blue morning glories and the plants known as "hens and chicks," which she grew in our lakefront garden in Toronto. I now include versions of these in pots on my deck.

I feel grateful for the love of solitude my mother passed on to me. I can now recognize the grace and selflessness she brought to my life, how much she believed in me despite her criticisms. Even in her eighties, she kept and displayed the ceramic figures I made as a child. She shared my letters and books with others. I appreciate all that she did, from helping me with homework and teaching me new things to worrying about my well-being.

Only now, in middle age, do I acknowledge how much my mom contributed to my life and character. For decades, she worried about the environmental impact of non-recyclables and donated to progressive groups and individuals from Jane Goodall to the charity Seva. Through her early to mid-eighties, she continued her love of gardening, made family scrapbooks, cooked enviable meals every day, and created simple, elegant flower arrangements.

My heart can now more readily appreciate her thoughtful and loving gestures in my childhood, from the miniature pancakes she'd make as treats for me out of tiny glops of batter to the cocktail mini-umbrellas she would bring back from a party as a coveted accessory for my dolls. She made countless clothes for me, including a sumptuous, full-length, blue cape with satin lining and a hood.

When I left home at seventeen, my mom regularly sent cards and long letters, often with newspaper clippings about books or topics she thought would interest me. I hardly showed gratitude for such gestures. When she could no longer write at all, I missed receiving her letters. She was the first person to encourage my literary efforts and inspire my interest in stories and the written word.

At age fifty-one, I felt grateful to give my parents help and support in 2010 in coping with daily tasks, more challenging due to their lack of memory. As my dad struggled with reduced strength and mobility, I watched my parents stubbornly cling to their familiar habits. Both achievers, they were reluctant to admit their new limitations. I felt compassion for their efforts to cope with changing circumstances. Rather than reveal more of their hearts or find serenity, they sometimes chose surly belligerence. As a friend of mine, a palliative care nurse, says: "People die the way they live." At least, they could both still laugh about their predicaments.

My mother died in her sleep on Sept. 7, 2016.

* * *

Fully reclaiming the stuck piece of me did not occur until my fifties, when body-focused work in therapy helped me build new neurosensory connections, creating new responses and clarity to experiences. After some resistance, I finally agreed with my therapist that one-on-one talk therapy was not going to be enough to heal me. My body, rather than just my mind, had to be more directly involved in the process. She suggested that I try a combination of what's called bilateral stimulation with EMDR (eye movement desensitization and reprocessing). EMDR, as developed by Dr. Francine Shapiro in 1987, is said to unblock the stress or trauma related to a disturbing event, helping to create psychological wholeness. Body responses and neural pathways are reintegrated in a new, adaptive, and cohesive way, rather than locked in anxiety-based dissociation.

But the thought of re-entering my body trauma terrified me. I feared that this might reactivate my previous debilitating grief and sense of victimhood. So, with sheer avoidance, I stopped intermittent visits to my therapist. (She had called me a "textbook case" as an incest survivor.)

With skepticism, I gingerly returned to her office. In preparing for EMDR, I felt safe, not threatened, learning skills to soothe myself before working on the trauma. She engaged me in a series of controlled eye movements and/or sensory tapping of the body. This activated my body's left and right hemispheres, helping them to work in harmony again. My therapist and I adapted the bilateral part of the EMDR process with using pressure points from EFT (emotional freedom technique), adapted by Dr. Barbara Mallory. After using this combined treatment plan for at least three months, I found that my anxiety, grief, and worry had lessened markedly. With new neuro-pathways, it was truly as if more openness and trust had sunk into my bones.

I not only had to learn to tune into my body responses, connecting my mind and felt sense, but to feel safe, in the present, to feel my feelings. I began to realize that as an adult, I didn't have to feel overwhelmed and at risk—a piece of my childhood trauma was gone. This required a dual focus of telling myself "Be here now" and "Remember: the past is over and I survived." The more I healed and reconnected my emotional self with my mind and body, I was no longer triggered as much by events that might duplicate the power imbalance of the incest. This greater sense of wholeness, combined with new awareness from meditation and reframing my thoughts and attitudes, helped me learn to take greater control of, and responsibility for, my words and actions.

Learning to heal through abuse and its confusions has brought me new resilience. To internalize and bear the contradiction of secrecy and lies versus "Always tell the truth" proved more difficult to integrate, but that paradox resides within me, mostly at rest. My response to incest feels more serene and stable, moored on a calm sea. When recently watching the movie *The Stranger*, which had prompted such agitation in me before, I felt completely neutral towards the content. Some resentment is still there, but forgiveness of both my mother and father has brought increased peace.

CHAPTER TWENTY-ONE

KALI

Victory to you, O Mahakali!—To you Victory,
The primordial source of all beings—Victory!
The formidable-looking goddess—To you Victory,
Renowned as the mother of the world—Victory!
 —Munindra Misra, *Chants of Hindu Gods and*
  Goddesses in English Rhyme

MY CURRENT LIFE as a semi-retired writer, editor, and writing in-
structor/coach is deeply satisfying. Through my past workshops as a
trained facilitator in SoulCollage®, I have met many interesting
people. This creative technique, which allows me to let go of words
and focus solely on images, honours seemingly opposing personality
aspects as equal paths to greater self-awareness. For example, my
confrontational self holds the same value as my compassionate self;
one is no better or worse than the other. Intuitively selecting images
from magazines and discarded books, I have made a personalized
deck of more than 250 SoulCollage® cards, representing my inner
and outer self, archetypal influences, and those who have inspired or
influenced me. Making SoulCollage® cards that reflect my deepest
self has enabled me to open to greater joy, contentment, and appreciation for all that has happened to me. It has also strengthened my
understanding of life's interconnectedness and inter-being: we are all
multi-faceted creatures embodying light and darkness.

 While my father was dying, SoulCollage® became a refuge. After
creating a card to represent him, I shared it with my parents. Its

images included my dad as a boy and a statue of a lascivious-looking, bare-chested male clutching a younger female. The card silently told my father: "I know who you are and what you did, yet, I recognize the pure child in you and the love that we have otherwise shared." With my dad in mind, I also created a forgiveness and compassion card, respectively. Viewing them daily helped reinforce my desire to share more of these qualities each day.

The SoulCollage® cards I have created over the years to represent my mother convey my gradual shift in attitude towards her. The first one featured a black cloud and lightning bolt over her head, representing her criticisms, judgments, and Chicken Little perspective. Later ones show photo images of her and me smiling with each other, sharing love and closeness through her dementia.

In my late fifties and beyond, I am still learning that bringing greater mindfulness to any moment is significant in itself. Finally, I have opened my heart to the truth that both my father and Frank shared a key trait: they were high-functioning alcoholics, or in today's terminology, suffered from alcohol use disorder. Although both had stressful jobs, Frank sought professional help for his alcohol abuse. He was willing to face deep childhood grief and express repressed anger. My father never dealt with his drinking and disdained any psychological probing. (Only in recent years have I fully grasped that Frank and I shared childhood trauma. He suffered the identity conflicts of adoption, an emotionally and verbally abusive father, and the death of two close friends in a fire at age eight.) I like what Dr. Maté says in his book *In the Realm of Hungry Ghosts*: "Addictions arise from thwarted love, from our thwarted ability to love children the way they need to be loved, from our thwarted ability to love ourselves and one another in the ways we all need. Opening our hearts is the path to healing addiction—opening our compassion for the pain within ourselves, and the pain all around us."

Physically, I still get fatigued but am healthy. My greatest recent challenge, besides COVID isolation and fears, was striving to be a loving, compassionate caregiver for Frank. In March 2018, after two serious back-to-back infections, he was hospitalized for about a month. We were stunned to receive his diagnoses: liver disease, colon cancer, and diabetes. The doctor said he had a 50/50 chance of living for a year. I felt angry and shocked that Frank's drinking, which seemed no more severe than my father's, had helped bring on this result. My dad had lived to age eighty-five.

After his diagnosis, Frank replaced beer, wine, and liquor with low- or zero-alcohol radlers, then nothing. (A friend did bring him several IPAs while he was in hospice.) I struggled to integrate the reality of our love with the shadow of addiction. In the perceived safety of black-and-white thinking, I wanted to reject Frank. *Am I in denial? Was our love a lie? How could I not have realized that he was an alcoholic?* I have never shared with anyone else the depth of unconditional love that Frank gave me, even with a previous partner who had no issues with alcohol. *Am I still acting out my relationship with my dad?* Early on, I had stated and meant, emphatically, to Frank, "I will not be with an alcoholic." Yet, here I was, combining a state of knowing and not knowing, just as I had done with incest.

"The roots of a lasting relationship are mindfulness, deep listening and loving speech, and a strong community to support you," says Thich Nhat Hanh. This phrase was one of dozens that friends read aloud at the vows renewal ceremony that Frank and I held in August 2018. Thin and weakened after five months of mostly bedridden life, Frank emerged slowly with his walker, then sat next to me on a raised wooden deck in front of our guests. I thought then that he would likely be dead within a month but he held on for another nine months.

Amidst bouquets of flowers and a sprawling laurel tree in our side yard, we celebrated twelve years of marriage—"the best years of my life," said Frank—with heartfelt rituals, music, cake, champagne, and a seafood buffet. He told the story of cradling the infant me in his arms at age five, a doting second cousin. He insists that's when he first fell in love with me.

For months, while Frank languished at home, friends and neighbours brought us homecooked meals of delicious organic food, often from their gardens. Love filled our refrigerator. Seven months after our ceremony, Frank was in our local hospice, where he spent his last nine weeks in the spring of 2019. In those final months, friends and family, near and far, visited his bedside, shared food and stories, and listened to his many tales while he had the strength to share them.

While visiting Frank in hospice, my sister Wendy handed me some black-and-white photos from my childhood, which she had taken with her Brownie camera. One I had never seen before:

Family photo #12: Pictured from the back, my father and I are walking away closely, side by side, on a large, open expanse of clipped grass. No one else is visible. My dad's left arm stretches across my back, his hand at my waist. A long row of young conifers stands in the background. The photo is stamped March 1967. I am eight years old.

I don't know where this took place and have no memory of this encounter. Wendy says our family was on holiday somewhere, likely one of our camping trips. "I don't remember him ever going off alone with anyone else," she tells me. "Maybe you'll want to tear this picture up."

My adult eyes try to analyze the body language in the picture. Was my dad trying to be protective—or was this part of our inappropriate intimacy? No animal or other person was around us. I didn't need protection.

Recently, I was surprised to come across a small Bible with my father's inscription, dated Nov. 21, 1964—exactly ten months after my fifth birthday, the age when I believe incest began. My parents already had a number of Bibles, including one my mom had received for stellar Sunday school attendance as a child, so why did he buy another one that year? Did he need to keep this portable, pocket-sized version close by to appease his guilt? My critical mind chides: *You're reading too much into this.*

Such minutiae don't matter anymore. Frank is dying. Months before he leaves the earth, he drafts his own obituary, which includes these words: "Heather, wherever I am, I will treasure every moment we shared. Your limitless love sustains me, always."

With a deeply caring hospice volunteer across from me, I am with Frank when he leaves his bruised, thin body on May 30, 2019.

His essence still fills my heart. As it says on our weddings rings: Love, fly on.

* * *

I still suffer flare-ups or mini-relapses of chronic fatigue syndrome, which feel like a burst of the flu: sore neck glands, joint pain, low energy, and weakened arms and legs. But now mindful of my body's silent warnings, I heed these symptoms and slow down or eat a more restrictive diet. I have learned to say "no" to many requests.

Globally, fallout from incest, covert or otherwise, remains. Child victims continue to face disbelief from others. Many still bear invisible scars. I continue to find the frequent international stories of child incest and sexual abuse, whether sex slavery, Internet porn and exploitation, or abduction, rape, and murder, truly disturbing. As RAINN reports, 93 per cent of perpetrators who sexually abuse children are known to their victim(s).

One in six adult females has been sexually assaulted in childhood by a family member. Eight per cent of people in Canada, aged fifteen and up, reported childhood sexual abuse, according to self-reported data from the federal government's 2014 general social survey on victimization.

In the United States, a child is abused every six minutes; one in four girls and one in six boys has been sexually abused by age eighteen. A 2000 report by the Bureau of Justice Statistics in the U.S. states that almost seventy per cent of all sexual assaults are committed against children. Most such assaults occur at home, committed by fathers, stepfathers, and friends of the family. Only one in 10 sexually abused children tells someone. Most child victims are taught and groomed, as I was, to think they are the special one. Yet, if my parents had had another daughter after me, *she* would have likely taken on that status.

My heart aches for the Indigenous survivors of childhood sexual abuse at Canada's residential schools, their loved ones, and the thousands of children who died in anonymous graves after suffering abuse and neglect at these schools.

* * *

For an archetypal influence, I have drawn inspiration from a powerful symbol outside my own culture: Kali (Hindi for "time"), Hinduism's Divine Mother. Often portrayed as black or blue with many arms, she's a female principle who touches all. Revered as both kind and fierce, she's associated with darkness and destruction, death and rebirth. She has transcended ego and identification with the body. Whether as a shrivelled crone with wild hair or a terrifying young fury, she was and is a sacred symbol, "an affirmation of the unity of nature and all its powers," says gender activist Rita Banerji. Although initially considered the consort of the Hindu god Shiva, she came first, then he was created. Ergo, she wound up with a better gig than Eve did.

Kali's transformational energy reminds me to release my fear of change, the unknown, and beliefs and habits that hold me back. Only now do I recognize that her combined light and darkness represent qualities not only in my father, but in Frank and me—in everyone, in diverging degrees. She embodies rage and reconciliation, fire and forgiveness, and everything in between. Like a black hole in space, Kali is said to devour time: a void without form yet full of potential. For me, her symbolic power represents the need to surrender, let go, and accept what is: the despicable and the divine.

* * *

During my father's illness and mother's dementia, my sisters and I contacted each other more frequently, sharing care and decisions regarding my parents and their future. I felt relieved that we could handle these duties with easy cooperation and mostly mutual agreement. Rallying with my sisters to respond to my parents' conditions in their final years acted as a tremendous reminder to embrace each moment as if it is all that matters. As more people I know die or worsen in health, I remind myself: *Carpe diem*. While my dad lay in a hospice bed, receiving intravenous pain medication, and my mother wrestled to find the right word in each sentence, I recognized more than ever that kindness and love—unconditional love, if possible—ultimately matter, not memories.

At a family, community, and world level, I support and encourage safe and peaceful efforts to promote reconciliation and compassion, particularly among traditional enemies. I recently completed training in how to conduct a peacemaking circle, offered by our local restorative justice society. At a global level, I appreciate the efforts of California psychotherapist Arman Volkas, the son of Auschwitz survivors, and his non-profit project Healing the Wounds of History. He provides workshops for people who share a historical trauma and are traditionally in conflict, whether it's Palestinians and Israelis, or the offspring of Holocaust survivors and Nazis. Admittedly, these global, horrific issues have far broader ramifications than incest within a single family, yet, they all deal with victimization, abuse of power, denial, subjugation, and more.

Creativity became a vital force in my healing, transmuting pain into constructive action. If a victim so desires, this gradual process can lead to reconciliation with, or forgiveness of, a perpetrator. Volkas uses group creativity—drama, poetry, and other forms—for this purpose. In the spirit of reconciliation, he offers six steps to help change enemies into allies:

1. Break the taboo against speaking to each other.
2. Humanize each other through telling our stories.
3. Explore and own the potential perpetrator in all of us. (This one is a toughie. Rather than condemning someone as "evil" and apart from us, it requires

recognizing that we all have the capacity for some form of cruelty under extreme circumstances. This stance acknowledges that so-called evil is part of a continuum, one in which we all partake at varying degrees.)

4. Move deeply into the grief.
5. Create rituals of remembrance.
6. Make commitments to acts of creation or acts of service.

Here in Canada, I support the goals of the Truth and Reconciliation Commission, striving to bring amends to centuries of racist and abusive colonialist behaviour. This includes many decades of sexual and other abuse committed by nuns and priests against innocent Indigenous children at residential schools. Daniel Heath Justice, OC, a Cherokee professor of First Nations and Indigenous Studies and English at the University of British Columbia, says, "Reconciliation... was, and remains, a legal obligation assumed by the Canadian nation-state as well as a moral one. Reconciliation alone is simply another word for colonialism-as-usual, but even the compound of *truth and reconciliation* is inadequate if it's not realized in relations, in action, in purpose." Heath Justice reaffirms that truth is always central to Indigenous calls for reconciliation. He says that we need to change systems and circumstances and look after one another with love and not fear, hesitation, uncertainty.

To me, bearing witness as compassionate listeners is part of this process. I applaud the practice of restorative justice, but do not consider it a blanket solution. Each one of us must choose how, when, or if we want to heal. Sometimes, it's not always a case of *wanting* to heal. Some people's abuse is so horrendous that they cannot even approach healing without enduring a psychotic break.

I encourage victims and survivors to speak out, at least to one other person, if they can without risking their safety, and if they can afford it, to seek out trauma-informed counselling. Breaking silence with a safe, trusted person is truly liberating and empowering. If they have enough fortitude and support, they can go public and press charges; I strongly support such efforts. However, someone must feel ready for this step, and be prepared for others' denial, condemnation, and possible retribution.

After all, most societies have maintained a cultural norm of much older men pursuing, and often preying on, much younger women. For instance, Joyce Maynard revealed in her memoir how J. D. Salinger, beloved author of *The Catcher in the Rye*, wrote her letters when she was eighteen and he fifty-three, saying she was his soul mate and they would "live out their days together." The two did live together and discussed having a child. Yet, Salinger supporters and media outlets condemned Maynard for writing publicly about their relationship. Maureen Dowd of the *New York Times* even called her a "predator." Maynard writes: "I might as well have murdered Holden Caulfield. Many have never forgiven me." Since then, more than a dozen women have contacted her, saying that they, too, as teenagers, received similar letters from Salinger.

Maynard reminds us: "It's not simply about how our culture continues to shame, dismiss, humiliate, devalue, and demonize women. It's the injury—sometimes overt counterattack, often gaslighting—that an abused woman is virtually certain to endure when she breaks her silence to tell what happened to her. Call it a one-two punch."

In Canada, survivors can seek support from groups such as the national Ending Violence Association (EVA) and/or its provincial counterparts[1] and community agencies. Once any form of child abuse is reported, local chapters of the global nonprofit Bikers Against Child Abuse (BACA) will provide 24/7 support with a highly vetted friendship group, accompany a child to court to testify, provide security outside a home, if necessary, and maintain a committed allyship for as long as needed. The U.S. has Chicago-based PAVE (Promoting Awareness/Victim Empowerment), Survivor.org, and state and community organizations. Survivor-run

---

1. In full disclosure, I served as communications manager for EVA BC in 2020–21.

Incest Aware provides helpful resources and identifies outlets for advocacy and sharing your story.

Awareness and education must come before reconciliation is possible. To help avoid sexual abuse, I support educating kids at home and at school about safe and unsafe touch and unsafe secrets. We must encourage children to speak out if an adult attempts inappropriate behaviour with them. We must find more understanding and supportive adults who will believe them and take action to help them. Reporting of incidents is essential. We need to educate guardians and people in power so that they can prevent child sexual abuse or at least recognize the signs of it in victims. Little Warriors, an Alberta-based charity, is one national organization that focuses on the awareness, prevention, and treatment of child sexual abuse. As the U.S. nonprofit group Darkness to Light (D2L) says, "We must act as a community." This organization offers five steps to empower people to prevent child sexual abuse:

1. Learn the facts.
2. Minimize opportunity.
3. Talk about it.
4. Recognize the signs.
5. React responsibly.

If any adults learn that child sexual abuse has occurred, they need to give victims healthy care and support, rather than disbelief, shaming, and blame.

Programs such as Be More Than a Bystander and Mentors in Violence Prevention (MVP) educate youth at schools and adults in workplaces about sexually inappropriate language and behaviour. Participants learn to understand how sexist and bullying attitudes and ignorance regarding consent can lead to the violence of rape, battering, incest—and murder. To maintain silence about any form of abuse only builds the protection of one who has harmed another.

I like the MVP model because it encourages people to speak out against abusive behaviour before, during, or after an incident. This reinforces that any individual who has the courage to break silence can make a difference by challenging and changing social norms. It also helps to create a peer culture that makes sexist abuse unacceptable. The Be More Than a Bystander approach is effective because it moves beyond the victim-perpetrator model. If we view all men, for instance, as potential perpetrators as I did in my early twenties as a radical feminist—this outlook was popular in the 1970s and 1980s—this can cause men to shut down and not feel safe to engage in critical dialogue. If women primarily see themselves as victims, they, too, might be reluctant to discuss this issue, especially with men present.

I think that the MVP approach works because rather than demonizing males, it views everyone as empowered bystanders who can choose to confront their abusive peers and support friends who are abused. I support making an MVP program part of a school's required core curriculum.

We need to end the long-held patriarchal model of men defining, dominating, and controlling women's lives. We need inclusive models and safe, supportive groups that address the reality of everyone's lives, including those of LGTBQIA2S+ children and adults. I support the work of Canada's Moose Hide Campaign, co-founded by *Raven Lacerte*, part of the Carrier First Nation, and her father Paul, which calls on men and boys to work together to stop the cycle of violence towards women and children. This national grassroots organization asks all of us to wear one of the campaign's moose hide pins to show our commitment to honour, respect and protect the women and children in our life and to speak out against intimate partner violence.

Ideally, I hope that we can all end up feeling safe enough, eventually, to share experiences together, and to hear each other's perspectives. Otherwise, as a society, we will make little advancement.

Above all, it is essential that we take responsibility for any words or actions that demean people and promote sexual violence towards them. Perpetrators need to be made accountable. As individuals and societies, we must not accept that sexual assault and incest are inevitable. Historically, most advice has been oriented to curbing heterosexual females' behaviour and manner of dress as supposed preventative actions against sexual assault and abuse from men. We need more voices to stand up and challenge long-standing patriarchal views that reinforce "boys will be boys."

I applaud Erin's Law in the U.S. and hope to see it adopted, eventually, around the world. The law's proponent, incest survivor Erin Merryn, is leading a crusade to have a prevention-oriented child sexual abuse program made mandatory in U.S. public schools from pre-kindergarten through grade five. This includes teaching school personnel about child sexual abuse, informing parents and guardians about the warning signs of child sexual abuse, and having assistance, referral or resource information available to support sexually abused children and their families. As of the summer of 2022, Erin's Law is now in effect in thirty-seven states.

We need systemic change. We need trauma-informed approaches in our schools, courtrooms, law enforcement, workplaces, and communities with corresponding changes in attitudes, laws, and policies. Not enough programs, services, and trained social workers are available to help child survivors of incest and sexual abuse. And few programs exist for perpetrators. Under Canada's child welfare laws, everyone has the duty to report known or suspected child abuse. We need to overcome cultural barriers and break the cycle of silence and denial within families and communities. We need to learn and understand the impact of intersectionality.

* * *

For about four years, I have attended an informal weekly Buddhist *sangha* group, based around the teachings of Zen master Thich Nhat Hanh. His promotion of a simple smile as a symbol of connection and appreciation has allowed me to redefine the impact of one. Instead of fearing that smiling at a man might infer sexual interest or flirting, as I learned in childhood, I can now provide warm, nurturing smiles that convey genuine connectedness. I can smile at my body, my worries, myself.

Thich Nhat Hanh identifies four basic elements of true love: loving kindness, compassion, joy, and inclusiveness. I try to live this way through my words and actions. Helping my father as he was dying inspired me to become a hospice volunteer.

One statement within Thich Nhat Hanh's five mindfulness trainings especially resonates with me: "I will do everything in my power to protect children from sexual abuse and to prevent couples and families from being broken by sexual misconduct."

This goal inspired me in 2016 to work with MVP as a gender violence prevention worker and coordinate our local MVP program two years later. This initiative fuelled me to speak out against sexual harassment and abuse and encourage others to do so. By the end of 2019, I became communications manager for the nonprofit association Ending Violence Association of BC, which provides training, support, and education regarding sexual assault, sexual harassment, and domestic violence.

Doing Inner Child work helped me tremendously and I encourage survivors to seek this out if it feels right. In his book *The Wild Edge of Sorrow*, psychotherapist Francis Weller offers a powerful list of questions to help heal and bring to consciousness a dissociated and fragmented child self, inviting written responses. He calls it "working with the complex."

We all need to gain a sense of belonging, whether it's through our family, community, work, relationships—or body, says counsellor and trauma consultant Resmaa Menakem. He reaffirms how essential it is for survivors to learn to reconnect and become grounded in their body, finding new ways to soothe their jangled nervous system. Many simple exercises, such as humming and belly breathing, promote a "calm, settled body," he says. (See the body and breath practices in his book *My Grandmother's Hands*.) Menakem calls the energetic, ever-present "settledness" that he has learned to access Infinite Source. In his words: "This settling of nervous systems, and this connection to a larger Source, is vital to healing." I wholly agree.

POCKETS

The last suit that you wear, you don't need any pockets.
—Wayne Dyer

IN POOL, PLAYERS can call the pocket in which they plan to sink a ball. I like this notion that signifies intention, rather than happenstance.

Pockets carry secrets. They hide things but items can tumble out. "Empty your pockets," we're told as children, and as airline passengers, waiting to pass through security. Rules control our private places.

In many moments, interpreting news events, listening to music or laughing at the same cartoon, my father and I were in sync, like two jazz musicians. We were "in the pocket": flowing and riffing together on beat, not missing a note.

Yet, memories of his suggestive humour linger, like Mae West's line: *Is that a pistol in your pocket or are you just happy to see me?*

Some might find this pocket metaphor creepy and inappropriate. One manuscript reader told me to take it out. But I bear such dissonance, this shadow, within me. I have power over it now.

Thich Nhat Hanh suggests that people can carry a beautiful pebble, carefully washed, in their pocket. Every time they put their hand in their pocket, they touch the pebble and hold it gently. They use it as a nudge to bring awareness to their breathing, to focus on the moment. When someone is angry, the pebble becomes the person's dharma or Buddhist teaching: while holding it, calmly breathe in and out, and smile. Hanh admits that this might sound childish, but he acknowledges the value of this practice. Holding the pebble brings you back to yourself. It is a tool to create mindfulness. We can think of the pebble as a rosary or prayer bead; it reminds us that our teacher is always with and within us. The pebble allows love to be born inside us, he says. It helps us to keep that love, and our version of enlightenment, alive.

"When you drop a pebble in the water, there are ever-widening circles of ripples," writes Robert Anderson in *Tea and Sympathy*. "There are always consequences." Indeed, there are.

Family photo #13: I am four days old, wrapped in a fuzzy blanket in the hospital. Under a complete head of hair, with one eye scrunched half-closed, I stare at the camera, my tiny hands folded together under my chin. My expression seems to say: *I don't know about this place. Do I really want to be here?* The final addition to a family, I am a wary new bundle, ready for love. But are they ready for me, ready for this rough pebble in their quiet stream?

Dad, you were, and are, the pebble within my soul's still pond. I carry the ripple effect of your words and actions every day.

A few of your belongings fill my office: a painting of a Burmese Kayan woman wearing brass neck rings, an old floor-standing globe, and a framed print of *The Bookworm* by Carl Spitzweg, showing a white-haired man on a wooden library ladder amongst floor-to-ceiling books.

I have learned that overcoming suffering can lead to many healing gifts: greater mindfulness and authenticity, tremendous empowerment, and a far more fulfilling life and work path. My journey has opened me to greater love and joy, which allows more openness to others' suffering and today's many injustices.

Healing one's demons is the most profound, revolutionary act a person can make. The sexual assaults I endured in India launched a pivotal role in my healing: they began to shake me out of dissociation, begun in response to my father and other men in childhood. Unwanted talk and touching in India—what post-traumatic-stress clinician Bessel A. van der Kolk calls "contextual stimuli," and Freudians "repetition compulsion"—plus the similarities between a then-boyfriend and my dad and accompanying weird déjà vu experiences, started to jolt me out of my denial. Freud's term refers to relationships, behaviour, emotions, and dreams that seem to replay early trauma: people subconsciously put themselves in situations like the ones that caused the original trauma to learn new responses. At a physical level, the assaults I experienced in India helped trigger sensations or somatic memory stored in my body.

India was a country whose landscapes and people I loved overall. Many wonderful moments and events there helped form the most memorable seven months of my life in 1990–91. But this portion of my tale, by necessity, concentrates on my ordeals there as a thirty-one-year-old solo backpacker.

I share my experiences in the hope that others in my situation might find a semblance of connection, validation, and perhaps, inspiration. Anyone who moves into adulthood without validation for "felt" life experiences and perceptions, whatever they are, will emerge with spiritual and emotional wounds. Yet, this hardly needs to guarantee victimhood or lifelong suffering. We can all decide how, when or if we want to heal—ideally, with the right support, receptive brain pathways, and a profound sense of safety.

Dad, you were buried with no letter in your pocket. Instead, I keep it in my meditation hut, on my altar, folded under the small brass Buddha that you bought, perhaps in Myanmar, which sits on a small wooden stand. These spontaneous words spilled out of me one day:

> *Dear Dad,*
> *Thank you for all of the jokes and laughter that you gave, and for the wise counsel and values of kindness and generosity.*
> *I am proud of all that you achieved and the love and lifesaving that you provided to so many people.*
> *I will carry on your rebel spirit and your beloved sense of play and irony and mischief-making.*
> *I am grateful to have inherited your intellect, curiosity, and love of books, history, and travel.*

I carry the legacy of your life within me and am glad that I could be your advocate and witness when you were dying and died.

You were the healer of many and I, too, have healed myself and others. I will continue that gift of yours.

Thank you for all that you were and are.

I will honour you the best way I can in my book, while telling my own truth.

I love you and will carry you in my heart. Love, Heather

One editor commented that this note wasn't credible. But it was, and is, my truth in a moment, springing from my deepest Self. After I wrote it, my inner critic took over: *That's not how you're supposed to feel about an abuser. What's wrong with you? You're letting him off too easily.*

I have loved and condemned my father. I can live with these contradictions.

FIND THE STILL POND WITHIN

By Bernie Siegel, MD

To know all is to forgive all.
—W. Livingston Larned

I WORK WITH people with wounded lives and life-threatening illnesses. I call my form of therapy "carefrontation." I cared about, and for, the people I have helped, but also confronted them to get them to give up the victim role and be empowered, to become a "respant," or responsible participant. When we can forgive and create a new life for ourselves, we can no longer be abused by others. If we are to heal, we need to go within, find the cause, and treat and eliminate it instead of turning to drugs or other substances to reduce symptoms. As Heather says, "We can engage or ignore, accept or resist." Choose healthy alternatives and move forward.

My hope is that by reading my afterword and Heather's book about healing from incest, you can find your way and heal your own life and body. When I started reading Heather's moving account of her journey through hell and what she learned from it, I couldn't stop. When I finished her story, my first thoughts for this afterword were to focus on the meaningful points we can all learn from. Then it occurred to me that, because I am a surgeon, I have some shared similar life experiences with her father. I wanted to share these, not to make an excuse for his abusive behaviour, but to help everyone understand: when we are trained as physicians, we receive medical information but not an education. We are taught to treat the result but not to understand and treat the cause.

Doctors at work: buried feelings take their toll

Physicians are not trained to care for people, either themselves or their patients. So, our feelings are buried within us and take their toll. We are not asked, in a meaningful and therapeutic way, why we chose medicine or our particular specialty so that we can better understand ourselves, our feelings, and our behaviour. None of my five children are doctors because they saw the pain I experienced on my own journey through hell in the medical field.

What does it say about Heather's dad that he was an anesthesiologist? That specialty renders people unconscious and numbs them; it truly does not deal with their feelings and emotions. I think his personality and the profession he chose offers us some understanding of his behaviour, related to his unhealthy and untreated needs. As physicians, we need to be taught how to deal with our feelings and the knowledge that you can't cure every patient. They do die and we need not see their death as our failure. I learned from one of my cancer patients that what we all need is the knowledge of how to live between office visits.

Doctors have a higher rate of addictions and suicide because they were not coached and educated properly. Heather's dad did not get emotionally involved with patients because he couldn't handle his emotions. I have been through that and found help by uncovering what was within me. I began a spiritual journey. We need to stop burying the pain and numbing ourselves through addictions.

We learn from our life coaches

A woman named Susan Duffy, who had alcoholic parents and whose sister committed suicide, has been my teacher. She survived an illness she was expected to die of decades ago. I met her as she came looking for support and healing. Her words in a letter to me related her lack of control over her parents and her life's circumstances. She wrote: "But when I let love into my prison, it touched every negative item in it, meaning the experiences in my life, and turned them into something meaningful." When I asked her for a picture of herself as a child, she said her parents never took one. She wrote: "All these years I would write him [her alcoholic father] letters but he would never reply. When I asked why, he said he had nothing to write me, that I already knew that he loved me."

My response to Susan applies to Heather and anyone else with a wounded relationship with a parent:

> *You can become a love warrior and heal through love. Your dad knows what you are consciously sharing. His body may have died but his consciousness is still present and can communicate with you through meaningful symbolic signs and coincidences. You may find a message from him, or your sister, through a symbolic sign, which comes into your life and reminds you of them. So, keep an open mind, one which is not thinking all the time. It is in the quiet moments that voices speak to us and miracles happen.*

When we know how to live in a healthy way, everyone benefits from our wisdom and insights. Heather shares her trauma and, in a sense, labour pains of self-birth. We can all benefit by reading about, and learning from, her experience. We know, for a fact, that memories are stored in our bodies. If we do not bring them forth and heal our wounds, we evade the truth. The body will present us with the bill as a dis-ease. As psychoanalyst Alice Miller has said, the wounds are like a child who will not stop tormenting us until we stop evading the truth.

Heather creates two sections in her book for the purpose of sharing her experiences with us. However, when dealing with life's traumas, we all must understand that we need to create internal unity, not be a duplex or triplex entity. Our mind, body, and spirit need to be healed and united. As Heather shows us, the journey to a healed life and body is not an easy one but the potential is there for all of us.

It's far better to learn from those who can be our life coaches than become enlightened through our own curse. Those who contemplate suicide and then turn away from that choice become our therapists and teachers. They chose to eliminate what was killing them and preserve their lives. They show us what can happen, what is possible, and our own potential to heal.

Many years ago, a dying friend started calling me "Journey" instead of Bernie. He awakened me and helped me to see how the events in my life were all part of the process of who I was becoming. A curse can become a blessing when I am willing to ask myself: What can I learn from my painful journey and experience? We all need to understand that everything we experience is part of what creates who we are. The younger we are, the more hypnotic it is and the harder it becomes to alter any negative ways of thinking and feeling. Only when we truly understand why, be it abuse from our parents or another painful experience, can we find peace.

We are each the keeper of the zoo

We all have our own definition of truth. It becomes a relative term because we are busy thinking and creating what we think is the truth. The only truth we can know is what is true for us as individuals. When I ask people to describe their disease experience, the words they use are invariably about something else going on in their lives. Carl Sandburg wrote about all the animals within us, whom I would call our multiple or sub-personalities; he shares that we are the keeper of the zoo. We make the choice about how, when, and if we want to heal or gain attention through our dis-ease.

When we develop multiple personalities, in Sandburg's sense, it is often to protect ourselves and gain the attention we do not get in healthy ways. It is empowering to know that we are all actors and can change who we are by practicing new thoughts and behaviour. When we become our authentic self, our body responds to the new and healthy internal chemistry and the life we can now truly love.

Just as Heather's dad kept a diary, so did I. One night, when I forgot to hide it, my wife read it and said, "There's nothing funny in it." I told her that my life wasn't funny. Then she told me many stories I had shared at the dinner table about funny things that happened in the hospital that had the whole family laughing. Yet, they never became a part of my journal as the pain did. Her comment was very therapeutic. As you read Heather's experience, you get the same sense about what she was storing in her body, which desperately needed to come out. The pages are filled with her pain and the courage she had to feel her experiences, change who she was, and stop leading a double life.

It is not easy but when the journey leads us to the discovery of divine love, forgiveness, and compassion, the healing begins. In no way is that easy for children to do unless someone re-parents them and they find a chosen dad or mom. When we can breathe in our pain and the pain of those we are interacting with, and breathe out compassion, the change begins.

Use anger in healthy, appropriate ways

Yes, anger is appropriate when we are not treated with respect. But I am not talking about what fills the headlines, when the abused seeks revenge and then experiences guilt. We need to speak up, express suitable anger, and listen to our coaches too. We can all stop being a victim. We control only one thing: our thoughts and associated feelings. We can empower ourselves to heal and find happiness, not through addictions, but in a healthy, life-enhancing way.

When I was getting overbearing, my children would quiet me

down by saying, "Dad, you're not in the operating room now." When our kids were driving me nuts, I also brought in healing humour with comments like "Do you know why your mother and I will never get a divorce? Because neither one of us wants the children." They laughed and quieted down because they knew they were loved.

When we are brought up storing unhealthy anger and being submissive, we self-destruct. Our children would tell me when they felt I didn't love them as much as their siblings. We would talk about why they felt this way and I explained the reasons for it. I gave them credit for speaking up rather than feeling unloved.

Aggression and anger can be used in healthy ways; how we apply them is the key to our life. As a surgeon, I cut people up to help them heal and be cured. We can all act that way with a knife, rather than destructively, whether it's metaphorical or not.

Re-parent yourself: Self-love is the key

When we do not need an illness, mental or physical, to get attention, we are on the road to recovery. In her tale, Heather often blames her father but I think they are so alike. We judge others but before we do, we need to understand what they have experienced and what created them. As an adult, we can change ourselves and our reactions to what our child self experienced and help ourselves to heal. Step up and accept responsibility.

Although we might feel powerless as a child, once we grow up, we need to realize that we are both the problem and solution. We need to forgive ourselves and accept that our own thoughts and feelings, not our parents, are now the problem. Heather seems to judge herself and be tougher with herself than she is with her dad. She is in control of only one thing, her thoughts, and can solve her problem by changing them.

Self-love is the key. Why blame your dad for your not loving yourself? Yes, how you were treated, and spoken to, by your parents had a hypnotic effect on you, as it does to all young children.

However, you can reprogram the negative mottoes and messages you received. You can re-parent yourself. Create shrines where you live and work that contain pictures of yourself as a child. Love that child every time you walk by the picture. Stop thinking and start feeling. Let your heart make up your mind. Sex and power can be yours and become a positive part of your life.

All parents need help and love. Relationships are not about one's personal desires but about what will help the relationship. Rather than life-enhancing messages, Heather's parents grew up with mottoes to die by, like "Be strong." This affected their relationships as father, mother, husband, wife, and doctor. Relationships are a struggle and they were not prepared for that.

Parents need to instill a reverence for life in their children and not a desire for upper-class or higher-income privileges. Material things are to improve life for us all, acting out of kindness, not just to have an elegant life and costly education.

Remember: Our parents had parents too. Stop blaming and criticizing! Adam and Eve didn't get it right and we are still learning. A perfect world is not creation. We are here to live and learn and become teachers for others, as this book can do for you all.

When done reading this story, all parents are to tell their kids they love them and are sorry for any pain they caused them. All children, wounded or otherwise, are to call their parents and say: "I love you." It is never too late to heal a broken heart.

A still pond: the secret to the solution

Consider the symbol of the still pond. Heather mentions her dad as a pebble; pebbles can cause the problem. By dropping a pebble into the pond, you create turbulence and ripples, which make it impossible for you to see the truth reflected back to you. Only when we quiet our minds, like a still pond, do we see and become aware of the truth about ourselves.

In this still-pond state of mind, you will hear voices from the greater consciousness, guiding and directing you to the new future you are creating for yourself. No longer will you have the need to lose your life to please others and live the life they choose and impose upon you.

The early part of Heather's book describes a turbulent time when the truth is hard to see. We can help ourselves move into a new reality by creating a mantra that contains positive words and messages. By meditating on it several times a day, we interrupt our negative moments with it. Meditation helped Heather create a still pond, see her truth reflected back at her, and heal her wounds.

When we stop thinking about the wounds of our past, we abandon them and heal. Memories are a choice, as are your thoughts and feelings. Stop thinking and move on with hope, knowing your potential. Again, this happens when the thinking mind is quiet and the still pond, such as yoga and meditation for Heather, come in. We ask ourselves what we are to learn from our experience and stop whining. Quotes and experts may help but you must also believe what you experience and not be limited by your negative beliefs and things you can't explain.

Feelings aren't right or wrong. They are to be used to help you eliminate what is killing you and find what heals you and others. When you choose life-enhancing behaviour, wonderful things will happen for you and everyone in your life. Ending your life is no longer an option of interest.

Let love become our weapon

Love is the weapon of choice. As Helen Keller said, "Far more than sight, I wish for my ears to be opened. The voice of a friend, the imaginations of Mozart: life without these is darker by far than blindness." To help yourself and others, listen. You and they will then know what you and they need to do. Don't tell others what to do but listen, just as Heather speaks to herself through her book. They will thank you.

Heather shares that to heal the inner child, we must integrate the shutdown child with the adult self. Again, I call it re-parenting one's self. To live in constant fear is self-destructive. It stops growth and healing. Fear is meant to protect us from danger. But if you think that every moment is dangerous, you will suffer the consequences of the damage to your mind and body. We need to be touched to grow and heal. I created the word "meassage" to define being massaged or touched in a therapeutic, loving way. It enhances our growth and health.

What we see in others is what resides within us; it is easier to project problems onto others than admit they are our issues too. See in others what your issue is and stop blaming them. Take responsibility for your life. Seek nature to help you to heal. Stop making excuses and explaining via therapists' words. We all have choices. The opposite of love is indifference, rejection, and abuse, which lead to a desire for revenge and guilt. Those actions are the headlines today.

A focus on sex needs to be dealt with. As an alternative to her story, Heather could have discussed life with those she developed a relationship with and not over-analyzed everything again and again, asking: "Who is this man? Why am I here?" Yet, she let go as she knew she needed to. As Heather shares, true emotional expression is an elixir to an emotion-starved heart.

There is always the potential to heal and we must believe it to have it happen. When we are ready to let love become our weapon, we can change others through the power of love. We need to seek out and be life coaches for each other. The right path for all of us is to follow our hearts and do what makes us happy so that we do not lose our lives to the desires of others. We are to choose how we contribute love to the world and have an authentic life. As Heather says, "Nothing external will ever bring me happiness." Yes, and the pain is continually buried within, where it causes more pain and dis-ease. Heather's family did not have a healed and healthy relationship.

Nature awakens us and helps us to be aware of our body and creation. It answers our questions by teaching us about survival.

Life's mountains teach us how to climb. We need to accept our mortality and enjoy the time of our life. Self-guilt, worrying or explaining doesn't heal the issues. Using sex as a way to prove you're a worthwhile person doesn't resolve the problem. We all need to deal with our multiple personalities and the need to win approval and find self-love and esteem. To choose life, be creative and unify mind, body, and spirit. Don't be denied a true, authentic life.

As Gandhi and Mother Teresa teach us, we are to become non-violent warriors. We need to stop letting the past control our present, separating our heart and head, and losing our identity. These are all self-destructive, along with rejection and self-criticism. In my own life, I learned, after being robbed and knowing who did it, that the time I spent resenting this person and wanting revenge allowed him to still rob me of my life's time. Only then did I let go and forgive him. Through my thoughts, I sent him a desire for him to find happiness. Then I was free and no longer being abused by him.

Abandon your past or replay it, heal it, and move on. Find a self-identity that doesn't need something to be wrong to get attention. You can turn a curse into a blessing. Stop the abuse. Plant trees. Send gifts. Create love and friendship, connecting everyone through their hearts.

Wake up: We are all connected

We are all connected. As a surgeon, I am always sharing that we are all one family, the same colour inside. Children sense this while adults feel separated from each other. If you don't like being in India, leave—whatever your metaphorical India might be. If I were the president, I would use love as my weapon and offer love and money to our enemies to improve their homelands and not spend it on weapons of destruction. I would prefer to die loving my enemies rather than hating them. If I were surgeon general, I would start programs to be sure that every child grows up feeling loved.

When you find your spiritual path and start that journey, you will feel oneness and compassion for all living things, including your father and others who have wounded you. Then you will experience a freedom like never before, like Nelson Mandela. When he left prison, he knew what he needed to do to be truly free of his imprisonment.

I love Heather's phrase "a healthy way to become vulnerable." Yes, the inner child who has a sense of childlike humour and self-worth can do that. You can be coached and grow rather than make excuses. The self-empowerment comes from divine love, wisdom, suffering, and survival. When you have the courage to confront the demons or monsters within you, they shrink and are no longer anything to fear. The dragon becomes only a lizard.

Heather has written a book as a witness to her experience. We can all benefit from writing a book, or journal, of our life experience and help ourselves to heal. But don't write it to get sympathy, be understood, or admired. Do it to heal yourself and help others. If other benefits come, that's fine, but do it to heal your wounds and help others, not to show your scars to get attention. Remember: In love's service, only the wounded soldier can serve.

When spirituality and compassion enter your life, healing will occur. You can stop carrying the cross. Don't just put it down—use the lumber to create something better. In a sense, Heather is doing this by sharing her wounds and burden. Learn from her by paying attention, not just to her troubles, but to her abilities and the ways she found to survive and thrive. The question for us all to consider is: What is the truth?

Wake up from your unconscious state. Let the anesthesia wear off. Stop comparing, numbing, distracting, making excuses, living the unhealthy messages of your past and more. Practice becoming the loving and compassionate person you want yourself and others to be. Healing is a process and death can be a great teacher. Graduations are commencements and that is what life is about: beginnings. Death and dying can be great teachers and commencements too.

How do you want to be remembered?

In closing, I'd like to say: Keep learning. Realize that life is about what we have learned, what I call the labour pains of self-birth. What makes it all worthwhile is that you *do* give birth to your new self. All the discomfort and pain become worthwhile. Most important of all, be kind to yourself. Love and forgive yourself.

Now is the time for us all to write a letter to our dad figure, whoever that may be, and move on. This will begin the process of re-parenting yourself. Never stop writing those letters and moving forward in your life, as Heather has. The only thing of permanence, which makes us immortal, is experiencing and sharing love—not incest. Which do you want to be remembered for? So, write your books and letters and choose life, as Heather did. When you do, you will receive your letter of reward, and your immortality.

Here is one of the letters I carry in my pocket from one of our sons:

> *Dad, I just wanted you to know that all my life you have been my hero. From the time I was a little boy throughout my whole life. All the times you came to school for show and tell and brought my pets in and all the classes you visited with body parts that fascinated and put in awe the entire school. All the pets you let me have and all the understanding and love you gave me no matter what. All the people you put back together when they were broken.*
>
> *I was always so proud to be your son and I always will be. I don't think there is anyone else in the world that will ever know what it means to have a father like you and a mother like mom. I just wanted you to know this so if some day comes that I can't tell you how much you both mean to me. You will know because I put it into words way before that day came.*
> *Love, Jeff*

Peace, love, and healing.

Bernie Siegel, MD
Woodbridge, CT
August 2019

Acknowledgements

THANK YOU TO all who nudged me to make revisions at different stages. More than anyone, Erin Parker, my editing angel, helped to elicit the story's current structure. She offered the kindest and most insightful suggestions imaginable. Nancy Barr and Deena Metzger provided frank feedback when needed most. The understanding, expertise, and support of four mentors—Suzannah Lessard, Diana Hume George, the late Richard Todd, and Webster Younce—in the Master of Fine Arts program in creative nonfiction writing at Goucher College in Baltimore helped me shape early drafts in important ways.

I am grateful to many friends who read all or parts of my manuscript. I truly needed and appreciated Steve Rosenberg's early enthusiasm and Judy Slattery's thoughtfulness. I gained valuable insights about betrayal trauma from Laurie Kahn. David Roche shared soulful perspectives. Encouragement from Marlena Blavin and her explanation of kinesthetic memory were timely. Glo McArter requested clarifications. Katrina Dennis kept me uplifted with her humour and feminist viewpoint. Mukesh Bhardwaj helped with sensitive appreciation and fact-checking. I benefited from the late George Payerle's editing and his recommended readings. Persephone Dimson's appraisal came with unconditional love. Annie Huston gave a blunt assessment of India-related content while Petra Long critiqued unnecessary repetition. Many thanks to Janice Williams for her words of support and encouragement along the way.

While artist-in-residence at Historic Joy Kogawa House in Vancouver, Susan Crean invited me to explore the theme of reconciliation, to re-examine my narrative voice, and expand the descriptions of my spiritual journey. Others who provided helpful comments on specific sections include Constance Brissenden; Georgeanna Drew; Colleen Friesen; Stewart Green; Eric Hellman; Lee Holmes; Howard Katz; Bonnie Sherr Klein; Linda Lawson; Betty MacPhee; Catherine McNeil; Sylvia Matthies; Andrea Nicki; David Swick; Raj Uppal; and Deb Vail.

I am grateful to Bernie Siegel for his inspirational words of "carefrontation" and his willingness to collaborate with a stranger. Much appreciation to Michael Mirolla at Guernica Editions for his caring, understanding, and support of me and my writing, and to David Moratto for his cover collaboration.

Thank you to everyone who heard me read excerpts prior to publication, especially women who had the courage to approach me and reveal a similar story. I would like to applaud Donna Besel for sharing part of that public journey with me, for her brave writing, and for providing support along the way. This book rests on the boldness of all authors who have written about their own struggle through incest or sexual abuse. Bearing witness to the inner strength of my writing students, past and present, who have brought a voice to their own trauma and vulnerability remains a deep satisfaction. Many thanks to you all.

Receiving the support of my three sisters, who believed my story when revealing it felt terrifying, was a crucial blessing. I appreciate their willingness to share their memories.

The unending love, patience, understanding, grace, wisdom, generosity, support, and endurance of my late husband Frank provided a nurturing sanctuary from which to write. For all of these gifts, I am grateful.

End Notes

Book's Front Epigrams

The quotation from playwright George S. Kaufman is cited by John Heilpern in "Host with the Mots" on page 114 in *Vanity Fair*, New York, NY, December 2010.

The Jean Houston quotation appears on page 8 in *A Mythic Life*, Harper Collins, San Francisco, CA, 1996.

The quotation by Richard Brautigan appears on page 7 in *Sunbeams: A Book of Quotations*, edited by Sy Safransky, North Atlantic Books, Berkeley, CA, 1990.

The Tori Amos quotation comes from page 156 of *Tori Amos: Piece by Piece* by Tori Amos and Ann Powers, Broadway Books, New York, NY, 2005.

Author Note

Stephen King's quote appears on page 18 of *On Writing*, Scribner, New York, NY, 2010.

Prologue: GONE

The epigram, from Salman Rushdie's *The Satanic Verses*, is taken from the *Honesty Quotes* section of the website Notable Quotes (notable-quotes.com/h/honesty_quotes.html).

For Aung San Suu Kyi's stance regarding Myanmar's Rohingya Muslims, the author drew from multiple media sources, including the 2017 documentary *The Venerable W.* by writer/director Barbet Schroeder; Oct. 29, 2017 article in *The Guardian*, "Rohingya crisis may be driving Aung San Suu Kyi closer to generals," theguardian.com/world/2017/oct/28/myanmar-fears-junta-return-rohingya-suu-kyi; and the Nov. 19, 2017 Al Jazeera article "Aung San Suu Kyi honours revoked amid Rohingya backlash" by Anealla Safdar and Shafik Mandhai, aljazeera.com/news/2017/11/aung-san-suu-kyi-honours-revoked-rohingya-backlash-171119052610172.html.

An image of Paul Peel's 1892 painting *Before the Bath* can be found at tumblr.com/search/Before+The+Bath+Artwork+by+Paul+Peel.

The lyrics to *Bei Mir Bist Du Schon*—this work is in the public domain in the United States because it was published in the U.S. between 1927 and 1977, inclusive, without a copyright notice—appear on the website International Lyrics Playground (lyricsplayground.com/alpha/songs/b/beimirbistduschon.shtml). Benny Goodman's version of this song, with Martha Tilton singing in 1937 at the Madhattan [sic] Room, is available on YouTube youtube.com/watch?v=_0HX5GUlcbs.

The comments from John Coutlee, excerpted from a letter written to Marian H. Conn on Dec. 10, 2010, appear with his permission.

Tiger Woods: The Rise and Fall (45:02 min.) is a 2010 British documentary, co-produced by Channel 4 and Fresh One Productions, which aired Oct. 2, 2010 on *The Passionate Eye* on Canadian Broadcasting Corporation's News Network.

The television news regarding the Toronto anesthesiologist with 26 sex assault charges (Dr. George Doodnaught) at North York Hospital was broadcast Sept. 30, 2010 via Global Television News in Toronto (globaltoronto.com/story.html?id=2671478). The author saw the story aired at Vancouver International Airport as part of an evening news broadcast. Other news sources for this item include the Canadian Broadcasting Corporation and the Stamford Advocate. See the following respective websites: (cbc.ca/canada/toronto/story/2010 /03/11/toronto-doctor-charged-nygh-sexual-assault.html); (stamfordadvocate.com/news/article/Toronto-anesthesiologist -accused-of-29-sex-attacks-682247.php).

PART ONE
ADRIFT IN ASIA (1990–91)

The quotation by Emily Dickinson appears on the Part One title page of "Quotations About the Past," *The Quote Garden* (quotegarden. com/past.html).

Chapter One: CONFUSED

The quotation by Robert Frost in the epigram appears on the website *Finest Quotes*, finestquotes.com/select_quote-category-Confusion -page-0.htm.

Some descriptive detail of Bangkok and the boat cruise comes from the author's 1990 journal entries and these websites: luxurythai. com/hotel_orientalriver.html; bangkok.sawadee.com/canals.htm; tour-bangkok-legacies.com/famous-writers.html; people.com/people /archive/article/0,,20089296,00.html, and brief email correspondence with the Oriental Hotel.

Identification of Kuching as Malaysia's fourth largest city is taken from these tourism websites: Sundog Travel (sundogtravel.ca/location /Kuching); Visit Malaysia (sarawak.attractionsinmalaysia.com /Kuching.php), and Wonderful Malaysia (wonderfulmalaysia.com /kuching-city-malaysia.htm).

Comments from Nancy Conn are from a long-distance phone interview conducted by the author on April 1, 2013.

The definition of covert incest comes from pages 9–11 of *Silently Seduced* by Kenneth M. Adams, Health Communications, Inc., Deerfield Beach, Fla., 1991. This is referenced on the blog *Under Much Grace* by Cynthia Mullen Kunsman, who suffered abuse under various Christian ministries (undermuchgrace.blogspot.ca/2008/06 /distinguishing-overt-from-covert-adams.html).

Judith Herman defines covert incest on page 70 of *Father-Daughter Incest*, Harvard University Press, Cambridge, MA, 2000. Her definition of a seductive father appears on page 109 of the same book. A similar definition of covert incest appears on *Psychology Wiki* (psychology.wikia.com/wiki/Covert_incest) and in the online feature "Emotional Incest: What is it?" by Dr. Jim Gordon, Beverly Hills, CA, 2009 (emotional-incest.com/indexWhat.html).

The remarks from Wendy Conn are taken from a long-distance phone interview, conducted by the author on March 12, 2013.

Chapter Two: STUBBORN

The quotation in the epigram comes from the website *Wise Old Sayings*, accessed by the author on Dec. 29, 2019. http://www.wiseoldsayings .com/stubbornness-quotes/.

The Lupita Nyong'o account is from her *New York Times* op-ed "Lupita Nyong'o: Speaking Out About Harvey Weinstein," Oct. 19, 2017. Accessed by the author on Oct. 20, 2017. nytimes.com/2017 /10/19/opinion/lupita-nyongo-harvey-weinstein.html

Nancy Conn's remarks are from a long-distance phone interview conducted by the author on April 1, 2013.

The comments from Wendy Conn are taken from a long-distance phone interview, conducted by the author on March 12, 2013.

The comments from Mary Ann Conn-Brody are taken from a long-distance phone interview, conducted by the author on Feb. 27, 2013.

The author's sister Nancy Conn provided the history involving their father's hard-drinking ancestors in an email sent to the author on August 11, 2013. Other remarks from Nancy Conn are from a long-distance phone interview conducted by the author on April 1, 2013.

The military experience of the author's father appears in his biographical entry on page 259 in volume xliii of the *Canadian Who's Who*, edited by Elizabeth Lumley, University of Toronto Press, Toronto, ON, 2008.

The author's account of travelling as a youngster with her dad in his red MGA is an excerpt from her article "Colourful little car was a ticket to a wonderful fantasy world," published on Sept. 20, 2002 in *The Vancouver Sun*, Pacific Press, Vancouver, BC, Canada.

Chapter Three: SHARDS

The Laurens Van der Post quotation in the epigram appears on page 17 of *Sunbeams: A Book of Quotations*, edited by Sy Safransky, North Atlantic Books in Berkeley, CA, 1990.

The figure for New Delhi's population in 1990 comes from the working paper "World Urbanization Prospects: The 2005 Revision," Mega-cities: fact sheet 7, Department of Economic and Social Affairs, Population Division, United Nations, New York, NY 2006 (un.org /esa/population/publications/WUP2005/2005WUP_FS7.pdf). Other website sources include Gaia Environmental Information System (ess.co.at/GAIA/CASES/IND/DEL/DELmain .html) and "Delhi now second most populous city in world," by Yoshita Singh, posted July 12, 2014, Indian Express online (indianexpress.com /article/cities/delhi/delhi-becomes-worlds-second-most-populous -city-after-tokyo/#sthash.AIq4PbOL.dpuf).

The information about Naggar Castle Hotel comes from the third edition of *India: a travel survival kit*, edited by Geoff Crowther, A. Raj Prakash and Tony Wheeler, Lonely Planet Publications, Berkeley, CA, 1987.

Chapter Four: REMEMBERING

The Joyce Appleby quotation, used in the epigram, comes from the Brainy Quote website (brainyquote.com/quotes/authors/j/joyce _appleby.html). Accessed July 25, 2015.

The altitude figure for Leh appears on a web page of the U.S. National Library of Medicine/National Institutes of Health (ncbi.nlm.nih. gov/pubmed/16275509). It cites a multi-authored article entitled "Effect of aging on blood pressure in Leh, Ladakh, a high-altitude (3524 m) community, by comparison with a Japanese town," first published in *Biomed Pharmacother*, 2005 Oct; 59 Suppl 1:S54–7. This altitude also appears on the website for Leh Ladakh Tourism (lehladakhtourism.com/about-ladakh/ladakh-geography.html) and Leh Ladakh India (lehladakhindia.com/acclimatization/).

The description of the author's childhood backyard first appeared in "Nature's Secrets," page 17 in *Vancouver Parent* magazine, December 1992, Vancouver, BC.

The Heidegger quotation appears on page 61 of Mark Nepo's *Seven Thousand Ways to Listen*, Free Press, New York, NY, 2012.

Confirmation of Stok Kangri's height can be found in the article "Tall order: 6,000m trek up Stok Kangri, one of the world's highest climbable mountains," by Simon Cable, *Daily Mail*, London, Eng., Nov. 1, 2013). The peak's altitude appears on many adventure travel websites, including Lonely Planet (lonelyplanet.com/india/jammu-and -kashmir/leh), stokkangritrek.com, and intoindia.com/adventures /trekking/ladakh-trekking-peak---stok-kangri/.

The origins of the name "Ladakh" appear on page 14 in *A Journey in Ladakh* by Andrew Harvey, Houghton Mifflin, Boston, MA, 1983. Harvey's description of the face of Kangri is taken from page 37 of the same book. Ladakh's English translation can also be found on numerous travel and tourism websites including Leh Ladakh India (lehladakhindia.com/land-of-passes/) and Nomad Travels (nomad-travels.com/ladakh-land-of-high-passes/).

The Buddhist saying about looking down at your feet appears on page 385 in *God in All Worlds*, edited by Lucinda Vardey, Pantheon Books, New York, NY, 1995.

Sources vary on when the Chinese invasion of Tibet occurred; most say 1949, others 1950. The Tibetan Youth Congress (tibetanyouthcongress .org/facts_about_tibet.html) says 1949, as do Save Tibet (savetibet .org/resource-center/all-about-tibet/history-tibet-before-chinese -invasion-1949) and Friends of Tibet (friendsoftibet.org). The Dalai Lama's website provides 1949 as the invasion date (dalailama.com /biography/chronology-of-events). Thomas Laird's *Into Tibet: The CIA's First Atomic Spy and His Secret Expedition to Lhasa* (Grove Press

2002) cites the invasion dates as the winter of 1950–51. The following magazine article says the fall of 1950: "The Extraordinary Journey of a Simple Buddhist Monk," p. 62, *Lion's Roar*, July 2017, Boulder, Colo.

Many translations appear for the Tibetan Buddhist mantra *Om mani padme* (or *peme*) *hum*. Some website sources are "The Meaning of Om Mani Padme Hung," posted Jan. 12, 2014 by Tsem Rinpoche (tsemrinpoche.com/tsem-tulku-rinpoche/buddhas-dharma/the -meaning-of-om-mani-padme-hung.html); "Mantras," Ram Dass (ramdass.org/mantras/); and "Om Mani Padme Hum significance and meaning" by Merlyn Seeley (examiner.com/article/om-mani -padme-hum-significance-and-meaning).

The comments from Nancy Conn are from a telephone interview with the author on April 1, 2013.

The comments from Wendy Conn are taken from a long-distance phone interview, conducted by the author on March 12, 2013.

The comments from Mary Ann Conn-Brody are taken from a long-distance phone interview, conducted by the author on Feb. 27, 2013.

The lyrics of "On the Good Ship Lollipop," written by Richard A. Whiting and Sidney Clare, appear on a variety of websites, including Metro Lyrics (metrolyrics.com/on-the-good-ship-lollipop-lyrics -shirley-temple.html), Reel Classics (reelclassics.com/Actresses /Shirley/goodship-lyrics.htm), and Song Lyrics (songlyrics.com /temple-shirley/on-the-good-ship-lollipop-lyrics/).

The Anais Nin quotation is from page 210 of Nin's *Incest: from "A Journal of Love" The Unexpurgated Diary of Anaïs Nin, 1932–1934*, Harcourt Inc., Florida, 1992.

Chapter Five: ASSAULT

The quotation by Madeleine L'Engle in the epigram is from "Vulnerability Quotes," *Brain Quotes* (brainyquote.com/quotes/keywords/vulnerability.html).

The Gulol Gali Pass altitude is mentioned on the Himalayan Club website (himalayanclub.org/?s=Gulol+Gali+Pass&=SEARCH), in a citation from *A Visit to Nun Kun, 1934*, written by Lieut. J. B. Harrison and published in April 1935. It's also cited on Map Carta (mapcarta.com/33405546).

The advice to women travellers in India is taken from page 68 in *India: a travel survival kit* by Geoff Crowther, A. Raj Prakash, and Tony Wheeler, 3rd ed., Lonely Planet Publications, Berkeley, CA, 1987.

The quotation "I do believe ..." appears on page 44 of *The Church of 80% Sincerity* by David Roche, Penguin Group (USA) Inc., New York, NY, 2008. It is used with permission from the author.

The quotation about ahimsa appears on page 63 of *Amrit Yoga and the Yoga Sutras*, by Yogi Amrit Desai, Yoga Network International, Inc., Sumneytown, PA, 2002.

Most of the details about Gandhi's intimacy with young girls and his grandniece come from Rita Banerji's Oct. 15, 2013 article "Gandhi Used His Position To Sexually Exploit Young Women. The Way We React To This Matters Even Today." It appears on the Youth Ki Awaaz web page: https://www.youthkiawaaz.com/2013/10/gandhi-used-power-position-exploit-young-women-way-react-matters-even-today/. Accessed by the author on May 12, 2021. Other sources include Jad Adams' book *Gandhi: Naked Ambition* (Quercus 2010), particularly on pages 255 and 282. Similar information appears in "Thrill of the chaste: The truth about Gandhi's sex life," April 7, 2010, *The Independent* online (independent.co.uk

/arts-entertainment/books/features/thrill-of-the-chaste-the-truth -about-gandhis-sex-life-1937411.html) and in "The Gandhi Nobody Knows" by Richard Grenier, *Commentary* Magazine, March 1983 (commentarymagazine.com/article/the-gandhi-nobody-knows/).

Gandhi's response to the sexual harassment of women in his ashram is cited on page 280 in Rita Banerji's *Sex and Power*. The original source is "Satyagraha in South Africa," *Collected Works of Mahatma Gandhi*, vol. 34, p. 202, cited in David Hardiman, *Gandhi in His Time and Others*, London: Hurst & Co., 2003, p. 107. Gandhi's belief that raped women should consider suicide appears on the same page of Banerji's *Sex and Power*. The original source is "Gandhi on Women: Part I" by Madhu Kishwar in *Economic and Political Weekly*, Oct. 5, 1985, pp. 1693–94, cited on page 107 of the same Hardiman source noted here.

The quotation from Pema Chodron appears on page 67 of *Awakening Loving-Kindness*, Shambhala Publications, Boston, MA, 1996.

Chapter Six: SHAMED

The Brené Brown quotation in the epigram, taken from *I Thought It Was Just Me: Women Reclaiming Power and Courage in a Culture of Shame*, appears on web page one under "Quotes About Shame," *Goodreads* (goodreads.com/quotes/tag/shame).

The Taj Mahal history comes from page 245 in *India: a travel survival kit* by Geoff Crowther, A. Raj Prakash, and Tony Wheeler, 3rd ed., Lonely Planet Publications, Berkeley, CA, 1987. Websites consulted for research confirmation include Taj Mahal (tajmahal.org. uk/history.html); the online article "Taj Mahal: Was India's 'monument to love' built out of guilt?" by Geeta Pandey, BBC News, June 25, 2001(bbc.com/news/world-asia-india-27970693); and Encyclopedia Britannica (britannica.com/topic/Taj-Mahal).

The remarks from Wendy Conn are taken from a long-distance phone interview, conducted by the author on March 12, 2013.

The modern slang definition for "raspberry" appears in the online *Urban Dictionary*, posted Nov. 14, 2004 (urbandictionary.com/define .php?term=raspberry). A similar definition appears on *The Online Slang Dictionary*, submitted by editor Walter Rader on Sept. 27, 2009 (onlineslangdictionary.com/meaning-definition-of/raspberry). The term "blowing a raspberry" appears on the Wikipedia website (en.wikipedia.org/wiki/Blowing_a_raspberry).

The paperback book mentioned, *Love and the Facts of Life*, is by Evelyn Millis Duvall, Association Press, New York, NY, 1967. The reference to Christian missionaries removing Indians' lingam pendants appears on page 216 of Rita Banerji's *Sex and Power*, Penguin Books, Haryana, India, 2008.

The dates regarding the roots of India's caste system appear on page 162 of Sally Armstrong's *Ascent of Women*, Random House Canada, Toronto, 2013. Other sources for the origin dates include "Timeline: A brief history of India's caste system," *The Globe and Mail*, published Dec. 2, 2011 and updated June 21, 2012, (theglobeandmail .com/news/world/breaking-caste/timeline-a-brief-history-of-indias -caste-system/article641264/) and "Study reveals origin of India's caste system," The *Times of India*, Aug. 11, 2013 (timesofindia .indiatimes.com/home/science/Study-reveals-origin-of-Indias-caste -system/articleshow/21754499.cms).

The quotation "It the skin is white, it is love at first sight" appears on page 184 in *Holy Cow: An Indian Adventure* by Sarah Macdonald, Broadway Books, New York, NY, 2003.

The statistic of two-thirds of married women in India facing beatings or rape appears on page 117 of *One Hour in Paris* by Karyn L. Freedman, Freehand Books. Calgary, AB. 2014. Other sources for this data is the article "Two-third [sic] married Indian women victims of domestic violence: UN," Press Trust of India, posted Oct. 13, 2005 on the website Express India (expressindia.indianexpress.com/news /fullstory.php?newsid=56501); and "Law to protect Indian women from marital rape and abuse" by Justin Huggler, Independent, published Oct. 27, 2006 (independent.ie/world-news/asia-pacific/law-to -protect-indian-women-from-marital-rape-and-abuse-26362032.html).

The custom of killing so-called "stillborn" female babies at birth is mentioned on page 93 of *Journey Back to Peshawar* by Rona Murray, Sono Nis Press, Victoria, BC, 1993. The contrasting status and response to a male vs. female birth in India comes from page 144 of the same book.

The South Asian Association for Regional Cooperation (SAARC) declared 1990 the "Year of the Girl Child" (saarc-sec.org/userfiles /05-Maldives-5thSummit1990.pdf).

Numerous sources, from SAARC and elsewhere, document the rate of female infanticide in India. A recent example is *The Atlantic's* May 25, 2012 piece "Trash Bin Babies: India's Female Infanticide Crisis" "https://www.theatlantic.com/international/archive/2012/05 /trash-bin-babies-indias-female-infanticide-crisis/257672/, accessed Oct. 25, 2018. Other examples are Humanium's "India's Missing Daughters," posted March 15, 2018, accessed by the author Oct. 25, 2018 https://www.humanium.org/en/indias-missing-daughters -desire-male-child-female-infanticide-india/; and Al Jazeera's "Female feticide, India's 'ticking bomb', July 6, 2015, accessed by the author Oct. 25, 2018 https://www.aljazeera.com/indepth/features/2015/06 /female-foeticide-india-ticking-bomb-150629090758927.html.

Older examples on this topic are gendercide.org/case_infanticide. html and the *International Journal of Criminal Justice Sciences*, vol. 1, January 2006 (sascv.org/ijcjs/snehlata.pdf) and *Female Infanticide in India: A Feminist Cultural History* by Rashmi Dube Bhatnagar and

Renu Dube (for example, p. 137), State University of New York Press, Albany, NY, 2005. Bhatnagar and Dube's book draws from *British Social Policy and Female Infanticide in India* by Lalita Panigrahi, South Asia Books, 1972.

The 1991 RAHI (rahifoundation.org) study *Voices from the Silent Zone*, which revealed incest in India among uncles and nieces and cousins, is mentioned in "Incest in Nature" by William Saletan, posted April 16, 2008 on slate.com (slate.com/blogs/humannature/2008 /04/16/incest_in_nature.html). Statistics from this survey appear in "World: South Asia—India's hidden incest," Jan. 22, 1999, BBC Online (news.bbc.co.uk/2/hi/south_asia/259959.stm) and in "India's Hidden Incest Crisis, Evangelical Fellowship of India (efionline.org /the-news/efi-news/52-child/103-indias-hidden-incest-crisis).

The content about Rema Rajeshwari and "She Teams" in Telangana comes from an online transcript of the Jan. 15, 2018 Canadian Broadcasting Corporation radio story on *The Current*. It's titled "'Change is slow': Female superintendent of police in India tackles sexual violence and harassment," reported by Anna Maria Tremonti and produced by Lara O'Brien and Nazim Baksh. cbc.ca/radio /thecurrent/the-current-for-january-15-2018-1.4487410/change-is -slow-female-superintendent-of-police-in-india-tackles-sexual -violence-and-harassment-1.4487642. The author accessed it on Jan. 15, 2018.

The main components of India's 2011 bill Protection of Children Against Sexual Offences are outlined on the website PRS Legislative Research (prsindia.org/billtrack/the-protection-of-children-from -sexual-offences-bill-2011-1598).

Other sources include "House seal on law against child abuse," *The Telegraph*, Calcutta, India online, May 23, 2012 (telegraphindia. com/1120523/jsp/nation/story_15521691.jsp) and "Parliament passes bill to protect children from sexual abuse," updated post May 22,

2012, New Delhi Television (ndtv.com/india-news/parliament
-passes-bill-to-protect-children-from-sexual-abuse-484204).

The information on the conviction of Kuldeep Singh Sengar for
raping a teenager comes from a Reuters news item that appeared in
the Dec. 21, 2019 print edition of Canada's *The National Post* on
page NP5.

The comment by Chandramukhi Devi regarding a gang-rape victim
in India appears in *The Indian Express* in an updated Jan. 8, 2021
article "NCW member on Badaun gangrape case: Women shouldn't
step out alone in the evening" (https://indianexpress.com/article/
india/badaun-gangrape-case-ncw-member-chandramukhi-devi
-7137918/). Accessed by the author on Aug. 5, 2021.

The statistics regarding increased child sexual abuse in India appear
in *India Today*'s article "109 children sexually abused every day in
India in 2018: NCRB." Jan. 12, 2020 (updated Jan. 16). (https://
www.indiatoday.in/india/story/109-children-sexually-abused-every
-day-india-2018-1636160-2020-01-12). Accessed by the author on
Aug. 5, 2021. An additional source for similar info includes https://
www.ndtv.com/india-news/22-jump-in-cases-of-child-sexual-abuse
-in-2018-says-report-2162716, accessed by the author on May 6,
2022.

The increase of child marriages in India and related content comes
from the Sept. 18, 2020 BBC News online article "India's Covid
crisis sees rise in child marriage and trafficking" (https://www.bbc
.com/news/world-asia-india-54186709). Accessed by the author on
Aug. 5, 2021.

The ritual of planting trees for each girl born in Piplantri is cited in
"A village that plants 111 trees for every girl born in Rajasthan" by
Mahim Pratap Singh in *The Hindu*, April 11, 2013 (thehindu.com
/news other-states/a-village-that-plants-111-trees-for-every-girl

-born-in-rajasthan/article4606735.ece). Stephen Messenger's article "Village in India plants 111 trees every time a girl is born" appeared on April 12, 2013 on the Tree Hugger website (treehugger.com /sustainable-agriculture/village-india-plants-111-trees-every-time -baby-girl-born.html). The *Huffington Post* published a similar article by Ron Dicker on June 26, 3013 (huffingtonpost.com/2013/06/26 /india-girls-trees_n_3498172.html).

Chapter Seven: FAMILY

The epigram quotation by George Bernard Shaw, attributed to his novel *Immaturity*, is taken from page 2 of "Family Quotes" on the Brainy Quote website (brainyquote.com/quotes/topics/topic_family2 .html). It also appears on a variety of quotation websites, including aphorismsgalore.com, quotationspage.com, and goodreads.com /author/quotes/5217.George_Bernard_Shaw notable-quotes.com/s /shaw_george_bernard.html.

India's population figure of 844 million in 1991 appears on page 173 in "Population Growth and National Income," *An Economic History of India* by Dietmar Rothermund, second edition, Routledge, London 1993. Other sources include Gaia Environmental Information System (ess.co.at/GAIA/CASES/IND/DEL/DELmain.html); "India Population," Index mundi, indexmundi.com/india/population .html; and the graph "India Population 1950, 2016," Worldometers (worldometers.info/world-population/india-population/).

The comment that likens female Khajuraho statues to Playboy models is quoted from page 495 of *India: A Travel Survival Kit*. 3rd edition, Lonely Planet Publications, Victoria, Australia, 1987.

The Rita Banerji content about incest appears on page 51 of *Sex and Power* and the quotation is from page 52 of the same book.

The remarks from Mary Ann Conn-Brody are taken from a long-distance phone interview, conducted by the author on Feb. 27, 2013.

The comments from Wendy Conn are taken from a long-distance phone interview, conducted by the author on March 12, 2013.

Comments from Nancy Conn are from a long-distance phone interview conducted by the author on April 1, 2013.

The Marabel Morgan book cited is *The Total Woman*, G.K. Hall, Boston, MA, 1975.

The *Born Liars* book and reference are cited in "The real lesson of Weinergate? Lying is as human as walking, talking and sex(ting)" by Elizabeth Renzetti, page F3, *The Globe and Mail*, June 11, 2011, Toronto, ON.

The 2009 experiment by Adam Galinsky is cited in "The paradox of power" by Sonia Verma, *The Globe and Mail*, page A14, May 21, 2011, Toronto, ON. The information about Gene Abel's work is on page 230 of *Father-Daughter Incest* by Judith Herman, Harvard University Press, Cambridge, MA, 2000.

The poem "Wild Geese" is from *DREAM WORK*, copyright © 1986 by Mary Oliver. Used by permission of Grove/Atlantic, Inc. Any third-party use of this material, outside of this publication, is prohibited.

Chapter Eight: TOUCHED

The John Keats quotation in the epigram is from "Quotes About Touch," page one, Good Reads quotations website (goodreads.com /quotes/tag/touch), accessed July 7, 2014. The quoted phrase is from Keats' poem "To— ("What Can I Do to Drive Away") from ebooks. adelaide.edu.au/k/keats/john/poems/to--.html, accessed July 7, 2014.

An earlier version of the author's account of the bird sanctuary in Bharatpur and nearby guest house appeared in "Bird Sanctuary," page 84, *Women Write Home: Emails From India*, Seraphim Editions, Woodstock, ON, 2013.

Keoladeo National Park is identified as a World Heritage Site on UNESCO's World Heritage convention website (whc.unesco.org/en /list/340) and the Lonely Planet website (lonelyplanet.com/india /rajasthan/keoladeo-ghana-national-park). Its World Heritage status is also noted on the website of Trans India Travels (transindiatravels. com/rajasthan/keoladeo-ghana-national-park-bharatpur-bird -sanctuary/).

The endangered status of Siberian white cranes, and their dwindling numbers, are cited on these websites: International Crane Foundation (savingcranes.org/species-field-guide/siberian-crane/); "Saving Wetlands Across Eurasia: Inspired by the Siberian Crane," UNEP/ GEF Siberian Crane Wetland Project, a PDF publication (unep.org /dgef/Portals/43/publications/Saving%20Wetlands%20Across%20 Eurasia.pdf); and in the article "Last western Siberian crane clocks up 78,000 km with latest migrate south," *The Siberian Times*, posted Nov. 4, 2014 (siberiantimes.com/ecology/others/news/n0009-last -western-siberian-crane-clocks-up-78000-km-with-latest-migrate -south/).

Thomas Gainsborough's painting *The Honourable Mrs. Graham* appears on numerous websites, including that of National Galleries Scotland (www.nationalgalleries.org/collection/artists-a-z/g/artist /thomas-gainsborough/object/the-honourable-mrs-graham-1757 -1792-ng-332).

Chapter Nine: MOLE

The Oscar Wilde quotation in the epigram, taken from *The Importance of Being Earnest*, appears on the website *Goodreads* (goodreads .com/quotes/364-the-truth-is-rarely-pure-and-never-simple).

PART TWO
Healing At Home (1991–2011)

The epigram in the section heading comes from the foreword of Barbara Kingsolver's book *Small Wonder*, Harper Collins, New York, NY, 2002, cited on the blog Citizen Action Monitor (citizenactionmonitor.wordpress.com/2010/07/05/barbara-kingsolver-on-borders-between-the-haves-and-the-have-nots/).

Chapter Ten: RATS

The quotation used in the epigram is from Alice Miller's *For Your Own Good*, 2nd edition, Farrar, Straus, Giroux, New York, NY, 1984. It appears in the online book review alice-miller.com/books_en.php?page=2a. Bernie Siegel, MD, author of *Love, Medicine, and Miracles*, cites it (see berniesiegelmd.com/2011/05/the-truth-of-the-body/), as does Tara Brach in *Radical Acceptance*.

One source for the information on yoga and somatic memory is "Releasing Somatic Memory through Ayurvedic Yoga Therapy" by Janya Wongsopa, submitted to the California College of Ayurveda, November 2006 (ayurvedacollege.com/SomaticMemory.htm). Other related content includes "Yoga Psychotherapy: the Integration of Western Psychological Theory and Ancient Yogic Wisdom," by Mariana Caplan, Ph.D., Adriana Portillo, M.A., and Lynsie Seely, M.A., *The Journal of Transpersonal Psychology*, 2013, Vol. 45, No. 2, pp 139–158 (atpweb.org/jtparchive/trps-45-13-02-139.pdf), and "Treating Trauma with Yoga" by Nicki Mosleyon, Jul 12, 2013, *Elephant Journal* (elephantjournal.com/2013/07/treating-trauma-with-yoga-nicki-mosley/).

The mean age of victims at the onset of incest is cited on pages 69–70, *The Incest Perpetrator*, ed. by Anne L. Horton, Barry L. Johnson, Lynn M. Roundy, Doran Williams, Sage Publications, Newbury

Park, CA, 1990. Other related sources include "Who are the Victims?" Rape, Abuse, and Incest National Network ((rainn.org/get -information/statistics/sexual-assault-victims) and *Incest: a Family's Secret* (abstract), Life Skills Education, 1991, cited on National Criminal Justice Reference Service (ncjrs.gov/App/publications /abstract.aspx?ID=148056).

Content regarding varied ages of incest victims can be found at "A Comparison of Incest Offenders Based on Victim Age" by Philip Firestone, PhD, Kristopher L. Dixon, BA, Kevin L. Nunes, PhD, and John M. Bradford, MD, *The Journal of the American Academy of Psychiatry and the Law*, 33:223–32, 2005 (jaapl.org/content/33 /2/223.full.pdf).

Chapter Eleven: HEALING

The source for the Rumi quotation, used in the epigram, is the Goodreads website goodreads.com/quotes/103315-the-wound-is-the -place-where-the-light-enters-you.

The content about Gregor as a cockroach comes from "The Metamorphosis" by Franz Kafka, *The Metamorphosis, In the Penal Colony and Other Stories*, Simon and Schuster, New York, NY, 2000.

The quotation by Charles Whitfield appears on page 243 of his book *Memory and Abuse*. The Saul Schanberg quotation appears on page 244 of the same book.

Mention of the study revealing that 40 per cent of adult women did not remember or else denied proven sexual abuse from 17 years earlier appears on page 199 of Gabor Maté's *In the Realm of Hungry Ghosts*. He cites the original source as L. M. Williams' "Recall of Childhood Trauma: A Perspective Study of Women's Memories of Child Sexual Abuse," *Journal of Consulting and Clinical Psychology* 62: 1167–76.

The author watched the entire testimony by Christine Blasey Ford, before the U.S. Senate Judiciary Committee, on Sept. 27, 2018, live on MSNBC. Her account about needing two doors on her re-modelled home as an adult were made in her opening statement. Numerous media accounts addressed this. Two examples are "Christine Blasey Ford takes the spotlight, Mark Judge lurks in the shadows" by Denise Balkissoon from *The Globe and Mail* on Sept. 27, 2018 (https://www.theglobeandmail.com/opinion/article-christine -blasey-ford-takes-the-spotlight-mark-judge-lurks-in-the/) and "Reporter Questions Christine Blasey Ford's 'Two-Door' Explanation" by Ashe Schow in *The Daily Wire* on Oct. 2, 2018 (https://www. dailywire.com/news/36600/reporter-questions-christine-blasey -fords-two-door-ashe-schow.) The author accessed both of these on-line on Nov. 12, 2018.

The material from Marlena Blavin is a result of the author's in-person interview with her in Roberts Creek, BC on July 9, 2010.

Chapter Twelve: *VALIDATION*

The epigram by Jill Bolte Taylor is from her book *My Stroke of Insight: A Brain Scientist's Personal Journey.* It appears on the Good Reads website at https://www.goodreads.com/quotes/tag/validation. Accessed by the author on Jan. 1, 2020.

The first part of the quotation from Sylvia Fraser appears on page 128 of *The Book of Strange: A Journey,* Doubleday Canada Ltd., Toronto, ON, 1992. The latter part, following the ellipsis, is taken from pages 135–136 of the same book. These excerpts are used with permission by the author.

The statistic regarding the average duration of incest appears on page 7 of Christine A. Courtois' *Healing the Incest Wound,* 2nd edition, W.W. Norton and Company, New York, NY, 2010.

Chapter Thirteen: ANGER

The quotation in the epigram by Eckhart Tolle is from the website *Wise Old Sayings* at https://www.wiseoldsayings.com/anger-quotes/. Accessed by the author on Jan. 1, 2020.

The Eve Ensler excerpts are from page 7 of her book *The Apology*, Bloomsbury Publishing, New York, NY, 2019.

The mention of anger as the wounded child in us appears on page 21 of *How to Fight* by Thich Nhat Hanh, Parallax Press, Berkeley, CA, 2017. The information about Thich Nhat Hanh's views on rehearsing anger and making it habitual appears on page 44 of the same book. His comment about embracing anger and learning mindful responses appears in his teaching video *Taking Care of Anger*, https://www.youtube.com/watch?v=9OvLOna5_1A, posted April 17, 2020. Accessed by the author on July 26, 2021.

In several chapters in his book *In the Realm of Hungry Ghosts* (Vintage Canada, Toronto, ON, 2018), Gabor Maté addresses how childhood trauma can affect brain development and later, lifelong stress response in adults. See "Their Brains Never Had a Chance" (pp. 179–187) and "Trauma, Stress and the Biology of Addiction" (pp. 188–200).

Chapter Fourteen: FATIGUE

The Sylvia Plath epigram is from *The Unabridged Journals of Sylvia Plath*. It appears on the Goodreads website at https://www.goodreads .com/quotes/746671-i-feel-occasionally-my-skull-will-crack-fatigue -is-continuous. Accessed by the author on Jan. 1, 2020.

Leonard Shengold's label "soul murder" appears on page 235 of *Healing the Incest Wound*, second edition, by Christine A. Courtois.

The term is from Shengold's 1979 article "Child abuse and deprivation: Soul murder" in *Journal of the American Psychoanalytic Association*, 27, pages 533–559, cited in Courtois' book. The term "spiritual orphans" appears on page 19 of Mark Matousek's article "America's Darkest Secret," published in *Common Boundary*, March/April 1991.

The author drew from first-hand experience and the following source material regarding chronic fatigue syndrome in the 1990s: *Chronic Fatigue Syndrome*, Element Books, Boston, MA, 1997; *Chronic Fatigue Syndrome: The Hidden Epidemic* by Jesse A. Stoff, MD and Charles R. Pellegrino, PhD, Harper and Row, NY, NY, 1988; and *Recovering from Chronic Fatigue Syndrome* by William Collinge, MPH, PhD, The Body Press/Perigree Books, New York, NY, 1993.

The content regarding Bessel van der Kolk's view on stress hormones is taken from sources such as "A Revolutionary Approach to Treating PTSD," *The New York Times* by Jeneen Interlandi, May 22, 2014. www.nytimes.com/2014/05/25/magazine/a-revolutionary -approach-to-treating-ptsd.html?_r=0, accessed by the author on June 9, 2017. Another source includes Paul Kennedy's radio show *Ideas*, "All in the Family, Part 3," April 21, 2016, Canadian Broadcasting Corporation.

The content related to Dr. Ric Arseneau is taken from his article "Hope for patients with fatigue, pain, and unexplained symptoms," Oct. 13, 2015, on the webpage *This Changed My Practice (UBC CPD)*, University of British Columbia, Faculty of Medicine. Accessed by the author on April 14, 2017. Source: thischangedmypractice .com/hope-for-patients-with-fatigue-pain-and-unexplained- symptoms/. Various articles in psychiatric journals address childhood trauma and the risk for chronic fatigue syndrome, as listed on the National Library of Medicine (US) web page https://pubmed.ncbi .nlm.nih.gov/19124690/. Accessed by the author Nov. 18, 2021.

Chapter Fifteen: SHOES

The Terry Tempest Williams quotation in the epigram is from the online site *AZ Quotes*, accessed by the author on Dec. 29, 2919. https://www.azquotes.com/quotes/topics/red-shoes.html.

The Barbara Allyn content is from the article "Reframing trauma a step to healing" by Perrin Grauer on page 3 in the Nov. 6, 2018 issue of *Star Metro Vancouver*, Vancouver, BC.

A description of dissociation preventing integration of memories and a coherent narrative appears on page 105 of *One Hour in Paris* by Karyn L. Freedmann, Freehand Books, Calgary, AB, 2014. The relationship between trauma, dissociation, and memory is addressed in numerous sources in psychology and psychiatry. A few related websites are International Society for the Study of Trauma and Dissociation (isst-d.org/?contentID=76); American Psychology Association: "Questions and Answers About Memories of Childhood Abuse" (apa.org/topics/trauma/memories.aspx); and "The Spectrum of Dissociative Disorders: An Overview of Diagnosis and Treatment" by Joan A. Turkus, M.D. (fortea.us/english /psiquiatria/spectrum.htm).

The summary of the red shoes fairy tale is adapted from "The Red Shoes," by Hans-Christian Andersen, pages 75–80, *Anderson Fairy Tales*, Omega Books Ltd., Hertfordshire, Eng. [date of publication not listed].

Wendy Conn shared the comments about her mother during a phone conversation with the author on Nov. 2, 2018 and a follow-up email on the same day.

Some information about incest victims' self-doubt, freeze response, and dissociation was confirmed through email communications with Georgeanna Drew, MA, a registered clinical counsellor in

Vancouver, BC. The author received feedback, via email, from Drew regarding this content on Aug. 10, 11, 15, 2014 and on Sept. 1, 2014.

Additional selected websites that address the body's freeze response to trauma and related issues are "The Anatomy of Trauma," The Sexual Assault Prevention and Awareness Center, University of Michigan (sapac.umich.edu/article/anatomy-trauma-0); "The Freezing Response to Traumatic Threat," Lifecentre: Supporting Survivors or Rape and Sexual Abuse (lifecentre.uk.com/dealing_with_the_effects/the _freezing_response.html).

The dichotomies of a traumatized body are addressed on page 89 in *Living Beside: Performing Normal After Incest Memories Return* by Tanya Lewis, McGilligan Books, Toronto, 1999. The impact of trauma on the body is addressed in the article "Physical Health Problems After Single Trauma Exposure: When Stress Takes Root in the Body" by Wendy D'Andrea, Ritu Sharma, Amanda D. Zelechoski, and Joseph Spinazzola, *Journal of the American Psychiatric Nurses Association*, 17 (6), pp. 378–392, 2011 (traumacenter.org /products/pdf_files/japna425187.pdf).

"The shaking of a soul" reference is attributed to Gudrun Zomerland on page 38 of Francis Weller's book *The Wild Edge of Sorrow*, North Atlantic Books. Berkeley, CA. 2015. The reference to "slow trauma" appears on page 38 of the same book. Dr. Gabor Maté's view on trauma is available through his books and many videos, including *The Wisdom of Trauma*, viewed by the author on June 9, 2021.

The term "inability to regulate affect," as it refers to the overreaction of traumatized individuals, appears on page 93 of *One Hour in Paris* by Karyn L. Freedman. The tendency of trauma survivors to overreact to everyday situations is addressed on these websites: "Creating New Possibilities for Treating Post-Traumatic Stress Disorder" by Victor Carrion, MD, Brain and Behaviour Research Foundation (bbrfoundation.org/discoveries/creating-new-possibilities-for-treating

-post-traumatic-stress-disorder); "The Rocky Road to PTSD," by Rosemary K.M. Sword and Philip Zimbardo Ph.D., posted Oct. 16, 2012, *Psychology Today* psychologytoday.com/blog/the-time-cure /201210/the-rocky-road-ptsd; and "Adult Survivors," Family Service Agency of the Central Coast [California] (fsa-cc.org/survivors-healing -center/adult-survivors/).

The definition of a traumatic stressor from an American Psychological Association task force appears on page 30 of Maggie Scarf's *Secrets, Lies, Betrayals*, Random House, New York, NY, 2004.

The definition of a traumatic experience is adapted from one that appears on page 103 of *A Feminist Clinician's Guide to the Memory Debate*, edited by Susan Contratto and M. Janice Gutfreund. It's from an article by Joyce Sese Dorado called "Legal and Psychological Approaches Towards Adult Survivors of Childhood Incest: Irreconcilable Differences?"

The issue of a victim equating the freeze response with death is from Peter A. Levine's (with Ann Frederick) *Waking the Tiger: Healing Trauma,* North Atlantic Books, Berkeley, CA. 1997. In a free download version of this book, related content appears on pages 84–86 in chapter 7 "The Animal Experience." The author accessed a PDF version of the book at oplysning.org/uploads/9/1/4/3/9143605/waking _the_tiger_healing_trauma_the_innate_capacity_to_transform _overwhelming_experiences.pdf. A relevant quotation of Peter Levine's appears on the website of the Somatic Experiencing Trauma Institute at traumahealing.org/waking-the-tiger.php.

Joanne Harris's story "The Scarlet Slippers" is used with her permission. It appears in Harris's book *Honeycomb*, Saga Press, New York, NY, 2021. Conn found the story on the website of *Enchanted Living* magazine, accessed on Dec. 6, 2019: https://enchantedlivingmagazine .com/the-scarlet-slippers/.

Chapter Sixteen: LOVE

The epigram is from *Quotes About Love* on the Goodreads website, page one. Accessed by the author on April 14, 2017. Source: goodreads .com/quotes/tag/love.

The information about delayed recall appears on Jim Hopper's website jimhopper.com/memory/. It's also cited in "Amnesia, partial amnesia, and delayed recall among adult survivors of childhood trauma," by M.R. Harvey and J.L. Herman, *Consciousness and Cognition*, 4, pages 295–306 (jimhopper.com/memory/#jlh).

Clinical studies regarding forgetting rates (Briere & Conte, 1993; Herman & Schatzow, 1987; Loftus, Polonsky, & Fullilove, 1994; Rose & Schwartz, 1996) are cited in "What can subjective forgetting tell us about memory for childhood trauma?" by Simona Chetti, Robin S. Edelstein, Gail S. Goodman, Ingrid M. Cordon, Jodi A. Quas, Kristen Weede Alexander, Allison D. Redlich, David P.H. Jones, *Memory & Cognition*, 2006, 34 (5) 1011–1025, p. 1012.

A statistic of 50 per cent of abuse survivors experiencing some degree of amnesia appears on page 49 of *A Feminist Clinician's Guide to the Memory Debate*, edited by Susan Contratto and M. Janice Gutfreund. This figure appears in the article "Recovered Memories of Child Abuse: Fact, Fantasy or Fancy?" by Connie M. Kristiansen, Kathleen A. Felton and Wendy E. Hovdestad. Numerous related studies are cited within the article.

The author discussed betrayal trauma with counselor Laurie Kahn. Kahn defines the term in her article "The Understanding and Treatment of Betrayal Trauma as a Traumatic Experience of Love," *Journal of Trauma Practice*, vol. 5. no. 3., 2006, pp. 57–72.

The Pema Chodron quotation appears on page 73 of *Comfortable with Uncertainty*, compiled and edited by Emily Hilburn Sell, Shambhala Publications, Boston, MA, 2003.

The Gabor Maté quotation, used with his permission, is taken from page xxix of his book *In the Realm of Hungry Ghosts: Close Encounters With Addiction*, Vintage Canada, Toronto, 2018. Note: This is a revised version of his 2008 title.

The Lauren Artress quotation is from page 165 of *Walking a Sacred Path: Rediscovering the Labyrinth as a Spiritual Practice*, Riverhead Books, New York NY, 2006.

The Walt Whitman quotation is from his poem "We, Two, How Long We Were Fool'd." This excerpt appears on page 265 of Elizabeth Gilbert's *Committed*, Viking, New York, NY, 2010.

The general information about labyrinths comes from Artress' book *Walking a Sacred Path* and from Virginia Westbury's *Labyrinths: Ancients Paths of Wisdom and Peace*, Da Capo Press, 2003. The linking of labyrinths with compassion and acceptance appears on page 96 of Westbury's *Labyrinths* book. Another source is "What does a labyrinth symbolize?" Potsdam website, the State University of New York (potsdam.edu/studentlife/counseling/labyrinth/symbol.cfm).

Definitions of the *yoni* appear on numerous websites, including Miriam-Webster's online dictionary (mirriam-webster.com), the Oxford University Press online dictionary (oxforddictionaries.com), and Yoniversum.nl. Content regarding the *yoni*'s sacred significance can be found in numerous books and on websites. One reference is the website Feminist and Religion, affiliated with the Women's Studies and Religion program at Claremont Graduate University: "Honoring the Sacred Yoni," by Deanne Quarrie (feminismandreligion .com/?s=yoni&x=0&y=0).

Chapter Seventeen: COURAGE

The epigram appears on pages 18–19 in *Storycatcher: Making Sense of Our Lives Through the Power and Practice of Story* by Christina Baldwin, New World Library, Novato, CA, 2005.

The 1946 movie *The Stranger*, starring Loretta Young, Orson Welles, and Edward G. Robinson, was directed by Orson Welles and produced by International Pictures and The Haig Corporation. Screenplay by Anthony Veiller. More info available on the IMDB website imdb.com/title/tt0038991/.

The terms "opportunistic offender" and "predatory offender" appear on the website of the Pinehurst, Mass. community advocacy group The Mama Bear Effect: Building Stronger Families Educating Against Sexual Abuse (themamabeareffect.org/index.html).

The term "regressed abuser" appears on the website for the Center for Sex Offender Management, U.S. Department of Justice, under "Understanding Sex Offenders: An Introductory Curriculum," Section 4: Subtypes and Typologies, csom.org/train/etiology/4/4_1.htm.

The reference to Ghana's investigative journalist Anas Aremeyaw Anas comes from the author's viewing of the 2015 documentary *Chameleon*, written and directed by Ryan Mullins for Eye Steel Film. More information is available at www.anasaremeyawanas.org and www.chameleondoc.com.

M.E. Rice and G.T. Harris state in a 2002 issue of the *Journal of Abnormal Psychology* (issue 111, pp. 329–339) that incest offenders do not molest children outside their families and are not sexually oriented toward kids or adolescents. Their article is entitled "Men who molest their sexually immature daughters: Is a special explanation required?" The author found reference to their conclusions on page 95 of *Healing the Incest Wound*, second edition, by Christine A. Courtois.

Three sources for Howard Hughes' stay at The Bayshore in Vancouver are "Some Famous Visitors" by David Spaner, page 761, *The Greater Vancouver Book*, edited by Chuck Davis, Linkman Press, Surrey, BC, 1997; "This Day in History: March 14, 1972," *The Vancouver Sun*, March 14, 2012, A2; and the Lonely Planet website hotels.lonelyplanet .com/accommodation/-P126039.html.

Chapter Eighteen: SEXSOMNIA

The quotation in the epigram appears in Bernie Siegel's *Love, Medicine and Miracles*. It is cited in the online feature "Be Happy Zone," by Lionel Ketchian, June 4, 2003, which appears on *www.happinessclub .com/FairfieldCitizen/060403.htm*, accessed July 8, 2014.

The article "Sexsomnia: fast asleep and having sex," Oct. 19, 2007, page A2, *National Post*, Toronto, Ont., is available online at nationalpost .com/news/story.html?id=548a828d-d97b-4fd3-888c-302e5d2328e3, accessed July 11, 2014. A source for the first reported case of sexsomnia in 1986 is "Sexsomnia: What is sleep sex" by Jennifer Huizen, *Medical News Today*, Dec. 8, 2017 (https://www.medicalnewstoday .com/articles/320448#overview). Accessed April 7, 2021. The original source for this date reference appears to be "Masturbation during sleep: a somnambulistic variant?" by K.E. Wong, *Singapore Medical Journal*, 1986; 27: 542–543.

The incidence of sexual assaults planned in advance is cited on page 76 of Judith Herman's *Father-Daughter Incest*, Harvard University Press, Cambridge, MA, 2000. This book provides the original source as "Drinking, Alcoholism, and the Mentally Disordered Sex Offender" by Richard Rada, Robert Kellner, D.R. Laws, and Walter Winslow, *Bulletin of the American Academy of Psychiatry and Law 6* (1978): 296–300.

The Pema Chodron quotation comes from page 41 of *Awakening Loving Kindness*, Shambhala Publications, Boston, MA, 1991. Chodron's quote about ego appears on page 25 of *Comfortable with Uncertainty*, Shambhala Publications, Boston, MA, 2002.

Chapter Nineteen: WITNESSED

The James Baldwin quotation is from *Another Country*. It appears on the Goodreads website at https://www.goodreads.com/quotes/tag /witness?page=2. Accessed by the author on Jan. 1, 2020.

The mention of a perpetrator singling out only one family victim comes from Christine A. Courtois' *Healing the Incest Wound*, second edition, W.W. Norton and Company, NY, NY, 2010.

The Laurie Kahn quotation comes from an earlier citation (Kahn: 1999) in a pre-publication document that Kahn gave to the author: "The Understanding and Treatment of Betrayal Trauma as a Traumatic Experience of Love," by Laurie Kahn, *Journal of Trauma Practice*, vol. 5 no. 3, 2006, page numbers not indicated.

The Criminal Code definition of incest appears on Canada's Justice Laws website, accessed by the author on Jan. 21, 2018 (laws-lois.justice .gc.ca/eng/acts/C-46/section-155.html). Other definitions related to sexual assault come from the following websites: Department of Justice Canada (/laws-lois.justice.gc.ca/Search/Search.aspx?txtS3arc hAll=sexual+interference&txtT1tl3=%22Criminal+Code%22&h1 tsOnly=0&ddCOnt3ntTyp3=Acts); LEAF https://www.leaf.ca/news /the-law-of-consent-in-sexual-assault/; Calgary Legal Guidance, https://clg.ab.ca/programs-services/dial-a-law/sexual-assault-and -incest/; The Sexual Assault Centre of Edmonton (sace.ab.ca/non _flash/sa01b1.html); and Interpol (interpol.int/public/children /sexualabuse/nationallaws/csacanada.asp).

The author used these sources for the definition of sexual interference in Canada, accessed on Aug. 28, 2022: Government of Canada's Justice Laws Website, https://laws-lois.justice.gc.ca/eng/acts/c-46/section-151.html; https://www.legalline.ca/legal-answers/what-is-sexual-interference/; and https://vilkhovlaw.ca/is-there-a-difference-between-sexual-assault-sexual-interference-in-canada. Sources used for definition of sexual exploitation, accessed by author on Aug. 28, 2022, were Department of Justice Canada https://publications.gc.ca/collections/collection_2007/jus/J2-306-2005E.pdf; BC Government website https://www2.gov.bc.ca/gov/content/safety/crime-prevention/community-crime-prevention/exploitation; and Bayne Sellar Ertel Carter https://www.bsbcriminallaw.com/blog/2018/06/what-is-sexual-exploitation/.

Judith Herman's quotation appears on page 70 of *Father-Daughter Incest*, Harvard University Press, Cambridge, MA, 2000.

The content regarding Freud's seduction theory is taken from Jeffrey Masson's website jeffreymasson.com/books/the-assault-on-truth.html and pp. 9 and 10 from Christine A. Courtois' *Healing the Incest Wound*, second edition, W. W. Norton and Company, NY, NY, 2010. Author Heather Conn heard Masson speak on this subject at the University of British Columbia in Vancouver circa 1980.

The Eve Ensler quotation is from her online *Time* feature "Eve Ensler on Bill Cosby: Let the Mythical Daddy Die," July 16, 2015, Time.com (time.com/3957881/eve-ensler-on-bill-cosby-let-the-mythical-daddy-die/).

The reference to the Vatican harbouring pedophile priests is taken from the 2006 documentary *Sex Crimes and the Vatican* (39 min.) by Colm O'Gorman. The BBC first aired it, then the Canadian Broadcasting Corporation (CBC). See news.bbc.co.uk/2/hi/programmes/panorama/5389684.stm. Free downloads of the film are available at freedocumentaries.org. Many online sources for this info are available, including http://america.aljazeera.com/opinions /2014/2/the-vatican-stillprotectspedophilepriests.html, and https:// www.independent.co.uk/news/world/politics/vatican-kept-code-of -silence-on-paedophile-priests-claims-un-report-9109363.html, accessed by the author May 6, 2022.

The statistics regarding the low rates of reporting of incest and conviction of offenders are from an online fact sheet, updated August 2012, called "End Violence Together: For the Dignity of Every Woman." This document was developed by Ending Violence Association of British Columbia, with help from the Province of British Columbia, Canada. The original source for these statistics is cited as *Rape in America: A Report to the Nation*, National Center for Victims of Crime, 1997 (endingviolence.org/wp-content/uploads/2014/02 /urvivors_Childhood_Sexual_Assault_Fact_Sheet.pdf).

The 2014 Statistics Canada "5%" rate of reporting of sexual assault appears on the Sexual Assault Support Services web page of Carleton University, Ottawa, ON: https://carleton.ca/sexual-violence-support /what-is-sexual-assault/getting-the-facts/ and on the Canadian Government's Department of Justice web page: https://www.justice .gc.ca/eng/rp-pr/jr/jf-pf/2019/apr01.html. A Canadian Government web page for the Office of the Federal Ombudsman for Victims of Crime states that the reporting rate is "less than 5%": https://www .victimsfirst.gc.ca/media/news-nouv/nr-cp/2021/20210501.html.

Sites accessed by the author on Nov. 30, 2021. 2014 statistics regarding the low reporting of sexual assault in Canada appear on the Department of Justice website, accessed by the author March 22, 2020 (justice.gc.ca/eng/rp-pr/jr/jf-pf/2019/apr01.html).

The statistics regarding the low incidence of reporting sexual assault in general are from the online fact sheet "Reporting Sexual Assault: Why Survivors Often Don't," Maryland Coalition Against Sexual Assault (umd.edu/ocrsm/files/Why-Is-Sexual-Assault-Under

-Reported.pdf). The original sources cited are U.S. Bureau of Justice Statistics, M. Planty and L. Langton, "Female Victims of Sexual Violence, 1994–2010," 2013, and Wolitzky-Taylor *et al*, "Is Reporting of Rape on the Rise? A Comparison of Women with Reported Versus Unreported Rape Experiences in the National Women's Study-Replication," 2010.

It is common knowledge among therapeutic professionals that incest is a notoriously underreported crime. This point is reinforced in sources such as "America Has an Incest Problem" by Mia Fontaine, Jan. 24, 2013, *The Atlantic* (theatlantic.com/national/archive/2013/01/america-has-an-incest-problem/272459/). Statistics on incest in countries around the world are available on Eve Ensler's V Day website (vday.org/take-action/violence-against-women/incest.html#.VtCsmeYepQI).

There are numerous examples of judges world-wide being lenient on pedophiles, blaming their child victims. Here are only a few recent cases: "Judge lets pedophile David Barnes, 24, off easy after suggesting 13-year-old girl seduced him," April 5, 2011, *Daily News* (nydailynews.com/news/world/judge-lets-pedophile-david-barnes-24-easy-suggesting-13-year-old-girl-seduced-article-1.112250); "Pedophile who said a seven-year-old girl seduced him is finally jailed weeks after judge set him free," by Paul Sims, Nov. 30, 2012, *Daily Mail Online* (dailymail.co.uk/news/article-2241125/Paedophile-said-seven-year-old-girl-seduced-finally-jailed-weeks-judge-set-free.html); "So a judge said a 16-year-old groomed her teacher—that's nothing" by Julie Bindel, Jan. 15, 2015, *The Guardian* (theguardian.com/commentisfree/2015/jan/15/judge-16-year-old-groomed-teacher-judges-lawyers). Nicole Polizzi summarizes courts' leniency in sexual assault with "Rapists Are Blaming Their Underage Victims—and Judges Are Taking Them Seriously," Aug. 9, 2013, Policy.mic (mic.com/articles/58535/rapists-are-blaming-their-underage-victims-and-judges-are-taking-them-seriously#.3i64GPUEj).sun.

The definition of False Memory Syndrome appears on the website of the False Memory Syndrome Foundation (wfmsfonline.org/index.php?faq=faq). The lack of medical or psychological diagnosis of this syndrome is mentioned on page 20 in "Childhood Trauma: Politics and Legislative Concerns for Therapists" by Sherry A. Quirk and Anne P. DePrince in *A Feminist Clinician's Guide to the Memory Debate*, edited by Susan Contratto and M. Janice Gutfreund, Harrington Park Press, Binghamton, NY, 1996.

Thich Nhat Hanh's quotation about peace and reconciliation appears on page 47 of *Peace Is Every Step*, Bantam Books, New York, 1992.

The mention of victims not getting a full apology in South Africa under the Truth and Reconciliation Commission is from pages 103–104 in Ellis Cose's *Bone to Pick*. The info about what forgiveness requires vs. reconciliation, in Cose's point of view, comes from page 95 of the same book. General information on the Truth and Reconciliation Commission in South Africa appears on the official Truth and Reconciliation website (doj.gov.za/trc/ and doj.gov.za/trc/legal/act9534.htm), and in *Bone to Pick*.

Reference to Vancouver, B.C.'s Truth and Reconciliation Commission event in October 2008 can be found in the post "Seeking Truth and Reconciliation in Vancouver," *CBC News British Columbia,* posted Oct. 12, 2013 (cbc.ca/news/canada/british-columbia/seeking-truth-and-reconciliation-in-vancouver-1.2021663). General related information about the Commission can be found at the websites Truth and Reconciliation Commission of Canada (trc.ca/websites/trcinstitution/index.php?p=905) and National Centre for Truth and Reconciliation, University of Manitoba (nctr.ca/map.php).

Information about Prime Minister Stephen Harper's apology regarding Canada's residential school system is available on numerous online sources, including these: Indigenous and Northern Affairs Canada (aadnc-aandc.gc.ca/eng/1100100015644/1100100015649); Aboriginal

Peoples Television Network (aptn.ca/news/2015/09/10/harpers
-2008-residential-school-apology-was-attempt-to-kill-the-story-says
-ex-pmo-speechwriter/); and "A long-awaited apology for residential
schools," Digital Archives of Canadian Broadcasting Corporation
(cbc.ca/archives/entry/a-long-awaited-apology-for-residential-schools).

Justice Murray Sinclair's quotation appears on the home page of the
Truth and Reconciliation Commission of Canada website trc.ca
/websites/trcinstitution/index.php?p=3/.

The Christina Baldwin quotation regarding the Babema tribe in
South Africa is from pages 18 and 19 of *Storycatcher,* New World
Library, Novato, CA, 2005.

Chapter Twenty: FORGIVENESS

The source for the Henry Miller quotation that appears in the epigram
is quoteworld.org.

The entry for the author's father appears on page 259 in *Canadian
Who's Who*, vol. xliii, edited by Elizabeth Lumley, 2008, University
of Toronto Press. Toronto, ON, 2008.

The account of the Scottish peasant (Jock Howieson (Hotson)), said
to be the author's ancestor, appears on pages 2–3 in *From the Scottish
Borders to Upper Canada: the Hart and Hotson Families* by Nancy
Conn, self-published in Toronto, ON, 2008. Nancy's book cites Sir
Walter Scott's *Tales of a Grandfather* as her original source for this
story. The reminiscences of Isobel (Hart) Davey appear on page 152
of *From the Scottish Borders to Upper Canada.*

The remarks from Mary Ann Conn-Brody are taken from a long-
distance phone interview, conducted by the author on Feb. 27, 2013.

The Bell Hooks quotation appears on the BrainyQuote website: https://www.brainyquote.com/quotes/bell_hooks_186101. Accessed by the author on Dec. 24, 2021.

The author first learned about Ho'oponopono during a Zoom workshop on Oct. 15, 2021, offered by Australian SoulCollage® facilitator Debrah Gai Lewis, entitled: "From Shame and Regret to Forgiveness: Healing Through SoulCollage®." The definitions and information about Ho'oponopono appear on these websites, accessed by the author on Oct. 18, 2021: https://www.psychologytoday.com/us/blog/focus-forgiveness/201105/the-hawaiian-secret-forgiveness and https://graceandlightness.com/hooponopono-hawaiian-prayer-for-forgiveness/.

The quotation by Mary Jane Williams appears on page 124 of her book *Healing Hidden Memories: Recovery for Adult Survivors of Childhood Abuse*, Health Communications, Inc., Deerfield, Beach, CA, 1991.

Francis Weller's content appears on page 34 and 35 of his book *The Wild Edge of Sorrow*, North Atlantic Books, Berkeley, 2015.

Information about the Charter for Compassion appears on the namesake website (charterforcompassion.org/the-charter) and numerous other sites, including "Charter For Compassion Makes Surprising Progress" by Karen Armstrong, first posted March 27, 2012 and updated May 27, 2012, *Huffington Post* (huffingtonpost.com/karen-armstrong/charter-for-compassion-progress_b_1382844.html), and "Charter for Compassion: at one with our ignorance," by Karen Armstrong, *The Guardian*, Nov. 10, 2009.

Thich Nhat Hanh's poem *Please Call Me By My True Names*, written in 1978, was first read at a Buddhist retreat in Amsterdam. Published by Parallax Press in 1999, it has appeared in many sources. The author first encountered it during a *sangha* session and found it online at https://www.okcir.com/Articles%20VI%203/TNHCallMEByMyTrueNames-FM.pdf, accessed on Dec 27, 2018.

The basic information about eye movement desensitization and re-processing (EMDR) is from the website of the EMDR Institute, Inc., Watsonville, CA (emdr.com/general-information/what-is-emdr /what-is-emdr.html), accessed Aug. 8, 2014. The bilateral stimulation information is from Anxiety Release (anxietyreleaseapp.com/what -is-bilateral-stimulation/), accessed Aug. 8, 2014. Additional information came from emails from Georgeanna Drew, a registered clinical counsellor in Vancouver, BC, on Aug. 10, 11, 15, 2014 and on Sept. 1, 2014.

Further content about EMDR comes from email correspondence with Georgeanna Drew and from these online sources: "What is EMDR?" EMDR Institute, Inc. (www.emdr.com/what-is-emdr/) and EMDR-Therapy (emdr-therapy.com/emdr.html). Similarly, Drew provided information on the Emotional Freedom Technique (EFT) to the author by email. The author also drew from "What is EFT? Theory, Science, and Uses" (emdr-therapy.com/emdr.html) and "What is EFT?" theenergytherapycentre.co.uk/eft-explained.htm.

Chapter Twenty-one: KALI

The epigram, an excerpt of a chant to honour the Hindu goddess Kali, is attributed to Munindra Misra, author of *Chants of Hindu Gods and Goddesses in English Rhyme*. The quotation appears on *Goodreads* (goodreads.com/quotes/tag/kali).

More information about SoulCollage® can be found at Seena Frost's website, soulcollage.com, and at the author's website for Sunshine Coast SoulCollage®, sunshinecoastsoulcollage.ca.

The figure that 93 per cent of child sexual abuse perpetrators know their victim(s) appears on a RAINN web page, https://www.rainn.org /statistics/children-and-teens. Accessed by the author on Nov. 18, 2021.

Thich Nhat Hanh's quotation about a lasting relationship appears in Goodreads https://www.goodreads.com/work/quotes/41700783 -how-to-love. Accessed July 28, 2018.

Portions of the section about Frank and our vows renewal ceremony first appeared in my personal essay "A slow good-bye," from the anthology *New Beginnings*, ed. Erik D'Souza, Timbercrest Publishing, 2019.

The statistic of one in six women experiencing childhood sexual assault from a family member appears on page 19 of *Marilyn* by Gloria Steinem, Henry Holt and Company, New York, NY, 1986.

The reference to 8 per cent of Canadians, ages 15 and up, reporting childhood sexual abuse comes from this Statistics Canada web page: https://www150.statcan.gc.ca/n1/daily-quotidien/170216/dq170216b -eng.htm. Accessed by the author on Nov. 18, 2021.

The reference to "one girl in three or four" is abused is from page 3 of Whitfield's *Memory and Abuse*. The 2000 report by the Bureau of Justice Statistics is cited on page 240 in Meredith Maran's *My Lie*, Jossey-Bass, San Francisco, CA, 2010.

The Rita Banerji quotation appears on page 162 of her book *Sex and Power*. Additional information about Kali appears on page 161 of the same book. Other source material on Kali came from the author's own knowledge; online Encyclopedia Britannica (britannica .com/EBchecked/topic/310141/Kali); Stephanie Anderson Ladd's *In the Lap of the Goddess*; and the websites exoticindiaart.com, thebuddhagarden.com, and dollsofindia.com/kali.htm.

The information about Arman Volkas' Healing the Wounds of History project appears on his Living Arts Center website (livingartscenter .org/Healing-Wounds-of-History/Home.htm).

Regarding the reported incidents of sexual abuse against Indigenous children at Canada's residential schools, there are far too many sources nation-wide to cite. The author has viewed many related documentaries, videos, and online content. Here are only a few items: https://nationalpost.com/news/canada/why-so-many-sexual -predators-at-indian-residential-schools-escaped-punishment; Truth and Reconciliation Commission, https://www.rcaanc-cirnac.gc.ca /eng/1450124405592/1529106060525; https://ottawacitizen.com /news/national/beatings-rapes-a-reality-for-children-at-residential -schools, all accessed by the author on Oct. 12, 2021.

Daniel Heath Justice provided, by email, to the author the exact quotations from a free public talk he provided, via Zoom, attended by Conn on Oct. 2, 2021. This was the Clifford Smith Memorial Lecture "Stories as Good Relations: Imagining Together (and Apart) in Incurious Times," hosted by Elder College of British Columbia's Sunshine Coast.

The content about Joyce Maynard and J.D. Salinger appears in her article "Shame the Devil" on pages 32–33 in the June 2021 issue of *Vanity Fair*, Conde Nast, New York, NY. The quotations are used with Maynard's permission.

The content about Darkness to Light comes from d2l.org/atf /cf/%7B64af78c4-5eb8-45aa-bc28-f7ee2b581919%7D/FINAL _D2L_5%20STEPS%20BOOKLET.PDF.

The description of the Mentors in Violence Prevention (MVP) model and the Be More Than a Bystander approach are paraphrased from the MVP Strategies website mvpstrat.com/the-bystander-approach/.

The information about the Moose Hide Campaign comes from their website moosehidecampaign.ca and from Raven Lacerte's editorial "A tiny piece of moose hide, a mighty campaign," page A17, *Vancouver Sun*, Vancouver, BC, May 21, 2022.

The information about Erin's Law comes from page 228 in Erin Merryn's book *An Unimaginable Act* (Health Communications Inc. 2013), the Erin's Law website (erinslaw.org/what-is-erins-law/), and the Erin's Law Facebook page (facebook.com/ErinsLaw/?fref=ts). Statistics about the rate of child sexual abuse in the U.S. and its related secrecy appear on the home page of erinslaw.org.

My phrases about reconsidering a smile's impact first appeared in the feature "Thank You, Thay" on page 82 of a collector's edition on Thich Nhat Hanh, published by Lion's Roar, Halifax, NS, 2017.

The quotation regarding sexual misconduct appears in Thich Nhat Hanh's 2014 Five Mindfulness Trainings, available on the website of his Plum Village retreat in France (plumvillage.org/mindfulness-practice/the-5-mindfulness-trainings/).

Francis Weller's questions appear on pages 159–160 under "Freedom and Choice: Working with the Complex" in *The Wild Edge of Sorrow*, North Atlantic Books, Berkeley, CA, 2015.

The Resmaa Menakem quotations and content appear on page 152 of *My Grandmother's Hands* (Central Recovery Press, Las Vegas, NV, 2017). His body and breath practices appear throughout the book.

Epilogue: POCKETS

The Wayne Dyer quotation used in the epigram comes from the famous quotations portion of the website citaten.net (citaten.net/en/search/quotes-pockets.html).

The term "contextual stimuli," used by Bessel A. van der Kolk, appears on page 112 of *Victimized Daughters* by Janet Liebman Jacobs, Routledge, New York, NY, 1994. The original source of the term is

Kolk's "The Compulsion to Repeat the Trauma: Re-enactment, Revictimization, and Masochism," *Psychiatric Clinics of North America* 12, no. 2 (1989): 389–411, esp. 396.

The term "repetition compulsion" appears in Freudian, psychiatric, and trauma-related literature. One source is page 112 in *Victimized Daughters* by Janet Liebman, Routledge, New York, NY, 1994. Several contemporary online references include *The Neurobiology of Freud's Repetition Compulsion* by Denise K. Shull (traderpsyches. com/documents/Neurobiology_Freud_Repetition.pdf) and Dr. John F. Abess's website Glossary of Terms in Psychiatry and Neurology, abess.com/glossary.html.

The musical reference to "in the pocket" comes from The Urban Dictionary, urbandictionary.com/define.php?term=In%20the%20 Pocket.

Variations of Mae West's famous line, from the 1933 film *She Done Him Wrong*, appear in numerous online sources including Wiki Quotes (en.wikiquote.org/wiki/Mae_West).

The pebble in the pocket story appears on pages 64–65 in *Anger: Wisdom for Cooling the Flames* by Thich Nhat Hanh, Riverhead Books, New York, NY, 2001.

The quotation about ripples and consequences by playwright and screenwriter Robert Anderson appears in his 1953 play *Tea and Sympathy*. At the end of the 1956 movie version directed by Vincente Minnelli, Deborah Kerr's character Laura Reynolds writes this excerpt in a letter to Tom, played by John Kerr, the sensitive young man she tries to support. This excerpt also appears on subzin.com /quotes/Tea+and+Sympathy/There+are+always+consequences.

Bibliography

Adams, Ja. *Gandhi: Naked Ambition*. Quercus. London, Eng. 2010.

Adams, Kenneth M. *Silently Seduced*. Health Communications, Inc. Deerfield Beach, Fla. 1991.

Alec, Elaine. *Calling My Spirit Back*. Tellwell Talent. 2020.

Anderson Ladd, Stephanie. *In the Lap of the Goddess: Connecting with the Divine Feminine*. (self-published). 2012.

Anonymous. *The Incest Diary*. Farrar, Straus and Giroux, New York, NY. 2017.

Armstrong, Mary K. *Confessions of a Trauma Therapist*. BPS Books. Toronto, ON. 2010.

Armstrong, Sally. *Ascent of Women*. Random House Canada. Toronto, ON. 2013.

Artress, Lauren. *Walking a Sacred Path: Rediscovering the Labyrinth as a Spiritual Practice*. Riverhead Books. New York, NY. 2006.

Ashby-Rolls, Trysh. *Triumph: A Journey of Healing from Incest*. Mc-Graw-Hill Ryerson. Toronto, ON. 1991.

Baldwin, Christina. *Storycatcher: Making Sense of Our Lives through the Power and Practice of Story*. New World Library. Novato, CA. 2005.

Banerji, Rita. *Sex and Power: Defining History, Shaping Societies*. Penguin Books. Haryana, India. 2008.

Bass, Ellen. ed. with Louise Thornton. *I Never Told Anyone: Writings by Women Survivors of Child Sexual Abuse*. Harper Perennial. New York, NY. 1991.

Bass, Ellen and Laura Davis. *The Courage to Heal: A Guide for Women Survivors of Child Sexual Abuse.* Harper Collins. New York, NY. 2008.

Bedi, Rajesh. *Ladakh.* Brijbasi Printers Private Ltd. New Delhi. 1986.

Besel, Donna. *The Unravelling: Incest and the Destruction of a Family.* University of Regina Press. Regina, SK. 2021.

Bettelheim, Bruno. *The Uses of Enchantment: The Meaning and Importance of Fairy Tales.* Alfred A. Knopf, New York, NY. 1991.

Tara Brach. *Radical Acceptance: Embracing Your Life with the Heart of a Buddha.* Bantam Books. New York, NY. 2003.

Birkerts, Sven. *The Art of Time in Memoir: Then, Again.* Graywolf Press. St. Paul, MN. 2008.

Blakeslee, Sandra and Matthew Blakeslee. *The Body Has a Mind of Its Own.* Random House. New York, NY. 2007.

Bradshaw, John. *Family Secrets.* Bantam Books. New York, NY. 1996.

Branden, Nathaniel. A *Woman's Self-esteem.* Jossey-Bass, Hoboken, NJ. 1998.

Brown, Laura S. and Jennifer J. Freyd. "PTSD Criterion A and Betrayal Trauma: A Modest Proposal for a New Look at What Constitutes Danger to Self." *Trauma Psychology Newsletter.* Winter 2008. pp. 11–15.

Butler, Sandra. *The Conspiracy of Silence: The Trauma of Incest.* Volcano Press. Volcano, CA. 1996.

Chaplin, Heather. *Reckless Years: A Diary of Love and Madness.* Simon & Schuster. New York. 2017.

Chodron, Pema. *Awakening Loving-Kindness.* Shambhala Publications, Boston, MA. 1996.

Chodron, Pema. *Comfortable With Uncertainty.* Shambhala Publications, Boston, MA. 2002.

Chodron, Pema. *When Things Fall Apart.* Shambhala Publications, Inc. Boston, MA. 1997.

Clancy, Susan A. *The Trauma Myth.* Basic Books. New York, NY. 2009.

Coffey, Maria. *Explorers of the Infinite.* Tarcher/Penguin. New York, NY. 2008.

Conn, Nancy. *The Family History of William Heather and Sarah Morley—from England to Upper Canada: the Heather, Bramhall, Morley and Hall Families.* Self-published. Stewart Publishing & Printing, Toronto, ON. 2003.

Conn, Nancy. *From the Scottish Border to Upper Canada: the Hart and Hotson Families.* Self-published. Toronto, ON. 2008.

Cose, Ellis. *Bone to Pick: Of Forgiveness, Reconciliation, Reparation, and Revenge.* Washington Square Press. New York, NY. 2004.

Christine A. Courtois. *Healing the Incest Wound.* 2nd edition. W.W. Norton & Co. New York, NY. 2010.

Contratto, Susan and M. Janice Gutfreund, eds. *A Feminist Clinician's Guide to the Memory Debate.* Harrington Park Press. Binghampton, NY. 1996.

Crowther, Geoff and Prakash A. Raj and Tony Wheeler. *India: a travel survival kit.* 3rd ed. Lonely Planet Publications. Berkeley, CA. 1987.

Courtois, Christine A. *Healing the Incest Wound.* 2nd ed. W.W. Norton and Co. New York, NY. 2010.

Danica, Elly. *Beyond Don't.* Gynergy Books. Charlottetown, PEI. 1996.

Danica, Elly. *Don't: A Woman's Word.* Gynergy Books. Charlottetown, PEI. 1988.

Desai, Yogi Amrit. *Amrit Yoga and the Yoga Sutras.* Sumneytown, PA. 2002.

DeSalvo, Louise. *Virginia Woolf: The Impact of Childhood Sexual Abuse on Her Life and Work.* Ballantine Books. New York, NY. 1989.

Didion, Joan. *The Year of Magical Thinking.* Alfred A. Knopf. New York, NY. 2005.

Ensler, Eve. *The Apology.* Bloomsbury Publishing. New York, NY. 2019.

Faleiro, Sonia. *The Good Girls: An Ordinary Killing.* Penguin Random House. Toronto, ON. 2020.

Farber, Yaël. *Nirbhaya.* Live theatrical show at The Cultch. Vancouver,

BC. Nov. 12 performance of Nov. 3–14, 2015 production.

Finney, Lynne D. *Reach for the Rainbow*. Perigree Books. New York, NY. 1992.

Fraser, Sylvia. *My Father's House: A Memoir of Incest and Healing*. Ticknor & Fields. Boston, MA. 1987.

Fraser, Sylvia. *The Book of Strange: A Journey*. Doubleday Canada Ltd. Toronto, ON. 1992.

Freedman, Karyn L. *One Hour in Paris*. Freehand Books. Calgary, AB. 2014.

Ghetti, Simona. Edelstein, Robin S. Goodman, Gail S. Cordon, Ingrid M. Quas, Jodi A. Alexander, Kristen Weede. Redlich, Allison D. Jones, David P.H. "What can subjective forgetting tell us about memory for childhood trauma." *Memory & Cognition*. Psychonomic Society, Inc. 2006, 34 (5), 1011–1025.

Gilbert, Elizabeth. *Committed*. Viking Penguin. New York, NY. 2010.

Gilbert, Elizabeth. *Eat, Pray, Love*. Viking Penguin. New York, NY. 2007.

Gornick, Vivian. *The Situation and the Story*. Farrar, Straus and Giroux. New York, NY. 2001.

Grimm, Jakob and Wilhelm. *The Goose Girl*. Creative Education. Mankato, MN. 1984.

Grimm Brothers. *Favorite Tales from Grimm*. Four Winds Press. New York, NY. 1982.

Grimm Brothers. *Sixty Fairy Tales of the Brothers Grimm*. Weathervane Books. New York, NY. 1979.

Gutkind, Lee. ed. *Surviving Crisis*. Jeremy P. Tarcher/Putnam. New York, NY, 1997.

Hanh, Thich Nhat. *Anger: Wisdom for Cooling the Flames*. Riverhead Books, New York, NY. 2001.

Hanh, Thich Nhat. *Peace is Every Step*. Bantam Books. New York, NY, 1992.

Harrison, Kathryn. *Exposure*. Random House, New York, NY. 1993.

Harrison, Kathryn. *The Kiss*. Random House, New York, NY. 1997.

Harvey, Andrew. *A Journey in Ladakh*. Houghton Mifflin. Boston, MA. 1983.

Heche, Anne. *Call Me Crazy*. Washington Square Press. New York, NY. 2001.

Heilbrun, Carolyn G. *Writing a Woman's Life*. Ballantine Books. New York, NY. 1988.

Herman, Judith. *Father-Daughter Incest*. Harvard University Press. Cambridge, MA. 2000.

Herman, Judith and Lisa Hirshman. "Father-Daughter Incest." *Signs* 2 (1977)

Hoffman, Richard. *Half the House*. Harcourt Brace and Company. New York, NY. 1995.

Anne L. Horton, Barry L. Johnson, Lynn M. Roundy, Doran Williams, ed. *The Incest Perpetrator*. Sage Publications, Newbury Park, CA. 1990.

Houston, Jean. *A Mythic Life*. Harper Collins, San Francisco, CA. 1996.

Hudson, Kim. *The Virgin's Promise: Writing Stories of Feminine Creative, Spiritual and Sexual Awakening*. Michael Wiese Productions. Studio City, CA. 2009.

Jacobs, Janet Liebman. *Victimized Daughters: Incest and the Development of the Female Self*. Routledge, New York, NY. 1994.

Johnson, Janis Tyler. *Mothers of Incest Survivors*. Indiana University Press. Indianapolis, IN. 1992.

Johnson, Robert. *She: Understanding Feminine Psychology*. Harper Paperbacks. New York, NY. 1989.

Judd, Ashley with Maryanne Vollers. *All That Is Bitter and Sweet*. Ballantine Books, New York NY. 2012.

Kafka, Franz. *The Metamorphosis, In the Penal Colony and Other Stories*. Simon and Schuster, New York, NY. 2000.

Kahn, Laurie. "The Understanding and Treatment of Betrayal Trauma as a Traumatic Experience of Love." *Journal of Trauma Practice*. vol. 5 (3), pages 57–72. The Haworth Press, Inc. Binghamton, NY. 2006.

Kane, Evangeline. *Recovering from Incest*. Sigo Press. Boston, MA. 1989.

Karr, Mary. *The Liars' Club*. Penguin Group. New York, NY. 1995.

Paul Kennedy, *Ideas*. "All in the Family, Part 3." Canadian Broadcasting Corporation radio show. April 21, 2016.

Kincaid, Jamaica. *My Brother*. Farrar, Straus and Giroux. New York, NY. 1997.

Kincaid, James R. *Erotic Innocence: The Culture of Child Molesting*. Duke University Press. Durham and London, 1998.

King, Deborah. *Truth Heals*. Hay House, Inc. New York, NY, 2009.

Kogawa, Joy. *The Rain Ascends*. Alfred A. Knopf. Toronto, ON. 1995.

Levine, Peter with Ann Frederick. *Waking the Tiger: Healing Trauma*. North Atlantic Books, Berkeley, CA. 1997.

Lewis, Tanya. *Living Beside: Performing Normal After Incest Memories Return*. McGilligan Books. Toronto, ON. 1999.

Loftus, Elizabeth and Katherine Ketcham. *The Myth of Repressed Memory*. St. Martin's Press. New York, NY. 1994.

Elizabeth Lumley, ed. *Canadian Who's Who*, 2008, vol. xliii. University of Toronto Press. Toronto, ON. 2008.

Macdonald, Sarah. *Holy Cow: An Indian Adventure*. Broadway Books. New York, NY. 2003.

Malone, Caroline, Linda Farthing and Lorraine Marce, ed. *The Memory Bird: Survivors of Sexual Abuse*. Virago Press. London, GB. 1996.

Maran, Meredith. *My Lie*. Jossey-Bass. San Francisco, CA. 2010.

McCall, Catherine. *When the Piano Stops: A Memoir of Healing from Sexual Abuse*. Seal Press, Berkeley, CA. 2009.

Maté, Gabor. *In the Realm of Hungry Ghosts: Close Encounters with Addiction*. Vintage Canada. Toronto. 2018.

Matthiessen, Peter. *Nine-Headed Dragon River*. Shambhala Publications, Inc. Boston, MA. 1985.

Matousek, Mark. "America's Darkest Secret." *Common Boundary*. March/April 1991.

McNally, Richard J. *Remembering Trauma*. Belknap Press. Cambridge, MA. 2003.

Maynard, Joyce. "Shame the Devil," pp. 32–33, June 2021. *Vanity Fair*. Conde Nast. New York, NY.

Merryn, Erin. *An Unimaginable Act: Overcoming and Preventing Child Abuse Through Erin's Law.* Health Communications, Inc. Deerfield, FL. 2013.

Merryn, Erin. *Living for Today: From Incest and Molestation to Fearlessness and Forgiveness.* Health Communications, Inc. Deerfield, FL. 2009.

Merryn, Erin. *Stolen Innocence: Triumphing Over a Childhood Broken by Abuse.* Health Communications, Inc. Deerfield, FL. 2004.

Middleton-Moz, *Children of Trauma: Rediscovering the Discarded Self.* Health Communications, Inc. Deerfield Beach, FL. 1989.

Miller, Alice. *Breaking Down the Wall of Silence.* Penguin Books, New York, NY. 1997.

Miller, Chanel. *Know My Name.* Audible.ca.

Mines, Stephanie. *Sexual Abuse/Sacred Wound: Transforming Trauma.* Station Hill Openings, Barrytown, NY. 1996.

Moore, J. "Sociology and incest avoidance: a critical look at a critical review." *American Anthropology.* 94: 930–933 (1992)

Morgan, Marabel. *The Total Woman.* G.K. Hall, Boston, MA. 1975.

Murdock, Maureen. *The Hero's Daughter.* Fawcett Columbine. New York, NY. 1994.

Murray, Rona. *Journey Back to Peshawar.* Sono Nis Press. Victoria, BC. 1993.

Nin, Anais, *Incest: from "A Journal of Love." The Unexpurgated Diary of Anaïs Nin, 1932–1934.* Harcourt Inc. New York, NY. 1992.

Norberg-Hodge, Helena. *Ancient Futures: Learning from Ladakh,* Sierra Club Books, San Francisco, CA. 1992.

Ostis, Constance M. *What's Happening in Our Family? Understanding Sexual Abuse Through Metaphors.* Safer Society Press. Brandon, VT. 2002.

Pearsall, Judy, ed. *The Concise Oxford English Dictionary,* 10th edition. Oxford University Press. Oxford, GB. 2002.

Petry, Bob. *Bala: An Early Settlement in Muskoka.* Lynx Images, Inc. St. John's, NL. 1998.

Rainer, Tristane. *Your Life As Story.* Jeremy P. Tarcher. New York, NY. 1997.

Ratliff, Evan. "Déjà vu, Again and Again." *The New York Times Magazine*, July 2, 2006. page 39.

Rivera, Margo. Ed. *Fragment by Fragment: Feminist Perspectives on Memory and Child Sexual Abuse.* gynergy books, Charlottetown, PEI. 1999.

Roche, David. *The Church of 80% Sincerity.* Penguin Group (USA) Inc. New York, NY. 2008.

Ross, John Munder. *The Male Paradox.* Simon & Schuster. New York, NY. 1992.

Rothermund, Dietmar. *An Economic History of India.* Routledge, London, GB. 1993.

Rothschild, Babette. *The Body Remembers.* W. W. Norton & Company, New York, NY. 2000.

Safransky, Sy. Ed. *Sunbeams: A Book of Quotations.* North Atlantic Books. Berkeley, CA. 1990.

Scaer, Robert C. *The Body Bears the Burden: Trauma, Dissociation, and Disease.* 2nd edition. Routledge Taylor & Francis Group, New York, NY. 2007.

Scarf, Maggie. *Secrets, Lies, Betrayals.* Random House, New York, NY. 2004.

Siegel, Daniel J. *Mindsight.* Bantam Books. New York, NY. 2010.

Silverman, Sue William. *Because I Remember Terror Father I Remember You.* The University of Georgia Press. Athens, GA. 1999.

Singh, Kathleen Dowling. *The Grace in Dying.* Harper Collins. New York, NY. 1998.

Slater, Lauren. *Lying.* Penguin Books. New York, NY. 2000.

Stein, Robert. *Incest and Human Love.* 2nd edition. Spring Publications, Inc. Dallas, TX. 1984.

Steinem, Gloria. *Marilyn.* Henry Holt and Company. New York, NY. 1986.

Stern, Jessica. *Denial: A Memoir of Terror.* Harper Collins. New York, NY. 2010.

Terr, Lenore. *Too Scared to Cry.* Basic Books. New York, NY. 1990.

Terr, Lenore. *Unchained Memories.* Harper Collins. New York, NY. 1994.

Thich Nhat Hanh. *How to Fight*. Parallax Press, Berkeley, CA, 2017.

Thornhill, Randy and Palmer, Craig T. *Why Men Rape*. The New York Academy of Sciences. January/February 2000.

Todd, Richard. *The Thing Itself*. Riverhead Books. New York, NY. 2008.

Vardey, Lucinda. ed. *God in All Worlds*. Pantheon Books. New York, NY. 1995.

Verma, Sonia. "The paradox of power." *The Globe and Mail*. A15. May 21, 2011. Toronto, ON.

Waites, Elizabeth. *Memory Quest: Trauma and the Search for Personal History*. W.W. Norton. New York, NY. 1997.

Walker, Alice. *Anything We Love Can Be Saved*. Random House, New York, NY. 1997.

Walls, Jeannette. *The Glass Castle*. Scribner, New York, NY. 2006.

Warland, Betsy. *The Bat Had Blue Eyes*. Women's Press. Toronto, ON. 1993.

Weller, Francis. *The Wild Edge of Sorrow: Rituals of Renewal and the Sacred Work of Grief*. North Atlantic Books. Berkeley, CA. 2015.

Whitfield, Charles L. Whitfield. *Memory and Abuse: Remembering and Healing the Effects of Trauma*. Health Communications, Inc. Deerfield Beach, CA. 1995.

Williams, Mary Jane. *Healing Hidden Memories: Recovery for Adult Survivors of Childhood Abuse*. Health Communications, Inc. Deerfield, Beach, CA. 1991.

Williams, Terry Tempest. *Refuge: An Unnatural History of Family and Place*. Vintage Books. New York, NY. 1991.

Wisechild, Louise M. ed. *She Who Was Lost is Remembered: Healing from Incest Through Creativity*. The Seal Press, Seattle, WA. 1991.

Wolff, Geoffrey. *The Duke of Deception*. Vintage Books, New York, NY. 1990.

Yogananda, Paramahansa. *Autobiography of a Yogi*. Jaico Publishing House. Bombay, India. 1990.

About the Author

Heather Conn has written for more than 50 publications, including *The Globe and Mail*, *Vancouver Sun*, *Edmonton Journal*, *Canadian Encyclopedia*, and the U.S. Sierra Club magazine *Sierra*. Her nonfiction has appeared in numerous anthologies, including Harbour Publishing's *Raincoast Chronicles 22* (2013) and *Emails from India* (Seraphim Editions, 2013). She loves to write about social justice issues, the environment, travel, health, arts and culture, and people's self-actualization stories. Heather is the author of four other books: two nonfiction histories and two children's fiction, including *Six Stinky Feet and a Sasquatch* (Peppermint Toast Publishing, 2019). She is also the co-writer of two Bravo TV short films *Divine Waters* and *Corona Station*. Her writing has brought awards from the Writers' Union of Canada, Southam Communications, BC Festival of the Arts, and others.

A devoted west-coaster, Heather has taught creative nonfiction at University of King's College (Halifax), and in BC, screenwriting at Powell River Digital Film School, travel writing at Capilano University, and journalism and professional writing at Selkirk College. She has created and facilitated dozens of private and public workshops at multiple venues, including in the U.S., and in BC from the City of Port Moody to Vancouver Coastal Health and Vancouver School Board.

Heather has edited for both publishers and independent authors, polishing dozens of nonfiction books, and a variety of newsletters and magazines, including BC-wide *PeopleTalk*. She thoroughly enjoys helping writers shape and deepen their stories. She has worked as an oral historian, screenwriter, communications manager, publicist, trained SoulCollage® facilitator, and Mentors in Violence Prevention trainer.

Heather has a master of fine arts degree in creative nonfiction from Goucher College in Baltimore. Find out more at heatherconn.com, @SixStinkyFeetandaSasquatch, @Heather Conn.

Printed in November 2022
by Gauvin Press,
Gatineau, Québec